Contemporary Old Testament Theologians

by Robert B. Laurin

Judson Press, Valley Forge

CONTEMPORARY OLD TESTAMENT THEOLOGIANS

Contemporary
Old
Testament
Theologians

List of Contributors

Norman K. Gottwald, Professor of Old Testament and of Biblical Theology and Ethics, American Baptist Seminary of the West, Berkeley, California.

G. Henton Davies, President, Regent's Park College in Oxford University, Oxford, England.

John N. Schofield, formerly Lecturer in Old Testament Studies, Cambridge University, and Fellow of University College, Cambridge, England.

Ronald E. Clements, Lecturer in Old Testament Studies, Cambridge University, Cambridge, England.

Robert B. Laurin, Professor of Old Testament, American Baptist Seminary of the West, Covina, California.

John I. Durham, Associate Professor of Old Testament Interpretation and Administrative Associate to the President, Southeastern Baptist Theological Seminary, Wake Forest, North Carolina.

David A. Hubbard, President and Professor of Old Testament, Fuller Theological Seminary, Pasadena, California.

Abbreviations

ATD	*Das Alte Testament Deutsch*
BEvTh	*Beiträge zur Evangelischen Theologie*
BVC	*Bible et Vie Chrétienne*
BWANT	*Beiträge zur Wissenschaft vom Alten und Neuen Testament*
BZAW	*Beihefte der Zeitschrift fur alttestamentliche Wissenschaft*
CBQ	*Catholic Biblical Quarterly*
CollGand	*Collationes Gandavenses*
CT	*Concordia Theological Monthly*
DtPfrBl	*Deutsches Pfarrerblatt*
ET	*Expository Times*
EThL	*Ephemerides Theologicae Louvanienses*
EThR	*Études théologiques et religieuses*
EvTh	*Evangelische Theologie*
FRLANT	*Forschungen zur Religion und Literatur des Alten und Neuen Testaments*
IDB	*Interpreter's Dictionary of the Bible*

JBL	*Journal of Biblical Literature*
JBR	*Journal of Bible and Religion*
JSS	*Journal of Semitic Studies*
JTS	*Journal of Theological Studies*
KAT	*Kommentar zum Alten Testament*
LQ	*Lutheran Quarterly*
NKZ	*Neue kirchliche Zeitschrift*
NRT	*Nouvelle Revue Théologique*
OS	*Oudtestamentische Studién*
RB	*Revue Biblique*
RHPR	*Revue d'histoire et de philosophie religieuses*
RSPT	*Revue des sciences philosophiques et théologiques*
RThP	*Revue de théologie et de philosophie*
SJT	*Scottish Journal of Theology*
TDNT	*Theological Dictionary of the New Testament* (Eng. trans. of *Theologisches Wörterbuch zum Neuen Testament*, ed. R. Kittel)
ThLZ	*Theologische Literaturzeitung*
TS	*Theologische Studien*
TT	*Theology Today*
TZ	*Theologische Zeitschrift*
USQR	*Union Seminary Quarterly Review*
VC	*Verbum Caro*
VF	*Verkündigung und Forschung*
VT	*Vetus Testamentum*
VT Sup	*Supplement to Vetus Testamentum*
WMZANT	*Wissenschaftlichen Monographien zum Alten und Neuen Testament*
WTJ	*Westminster Theological Journal*
ZAW	*Zeitschrift fur die alttestamentliche Wissenschaft*
ZDPV	*Zeitschrift des Deutschen Palästinavereins*
ZZ	*Zwischen den Zeiten*

Foreword

THE IDEA FOR THIS BOOK developed from classroom need. As a teacher of the Old Testament I found myself facing the problem felt by all teachers, namely, not enough time to help my students become involved with the wealth of important material in my discipline. How, for example, could I help them to become acquainted with the theological contributions of von Rad, Eichrodt, Vriezen, Procksch, Jacob, van Imschoot, Knight, and others, and still have time for other aspects of Old Testament study? I needed something more extensive than the very helpful series of articles that appeared in *The Expository Times* during 1962-1963, and yet brief enough so that the students could have a sense of the whole. I also wanted something that could provide a review perspective for those who had finished their degree. This book is the result.

The men who have written the essays are all engaged in the task of teaching the Old Testament, and represent various Baptist denominations in different parts of the world. I wish to thank them for their cooperation and patience during the unexpected delays which arose in the production of the book. It has been pleasant working with them. The editors at the Judson Press, particularly Mr. Harold L. Twiss, have also been long-suffering and encouraging. My thanks are given to them as well. Finally, I would express my gratitude to my secretary, Mrs. Almeda McKee, and to her assistant, Miss Maxine Clark, for their willing help in manuscript preparation.

ROBERT B. LAURIN
Covina, California

Contents

Contemporary
Old
Testament
Theologians

Introduction

THE IMPORTANCE OF THE OLD TESTAMENT for contemporary man is becoming increasingly recognized. This growing interest can be seen not only in the marked growth of writing within the Old Testament field itself, but particularly in the expanding discussion about the place of the Old Testament in interdisciplinary studies which speak to current theological, philosophical, and sociological concerns. H. Miskotte, *When the Gods Are Silent,* is a good example,[1] as well as the growing list of volumes and articles dealing with hermeneutics and history. The reasons for this attention are varied, but undoubtedly the Old Testament's profound sense of a historical process and its probing search of man's basic existential questions are among the most important. James Robinson has even claimed that Old Testament scholarship could well become the central base for all theological discussion in the coming generation.[2] The present volume is intended

[1] See Kornelis H. Miskotte, *When the Gods Are Silent,* trans. John W. Doberstein (New York: Harper & Row, Publishers, 1967).

[2] J. M. Robinson, "The Historicality of Biblical Language," in *The Old Testament and Christian Faith,* ed. B. W. Anderson (New York: 1963), p. 150.

15

to contribute to this by providing a compendium of recent important books on the structure and content of Old Testament theology.

Crowning Old Testament study is the elucidation of its theology,

> since the construction of a scientific theology of the Old Testament presupposes the results of all the other Old Testament studies and also because these varied studies require some further study to collate and synthesize their results so as to make them available to other branches of theological science and to the world of secular learning as well.[3]

If the Old Testament is going to take its necessary place in present-day debate, then its theological contributions need to be understood clearly and properly. The history of the church and synagogue shows us how often the Old Testament has been used for the confirmation of previously determined dogmatic positions. What does the Old Testament really say when investigated by means of the scientific methods of higher and lower criticism? Answers to this question are offered here by the major Old Testament theologies under review. The answers are not uniform, of course, for these books illustrate the commonly recognized problem of structuring the theology of the Old Testament. Do Christian dogmatics provide the proper rubrics with the standard divisions of revelation, God, creation, man, sin, and salvation? Is exposition presented around a common theme (e.g., kingship or covenant) the best way to give the answer? Or does a developing, historical methodology provide the most satisfying approach? Indeed, can one even speak of "a" theology of the Old Testament? These are questions to keep in view throughout the book.

There is a further perspective from which the reader of these essays must evaluate the ultimate worth of the contemporary theologies of the Old Testament: What should be the task of a writer on Old Testament theology? The usual answer has been something along the order of the words of Krister Stendahl: "The task of biblical studies, even of biblical theology, is to *describe,* to relive and relate in the terms and the presuppositions of the period of the texts what they meant to their authors and their contemporaries. To furnish the original." [4] Stendahl then points out that answering the question of

---

[3] Robert C. Dentan, *Preface to Old Testament Theology,* rev. ed. (New York: The Seabury Press, 1963), p. 97.

[4] Krister Stendahl, "Implications of Form-Criticism and Tradition-Criticism for Biblical Interpretation," *JBL,* 77 (1958), p. 38.

meaning for us here and now is the task of systematic theology. But can we rest content with an Old Testament theology that is merely "descriptive"? Dentan has expressed it correctly when he states that "it is necessary for Old Testament studies to be concerned with the value of the things with which they deal and to indicate their significance for the rest of life." [5] Are we, after all, simply antiquarians interested in the beliefs of an ancient people? Or are we modern men with modern concerns? Current writers are turning to the Old Testament to gain help in answering modern questions. Edmond Jacob has written that the Bible does not contain "a timeless revelation, but a word of God for particular men in particular circumstances." [6] While this is certainly true for men of Bible times, we are also "particular men" who long to know that "word" for our "particular circumstances." What part can the Old Testament play in giving us such a word? Must the biblical department remain dispassionate and objective in handling the Old Testament at this point, and leave the problem of contemporary meaning to the systematician? To express this concern is not to deny that we must clearly distinguish, as Langdon Gilkey writes, "between *Hebrew* recital (biblical theology) and *our* recital (confessional or systematic theology) if our confessions are to make any sense at all." [7] Our present Old Testament theologies have done a tremendous service in providing for us the distinctive beliefs of the Old Testament in readily available form. But can we really say that the task of the Old Testament theologian is only to provide the tools for someone else to ask the important ultimate questions? T. Vriezen seems to think so, for he writes that biblical theology "collects the materials supplied by the Bible as it has come to understand them in the light of history, so that the dogmatician, engaged in his systematic work, may know what the points at issue in the Bible are." [8]

---

[5] Dentan, *loc. cit.*

[6] Edmund Jacob, *Theology of the Old Testament,* trans. Arthur W. Heathcote and Philip J. Allcock (New York: Harper & Row, Publishers, 1958), p. 27.

[7] Langdon B. Gilkey, "Cosmology, Ontology, and the Travail of Biblical Language," *CT,* 33 (1962), p. 153.

[8] T. C. Vriezen, *An Outline of Old Testament Theology* (Newton, Mass.: Charles T. Branford Co., 1958), p. 119; see also E. Jacob in the preface to his second French edition, p. vii.

The question needs to be asked whether or not the usual descriptive approach to writing Old Testament theology has even been true to its stated task. The men of the Old Testament were not simply proclaimers of words dropped from heaven; they were not secretaries. They were men involved in their message, those who spoke a word out of certain cultural and ideational backgrounds. How have these elements shaped their thought, and so blunted or obscured the realities of their situations and beliefs? Edmond Jacob comments:

> The narration of history implies for the Israelite an interpretation of it, because he views God's action through faith and not by the methods of the archivist or the archaeologist. . . . the Hebrew mind has little awareness of the notion of history, for it is interested in history only to the extent in which in is *his et nunc* a present and dynamic reality.[9]

Thus when we describe Old Testament theology we cannot simply present what the Old Testament characters believed if we are truly to be descriptive of their thought and intent. Old Testament theology must be dialogical and judgmental if it is to be true to the Old Testament. It must also deal with the *hic et nunc* as well as the philosophical and cultural presuppositions that permeated the work of the Old Testament writers. These assumptions are also part of what they believed. Such an attempt is often made, of course, but it is not usually carried far enough. If Old Testament theology is truly to speak to modern man, the biblical theologian must describe Old Testament faith in contemporary terms and models. He will seek to expose what is provincial and merely historical in the thought of the Old Testament and will try to provide that which he believes must remain. He, too, must get involved and feel the relationship with God felt by the Old Testament writers. If he does so, he will inevitably search for new models by which to describe that faith which he discovers, but in the process he will truly have described Old Testament faith.

The period of separate disciplines in the theological curriculum is passing, and the sooner the better. It is true that we will always have to have separate areas of specialization, in order to handle the volume of work. But the day is past when an Old Testament expert can be content with thinking he has done his work if he has simply described

---

[9] Jacob, *op. cit.*, p. 184.

the facts in his field without relating them to the work of other departments. He will provide far more helpful material to his contemporaries if he comes to recognize that he is part of a community of scholarship embracing many disciplines. He must ask the question, for example, of the meaning of the Old Testament for the church and synagogue, indeed for all men. And he must give some answers, because he has lived with the text more intimately than others. He has the tools of language and history to open up the penetrating issues. He is a man concerned about the same issues of life that concern the confessional theologians. What does he, with his own special insight, think about the implications of Old Testament belief?

Each man, because he is a man, has common concerns with other men: Who am I? Where is reality to be found? What is the significance of existence? Yet each man has only a small area of knowledge in which he can gain some competence. His unique contribution to the common human concerns can come when he utilizes his expertise in that small area to show us how a solution there can help us to solve those concerns. We have, therefore, expected the wrong thing by waiting for the dogmatician or systematician to be the spokesman to our culture. Stendahl complains that biblical specialists always show up "amateurish and nearsighted" when they try to handle the questions of meaning, since these questions demand a technical competence in philosophy, epistemology, semantics, and systematic theology which cannot be expected of biblical scholars.[10] But what are we doing when we expect the systematician to be competent in Old Testament studies? The problem is the same for all of us. Interdisciplinary involvement, therefore, is a necessity, but not merely for the purpose of having the systematician or practical theologian interpret to the modern world the facts provided by the biblical theologian. Its purpose should be for each man—Old Testament scholar, New Testament expert, church historian, systematician—to bring the contributions and insights of his field to the common problems of mankind. The focus of interdisciplinary work, therefore, is not to be on one man who will answer contemporary questions, but on the questions themselves to which each discipline has something to say.

Too long we have labored under the false impression that we lose

---

[10] Stendahl, *op. cit.,* p. 33.

our "objectivity" in Old Testament studies when we affirm what we believe, what we consider to be correct or false in the biblical claims. As a teacher of Old Testament, I want a chance to engage in dialogue with the theological evaluations of others who write on common themes. I am more than an antiquarian. I am a twentieth-century man who believes the Old Testament can be a twentieth-century document. Old Testament theology can help us most when it challenges us by speaking to twentieth-century questions in the midst of describing pre-Christian approaches to common problems.

Most of the theologians discussed in this book have made a start in this direction. This is particularly true of Vriezen, von Rad, and Knight. And one finds a comparable concern in other areas of Old Testament work. In commentary writing there is a new mood, exemplified in the German series *Biblischer Kommentar* or *Das Alte Testament Deutsch*. Although often these commentators do not spend enough time on the questions of meaning, yet their interest is more than mere description. They constantly ask the question of the "Ziel" (goal, intent) of a given passage. The same can be said of other recent commentaries.[11] One can also notice this interest in the contemporary value of the Old Testament in the increasing discussion of the hermeneutical question by Old and New Testament theologians.[12]

The choice of the particular authors for discussion in this volume was determined by their importance, by their variant approaches, and by the availability of their work in a volume or two. It will be obvious that a host of writers on Old Testament theological themes has been omitted, as well as those with separate books on the subject. The works of Abraham Heschel, Wilhelm Vischer, and perhaps, Ludwig Köhler, would particularly merit extended examination. But space limitations required that only the present selection could

[11] James D. Smart, *History and Theology in Second Isaiah: A Commentary on Isaiah 35, 40-66* (Philadelphia: The Westminster Press, 1965) ; George A. F. Knight, *Deutero-Isaiah: A Theological Commentary on Isaiah 40–55* (Nashville: Abingdon Press, 1965) ; James M. Ward, *Hosea: A Theological Commentary* (New York: Harper & Row, Publishers, 1966).

[12] Cf. especially Claus Westermann, ed., *Essays on Old Testament Hermeneutics,* James Luther Mays, ed., English translation (Richmond: John Knox Press, 1963) ; Bernhard W. Anderson, ed., *The Old Testament and Christian Faith* (New York: Harper & Row, Publishers, Inc., 1963).

be included. Each of the essays deals with certain common concerns in critiquing the particular theologian's work: his arrangement of Old Testament theology, his understanding of the relationship between faith and history in the Old Testament, his concept of the relationship between the Old and New Testament, and his development of the details of the theology or theologies of the Old Testament. Each author, however, has been left free to arrange his essay in ways that best fit the particular theologian he discusses. The transliteration of Hebrew words in each essay is varied, for it reflects the methodology of the particular theologian.

It is hoped that this book will be useful as a text for classroom survey and discussion, or as a guide to the intensive examination of individual authors. Thus, each essay concludes with a bibliography of further writings by the particular theologian.[13]

---

[13] A helpful supplement to the present volume is R. Dentan, *Preface to Old Testament Theology (op. cit.)*. This book provides a discussion of the history and methodology of research on the theology of the Old Testament.

1
W. Eichrodt
Theology of the Old Testament

by Norman K. Gottwald

Walther Eichrodt was born on August 1, 1890, in Grensbach, Germany. He was educated at the universities of Greifswald, Heidelberg, and Erlangen, and received an honorary doctorate from the University of Glasgow. He taught first at Erlangen, and then became Professor of History of Religions and Old Testament at the University of Basel in Switzerland.

WALTHER EICHRODT's *Theology of the Old Testament* is the single most important work of its genre in the twentieth century. This is not alone because of its scope (the English translation exceeds one thousand pages). Eichrodt's importance lies in the working solutions he brings to those critical questions of biblical study and theological inquiry which the nineteenth century so sharply posed and so inconclusively dealt with. It is in the endeavor to unite exegetical/historical craftsmanship and theological reflection that Eichrodt makes his greatest contribution. By producing an amalgam of historical and theological inquiry on an architectonic scale, he forces us to judge whether our century has succeeded any better than the last in relating the apparently disparate attitudes toward the Bible represented by historical method and theological science.

ARRANGEMENT OF OLD TESTAMENT THEOLOGY

An author's method must be assessed both by what he says and by what he does, that is, in terms of his intention and his execution. Often the congruence, tension, or disjunction between methodological

25

theory and practice will tell us more than the actual conclusions reached.

Eichrodt is at pains to set forth his method in deliberate contrast to what had prevailed previous to his programmatic essay on Old Testament theology written in 1929 [1] and the launching of the first volume of his own theology in 1933 (volumes two and three in 1935 and 1939 respectively).[2] He believed that to date two basic types of miscontruction of biblical theology had occurred. One was "historicism" or "developmentalism," a simplistic and rigid view of history in which a tight, quasi-mechanistic, causal conception of the relation between events was linked with evolutionary views transferred naively from biology to history. So viewed, Israel's religion was seen mainly in terms of evolving ideas and institutions, with a stress on their variety and time-bound character. The other misconstruction, "naive orthodoxy," was in its own way similarly simplistic and rigid in its view of the subject matter, sometimes rationalistic in its treatment of Israel's religion as an arsenal of proof texts for current doctrine and at other times spiritistic in its belief that special guidance entitles the interpreter to find concealed meanings in the biblical text. In either form such orthodoxy substituted dogmatism for historical study and imposed a non-existent unity upon Israel's religion, thereby eliminating the distance between Israel's life and our own life necessary for genuine historical inquiry.

It seemed to Eichrodt that, in contrast to "historicism" on the one side and "orthodoxy" on the other, history must be allowed to stand on its own, that theology must be permitted to do the same, and that each, properly understood, contributed to the other. His Old Testament theology may be understood as a detailed attempt to show how historical and theological disciplines may properly CONVERGE UPON or EMERGE FROM the Old Testament without simply merging with or displacing one another.

[1] Walther Eichrodt, "Hat die alttestamentliche Theologie noch selbstandige Bedeutung innerhalb der alttestamentlichen Wissenschaft?" *ZAW*, 47 (1929), pp. 83-91.

[2] W. Eichrodt, *Theologie des Alten Testaments:* vol. 1 *Gott und Volk* (Leipzig: 1933); vol 2 *Gott und Welt* (1935); vol. 3 *Gott und Mensch* (1939). Eng. trans. by J. A. Baker, *Theology of the Old Testament* (Philadelphia: The Westminster Press, vol. 1, 1961; vol. 2, 1967). Volume 1 © 1961 S.C.M. Press, volume 2 © 1967 S.C.M. Press. All quotations are used by permission.

In the preface to the first volume, restated in his preface to the English edition in 1961, Eichrodt asserts his intention to examine the religion of ancient Israel as "a self-contained entity exhibiting, despite ever-changing historical conditions, a constant basic tendency and character" (I, p. 11).[3] This statement succinctly catches up the fundamental features of his method: an organismic view of history and culture, a significant allowance for historical development, and an ultimate subordination of development to the structural or typical character of the whole.

Accordingly, Eichrodt sees his theology as historical in the sense that it represents a synthesis of the results of mainstream historical study of the Bible. He dubs this synthesis "a cross section" which lays bare the dynamics of Israelite religious thought and practice. His theology is comprehensive in that it aims to encompass "the structural unity" of the religion and, in so doing, to distinguish the essential features from the nonessential.

The problem for Eichrodt is how this comprehensiveness can be achieved without repeating the past unproductive procedures, whose manner of generalizing from historical data must be rejected. It is not sufficient, for example, to describe the historical unfolding of Israel's faith punctuated by occasional summaries. For Eichrodt that would be merely history of the religion of Israel in a pejorative "historicist" sense. Nor is it sufficient to organize the historical data under general headings, such as God, man, sin, salvation, etc. That would be theology of the Old Testament in a pejorative "dogmatic" sense. Nor will it do to write about the essential features of the cross section apart from historical development. That would fall under the stigma of theology of the Old Testament in a "metaphysical" or "spiritistic" sense. All such undertakings he believes to be futile; a new course must be charted.

The only adequate method is for the cross section to be "a typical description of a living process." This means that it is vital *"to have the historical principle operating side by side with the systematic in a complementary role"* (I, p. 32). This would be imperative for the explication of any religion, but it is urgent for Israelite religion because of "the prominence of the personal and historical factors" in

---

[3] *Ibid.* All citations in the text are of the English translation, roman numerals indicating volumes and arabic numerals indicating pages.

it. Eichrodt commits himself to a primarily systematic form of arrangement for Old Testament theology incorporating extensive segments of historical analysis and synopsis in the systematic framework.

But is talk about a systematic treatment of historical data anything more than playing with words? Indeed, what basic principles will assure that the system does justice to the living process of Israelite thought? Eichrodt insists that it is necessary to draw the principles directly from the Old Testament itself and not from categories operative in philosophy of history or in systematic theology, for "we must plot our course as best we can along the lines of the Old Testament's own dialectic. This speaks of a revelation of the God of the People, who in his rule proves himself to be also the God of the World and the God of the Individual" (I, p. 33). This suggests that the best system is threefold: first, thoroughly to explicate Israelite faith under the category "God and the People" (Part I), and afterward, in what amounts to derivative subheadings, to explore the corollary categories of "God and the World" (Part II), and "God and Man" (Part III).

This system allows Eichrodt to emphasize two features of Israelite religion which, while often commented upon, have often been disregarded in the arrangement of biblical theologies. First, the primary topic of Israel's religious records is neither the religious consciousness of Israel nor the being of God. It is rather the intimate and abiding connection between the people and its deity. Therefore, all Old Testament theology must keep the reciprocal communion of God and people in constant view. It is always a matter of God FOR Israel and of Israel UNDER God. Secondly, it is not simply the general relationship between God and man which the Old Testament makes central. There is a peculiarly concrete and limiting focus on God and on the people of Israel. This is done in a deliberate manner, not as though God of the Old Testament simply grew up as the limited counterpart of Israel but rather as though a clearly superior Being limited his relationship to man by focussing it upon a particular segment of humanity which becomes, in that act of divine self-limitation, a corporate body and a congregation. From the primary divinely self-limited relationship with Israel stem implications for the relation of God to all his creation, both in the natural world and among the nations, as well as to individual Israelites. Eichrodt selects the cate-

gories and their sequence with care in order to stress that in Israelite thought God is seen IN RELATION TO MAN and seen, furthermore,
in the procedural order of his RELATION TO ISRAELITE MAN AS A
GENERIC COMMUNITY, followed by his RELATION TO MEN AT LARGE
and to INDIVIDUAL ISRAELITES.

Of course Eichrodt readily admits that this structural unity is not
something explicitly stated in the Old Testament, for he does not
believe that any theological propositions in the full sense appear there.
He argues rather that, taken as a whole, the living process of Israelite religion suggests this tripartite approach as the one way we
can best organize the data of the Old Testament summarily while
remaining in touch with the particularist mind of ancient Israel. The
cross section is a theoretical construct intended to illuminate the rich
detail of Israelite religion by pointing repeatedly toward the inner
unity of its view of reality.

To this point I have avoided speaking of "the covenant," the concept which supposedly best epitomizes Eichrodt's arrangement of the
material, and around which much controversy has swirled. I have
done so because the controversy has been so narrow and superficial
that Eichrodt's intention has been overlooked and any real assessment of the strengths and weaknesses of his approach has been
quickly lost in terminological wrangling. Since the controversy has
been so persistent, however, something must be said about it.

The fundamental category of "God and the People" is in Eichrodt's usage expressible by the linguistic cipher: COVENANT. In his
first edition, however, Eichrodt hardly mentions the concept of covenant in his discussion of methodology. In fact, where he attempts to
state the unity of the living process of Israelite religion and to con-
nect it with the New Testament, he speaks rather of THE RULE OR
KINGSHIP OF GOD, specifically *"the irruption of the Kingship of God
into this world and its establishment here"* (I, p. 26). In defending
the retention of the covenant cipher in the preface to the fifth revised
edition (1957), Eichrodt claims that the term is "a convenient symbol
for an assurance much wider in scope and controlling the formation
of the national faith at its deepest level, without which Israel would
not be Israel" (I, p. 14). By way of decoding the covenant symbol he
sees it as expressing "the explicit or implicit assumption that a free
act of God, consummated in history, has raised Israel to the rank of

the People of God, in whom the nature and will of God are to be revealed" (I, p. 14). That identical assurance or assumption can as well be described by the notion of the kingdom of God.

It appears then that Eichrodt's critics have a point. He could have been more consistent had he not used a term to organize the first part of his theology which, on his own admission, is not used throughout the Old Testament and is only one limited juridical symbol for a much wider belief. In defense of Eichrodt, however, it is hard to see what other term might have been used as a cipher symbol that would have been sufficiently brief and clear. To use either "kingdom" or "communion" (Vriezen's proposal) would have required considerable clarification to avoid certain notions which Eichrodt wants to oppose: firstly, that the kingdom of God can be equated with empirical Israel, and secondly, that the relationship between God and people is a natural connection. Whether those dangers, as accented and elaborated by Eichrodt, are properly the concern of Old Testament theology is a matter of dispute. If we assume that they are, however, then Eichrodt has probably chosen the best available single cipher/symbol for his cross section.

Perhaps the real concern of critics who have questioned Eichrodt's use of covenant typology is the issue of whether the religion of Israel can be regarded as a unity and as somehow normative for contemporary religion. Wherein does its unity consist and how are we the interpreters to regard its truth-value? But these questions would persist under any scheme informed by Eichrodt's presuppositions, and would apply equally to any alternative cipher/symbol he might have chosen. The objections, I am suggesting, ought more clearly to have been directed against his presuppositions about the unity and normativeness of Israel's religion rather than against the one emotionally-charged term. I am inclined to think that the dispute over "covenant" has often masked the deeper question of the ground on which the Old Testament theologian stands when he does his work. To that question we shall return. At the level where the covenant dispute is usually cast, Eichrodt comes off reasonably well. Although he may be faulted for some inconsistency, it is doubtful that any of his critics have shown a more suitable substitute.

Since we have referred to the broad questions of unity and truth-value in Israel's religion, it is pertinent to comment on the relation between Eichrodt's method and wider historical and sociological inquiry. Eichrodt struggles with the baffling question of how the discrete and ambiguous data of history are to be brought into the purview of orderly interpretation. Sociology of religion reaches for the identification of constant features and for the structural arrangement of these features. It seeks for "laws." In spite of Eichrodt's disclaimers about the irrelevance of scientific laws as "bloodless abstractions," there is no doubt that his structural cross section is an effort at scientific description. His "typical description of a living process" is broadly within the orbit of Max Weber's "ideal type." In his *Ancient Judaism,* Weber the unbeliever—like Eichrodt the believer—tries to cope with what it is that gives unity and distinctness to the multi-faceted culture of ancient Israel. The biggest single difference between them is that Weber pierces through the theological superstructure and looks for the socio-cultural ground, whereas Eichrodt treats the theological structure as a meaningful ground in itself. Nonetheless, Eichrodt uses an ideal type which no more totally exhausts the historical data than does Weber's.

Eichrodt has formulated a type something like this: Israelite thought is dominated by the conception of a God who is free, transcendent, ordering will, and whose explicit aim is the creation of a freely responsive and ordered community of men. When we hold up that model to the Old Testament materials much of their diversity and opaqueness is illuminated. That model may indeed account for more of the data than any other. By accepting his model we can appreciate Eichrodt's inquiry as an experiment undertaken by a vastly informed and well organized mind. Naturally, other models are possible which may supplement or replace Eichrodt's. However, to accept his model provisionally as one way of approaching the materials is not in itself to consider the purposes for which such a model can be used. Yet, in the final choice of ideal types we are inevitably led to consider what interests of ancient Israel and what needs of our own either can or cannot be met by the optional types available to us.

CONTENTS OF OLD TESTAMENT THEOLOGY

We have already noted that the skeleton of Eichrodt's theology is his manner of articulating the ways in which God is related to man in ancient Israelite thought. This includes both the persons and groups with whom God is related and the means by which he relates himself to them and they in turn to him. "The irruption of the Kingship of God into this world and its establishment here," the leading theme of the Old Testament, is made tangible in the union of Yahweh and the Israelite congregation, conceived as an organic historical entity but not simply identical with the social and political forms in which the congregation appeared from time to time.

By far the longest section of the *Theology* (511 pages in the English translation) delineates the relation of God to the community of Israel conceived as a people who experience the divine revelation and who live responsively to the God who is revealed. Almost the same space is divided between describing how the God of the covenant is related to nature and to generic humanity (228 pages) on the one hand, and to individual Israelites (298 pages) on the other hand. It is apparent that the fuller treatment of Part I stems from the author's conviction that this is the primary category of Israelite religion, whose proper understanding is the precondition for understanding its secondary and tertiary features. Some of the disproportion is explainable, however, by the fact that aspects foundational to all three sections, or aspects recurrent in all dimensions of the divine-human relationship, are developed only once in Part I and simply referred to at relevant points in Parts II and III. Inevitably the same theme is sometimes treated two, three, or more times. Eichrodt often manages to impart a new perspective which sets the repeated features in a new light, creating suggestive interconnections and reinforcing reader learning; but too frequently there is a redundance of subject matter which the preciousness of style only exacerbates.

In a sense, Eichrodt keeps a firmer hand upon the details of his theology than does von Rad, who deliberately chooses to let the literary traditions stand by themselves and speak in their singularity. Eichrodt's generalizing and summarizing hand dominates the whole, so that, in spite of its bulk, the work reveals a main line of argumentation which stands out with general clarity. The constant reference back and forth among the main sections, as well as within them, serves to focus attention on Eichrodt's central affirmation that Israel's theology is unified by its manner of conceiving God's relation to his creation. No matter how complex or seemingly tangential the matter under discussion may be, Eichrodt repeatedly points out that it is in some way finally connected with a God who is seen in relation to humanity, to nature, and to individual Israelites almost wholly through the Israelite religious community, i.e., ancient Israel regarded as a covenanted body.

Let us note now the more detailed articulation of the subparts, tracing the main line of Eichrodt's exposition and finally assessing how he integrates detail into his intellectual grasp of the subject. Part I, "God and the People," sets forth the pivotal model of the sovereign suprahistorical Yahweh who enters into communion with a people, a communion which both manifests God's nature and elicits a particular quality of life and thought from the covenanted people. This model is contrasted with conceptions of God which are intellectualistic or pantheistic, and conceptions of the people of God which are nationalistic or naturalistic. He sees the history of Israel's religion as the history of a people's struggle to maintain and to develop that relationship in a manner faithful to the revelation and in a manner relevant to changing historical circumstances. It is a history of struggle and challenge, of mutation and elaboration, of departure from Yahweh's revelation and of renewed revelation and commitment. To dramatize the historical character of the revelation and the response, Eichrodt offers an extended account of "the history of the covenant concept" in which he shows the unity of belief about the covenant running through Israelite history and the manifold variations and accents of view which followed one another or existed concurrently. His stress is upon the ultimate unity which permeates the admittedly rich, complex, and often contradictory course of Israelite thought about Yahweh and his people.

Eichrodt next proceeds to fill in details of the covenant conception. He opens the exposition with an analysis of the covenant statutes, first the secular laws and then the cultic laws. He is careful to stress the interconnection of "secular" and "cultic" in Israel's understanding. Again, he incorporates a considerable section where the nuances in attitudes toward law peculiar to different periods and layers of traditions are underscored. Cultic law is shown to be *the medium by which divine power is presented* to men for their participation" (I, p. 99), and the particular ways in which Israel accommodated cult to her covenantal view of God are indicated in topical sections on sacred sites, sacred objects, sacred seasons, and sacred actions (including consecration and purity rites, sacrifices, and prayer). This entails a survey of the main theories about the meaning of sacrifice, in all of which he finds elements of truth. He concludes that the significant thing in Israel is that sacrifice became a bearer of historical religion, was challenged for its abuses, and was finally rendered meaningless by trends toward eschatology, mysticism, and Christian incarnational theology. He stresses that the pagan aspects of the cult were held in check by Yahwism. At the same time the cult served to remind Israel of its concrete ties to a spiritual and personal God. In this section Eichrodt combines topical, historical, and synthetic treatments of the covenant statutes. This approach permits him to move back and forth from fine detail to comprehensive summaries and evaluations.

The angle of approach next shifts from requirements laid on the community to the God who reveals the requirements. He is considered first under the names by which he is called and secondly in terms of the affirmations Israel makes about his being and his activity. The names of God are arranged in three groups: names for God which Israel shares with the Semitic world (El, either alone or in its various compound forms or in the plural), names of God peculiar to Israel (Yahweh, or its short form Yah, or the compound Yahweh Sebaoth), and epithets of God which never became proper names (Melek, Baal, Adon[ai]). This section includes much technical information on etymologies and linguistic constructions. Eichrodt regards "Yahweh" as a probable Mosaic expansion of the shorter "Yah," and for Moses the name probably meant "He is" or "He is present." The important thing for Israel is that the name expresses God's active presence and his *"opposition to all that is merely naturalistic* and part of the phenomenal world" (I, p. 191). As in his treatment of cult, Eichrodt stresses that the multiple names for God were different ways of conceiving the same divine reality.

In moving on to a substantive discussion of the covenant God, Eichrodt distinguishes between affirmations about the divine being and affirmations about the divine activity. Since the author fulminates against the view that speculative theology is to be found in the Old Testament, this distinction is surprising, the more so in that he does not try to justify it. Apparently, Eichrodt means to say that the affirmations about the divine being are those deep underlying assumptions about God which suffuse all the descriptions of his deeds and all the qualities ascribed to him. These affirmations are that God is PERSONAL, SPIRITUAL, and ONE. The active, humanizing way in which God is pictured leads Eichrodt to conclude that "it is not the spiritual nature of God which is the foundation of Old Testament faith. It is his personhood—a personhood which is fully alive, and a life which is fully personal" (I, p. 211). The spiritual qualification of personhood arises to assert that the divine personality is not limited as is the human personality. The two interpenetrating conceptions "point unmistakably to a *superhuman* personality" (I, p. 213). The superhuman personality of Israel's God is also One. This oneness is rooted in the Mosaic conviction that Yahweh rules out all rival deities for Israel and that his reality is not restricted to the official cultus. This belief maintained itself with such shattering force throughout Israelite religious history that an effective monotheism existed long before God's oneness was formally proclaimed. Consequently, the three aspects of divine being are intertwined so as to demonstrate that "the essential factor in the emergence of a vital and moral monotheism was not philosophical speculation, but the experience of God's close and living reality" (I, p. 227). The Israelite outlook is contrasted with nature religions and also with other formal monotheisms or monisms such as the Egyptian belief in Aton and the Hindu belief in Brahma.

The underlying "being" of God is expressed in his many activities which are "couched in precise and concrete terms, adapted to express *the note of personal decision* which marks the Old Testament revelation of God" (I, p. 228). Activities of God which reflect one or more of the attributes of power, lovingkindness, righteousness, love, wrath, and holiness are shown by Eichrodt to be varied ways of indicating his single superhuman personality. In his fairly extended expositions of the affirmations, Eichrodt gives attention to the wide range of attitudes and emphases in Israel's picture of deity. He shows, as an example, that in Deuteronomy divine love upholds the present order of the world, while in the prophets divine love presses toward a wholly new order. He also engages in a polemical defense of the attributes, as for instance, when he insists that neither wrath nor holiness is conceived in the impersonal and capricious way exhibited in other religions. He goes so far as to claim that the wrath of God is not a permanent attribute of Yahweh but only a transient expression of his displeasure with particular human abuses. In synthesis he sees the many strands in the Old Testament picture of God as working toward "increasing logical consistency" along the lines of the model of *a being without limitation who chooses self-limitation in covenant with Israel and who operates from beyond history within history in order to work toward historical goals.* The result is both LOGICAL in the sense that it reaches out to incorporate disparate and ever larger tracts of experience and PARADOXICAL in that it rests upon a belief that the God who overarches all combines apparently opposing features and is, in the last analysis, inexplicable by human standards. Once more, Eichrodt's skill in combining topical, historical, and synthetic approaches to Old Testament faith yields a rich and appealing series of designs within designs in which many types of description and assessment operate on several levels. It is clear that any critique of his work has to take these many levels and modes of argument into account.

Eichrodt next doubles back to the community and examines its leaders under the category of "instruments of the covenant." The charismatic leaders are Moses, the seers (Balaam, Deborah, Samuel), Nazirites, judges, early prophets *(Nabism* before Amos), and classical prophets. The official leaders are priests and kings. Moses is seen as the archetypal mediator from whose many roles the specialized functions of later leaders developed. Attention is given in each case to the activities of the office, as well as to an occasional historical account of the origins and development of the office (e.g., he offers his view of the much debated Levitical office, I, pp. 392-402). The overwhelming weight of this section falls on theological exposition, for Eichrodt tries to construct the outlook on God and man reflected in each of these offices. He works back and forth between the common presuppositions of two or more of the offices and the distinctive features and outright conflicts which separate them.

The personal and historical factors in Israel's religion are brought to the fore as Eichrodt shows the particular mixtures of affirmations about God and assertions of his claims on Israel which were concretized in her official spokesmen. The section on classical prophecy is a *tour de force* defying simple summation. Here the masterly synthesist communicates the dynamic sense of God as a supportive and menacing presence in prophetic consciousness, an accomplishment similar to von Rad's in its passion, incisiveness, and intellectual scope.[4] There is a brilliant grasp of the urgent social and political crises in Israel and Judah which evoked and shaped the prophetic response. That Israelite prophetic thought was an attempt to see communal crises in terms of the demand for a totally new orientation toward the future is powerfully expressed. Eichrodt synthesizes prophetic thought in terms such as these: *"the overall spiritual pattern of classical prophecy as that of a dynamic power released by a new sense of the reality of God"* which "unleashes a forward movement which can no longer be restrained" (I, p. 387). Or he speaks of "the absoluteness of a sovereign authority embracing the whole world" (I, p. 388), one which "calls for steadfast endurance in the fierce tension between present and future . . . between the God who has come and the God who is yet to come" (I, pp. 389-390).

The final two sections of Part I deal with "Covenant-Breaking and Judgment" and "Fulfilling the Covenant." They posit the problem of how the covenant between God and man can continue when Israel has failed repeatedly to live in consonance with the revealed will of Yahweh. The problem poses itself sharply at the close of the monarchic age and supremely in the exile. Then, the early exuberance and naïveté had faded and the only way in which the covenant could be seen as viable would be if God initiated it anew from his side. Thus, the key notion of the kingdom of God intruding itself into history is reintroduced. The covenant with Israel is the bridgehead of the divine dominion but Israel's sedition against the ultimate king threatens collapse of Yahweh's provisional government. Yet, because Yahweh is ruler of the world, he can extend the salvation-hope to Israel on the basis of his grace. Eichrodt shows how Old Testament materials divide over the possibility of the covenant's annulment as they also divide over the radicalness of the measures called for to assure the covenant's continuance. On the whole, however, he describes an increasing somberness in Israel's evaluation of her plight before Yahweh, especially as a result of the prophetic critique of the national self-confidence.

[4] Gerhard von Rad, *Old Testament Theology*, vol. II (New York: Harper & Row, Publishers, 1965), pp. 3-315.

As an integral part of his sketch, Eichrodt lays out the principal forms of the Old Testament hope of salvation in their "bewildering diversity," whether warlike or peaceful, whether cultically or ethically oriented, whether with or without a messianic figure, whether for Israel alone or for all nations, whether looking more to the past or to the future. He sees postexilic Judaism as incorporating elements of the popular salvation-hope and of the prophetic salvation-hope in an unstable and inconclusive manner. This leads Eichrodt to inquire into the origins of the salvation-hope which he locates primarily in the broadly messianic impulses of Israel's early communal experiences as expressed by judges and seers, thus antedating classical prophecy. Myth and cult helped to give vesture to the basically communal and historical hope. Eichrodt distinguishes between national-political hope and communal-religious hope. The two kinds of hope were inter-mixed, but the latter was somehow normative and determinative in Eichrodt's judgment. The basis for this distinction is not altogether clear, but it seems to have to do with the supposed motives of the persons who entertained this or that salvation-hope. Eichrodt closes with the contention:

> It was not because men wished to become a nation, or sought with sorrow a national status that had departed, that they ascribed to Yahweh a restoring action in the future. It was because they knew God, and had made living trial of his sovereign power and his claim to dominion, that in times of crisis they were able to turn their eyes toward a consummation of history that would take the form of the setting up of God's kingdom. It is the man who knows God, who knows God's future (I, p. 501).

This moving passage is nonetheless obscurantist. The Old Testament itself does not discuss the origins of the salvation-hope with any great degree of self-consciousness. Certainly no Yahwist, however "nationalist" his hope, would have conceded that his hope in Yahweh was a form of psychological wish-fulfillment. Therefore, to say that the proper salvation-hope is the one based on knowledge of God is simply not to treat the problem of the source of that hope. This example is one of a considerable number of instances where Eichrodt has mixed the operations of faith and history.

The mixing of genres is further evidenced by Eichrodt's explora-tion of the relation between Old Testament "prediction" and New Testament "fulfillment" at the close of Part I. He rejects the old traditionalist view and instead finds similarities in the texture of Old Testament hope and New Testament salvation. In both *"redemption is linked to time and history, to space and form"* and has to do "with *a once for all, decisive event"* (I, p. 505). Real communion between God and man in history, the kingdom of God on earth, links Old Testament and New Testament. Yet the inexplicability of the early Christian salvation-affirmation lies in the fact that the earth is not yet the Lord's. Only in the mystery of faith can it be asserted that Jesus is the Christ, the culmination of Old Testament salvation-hope. But what sort of logical and scientific claims can be based on faith-knowledge?

We must give much less coverage to the remainder of Eichrodt's *Theology,* confining ourselves to the general structure and to those points which introduce distinctively new elements.

In the second major portion of his *Theology,* "God and the World," Eichrodt examines the modes of God's communication with the world, beginning with the theophany, both in its most physical sense and in its spiritualized forms of the *mal'āk* (messenger) of Yahweh, the *kābōd* (glory) of Yahweh, the *pānīm* (face) of God, and the Name of Yahweh. He then moves on to the cosmic powers of God: his Spirit, his Word, and his Wisdom, which are regarded as more complicated and sophisticated ways of conceiving the divine activity in the world. He tries to mark off the scope and peculiar flavor of each way of conceiving God's connections with the world. Spirit, for example, is examined in its cosmological, soteriological, eschatological, and ecclesiological usages. The differing but related psycho-conceptual functions of spirit and word are described respectively as "animating power" and "expressed thought and will."

Eichrodt next turns to cosmology and creation, which brings him back to the central Israelite model of God as a free spiritual and personal being who posits a world over against himself but maintains close communion with it. He stresses here that "creation" is simply a more general way of regarding the activity of the God of Israel; the creation concept is not an alternative to the covenant concept since it overlaps, elaborates, and supports the covenantal view of God. He shows formal and even substantive similarities between Israelite and Babylo-Canaanite cosmologies but stresses in the end the radical independence of the creation *gestalt* in Israel. His theological temper shows in the argument that the later theologoumenon of *creatio ex nihilo* grew logically out of Israel's view of the creator's sovereignty, while his historical sense concedes that the precise doctrine is not present in the Old Testament, nor could it have been in the absence of metaphysical ways of putting and answering ultimate questions. His section entitled "The Place of Man in the Creation" leads to an analysis of the components of human nature which are shown to be varying ways of describing the one psycho-physical totality (*rūah, nepeš,* etc.). He leans sharply away from H. W. Robinson's view of diffused consciousness toward A. Johnson's analysis of a human totality focused now in this and now in that particular bodily member. So-called "providence" in maintenance of the world is shown to be simply an aspect of the continuing creative activity of God. "Natural law" is the dependability of God's activity. "Miracle" is God's freedom to do amazing things and, more often than not, refers to common events which signifiy God's presence to the faithful. A treatment of the celestial world (Yahweh's heavenly home, angels, cherubim and seraphim, satan) and the underworld (Sheol, the grave, demons) rounds out the section. These somewhat loosely articulated sections allow Eichrodt to explore several atypical or arcane aspects of Israel's religion, such as the role of satan and the problem of ancestor worship. He sees these realms with their strong mythological rootage in the ancient world as sharply restricted in Israel by stress on the single sovereign will of Yahweh.

The final division opens with a complexly nuanced analysis of "The Individual and the Community in the Old Testament God-Man Relationship" in which Eichrodt sets forth a cross section of the relation of individual and community in the various historical periods from Moses to the post-exilic age. He argues that while individualism in the sense of personal responsibility was never lacking in Israel's historical religion, it was brought to the fore by the breakdown of monarchy and the reconstituted community both in its exilic and its restored Palestinian forms. His view of the relation of Old Testament collective piety to individualism is well summed up as follows:

> The religious faith of the Old Testament helped religious individuality to come to life in a context of strong collective ties, because it understood God's demands to the nation as at the same time a call to the individual,

imposing upon him an obligation of unconditional loyalty even when the call ran counter to the natural bonds of community (II, p. 265).

This section contains cogent summations of the collective-individual dialectic in the Old Testament, but parts of the discussion are blurred by an overly-rhetorical style, e.g., "the community called to such a task [eschatological fulfillment] is *from the outset intolerant of any arbitrary restoration of the nation-state by taking advantage of a favourable whim of destiny*" (II, p. 255) ; and also by an annoying tendency to rebut movements of thought and practice in the community by appealing to the pure will of God, e.g.:

> Except where men [late Jewish sectarians], with the help of alien forces, were moving toward a deliberate breakaway from this basis [fundamental principles of the community], the wave of individualism broke against the rock of the strict demand that the whole of life be related to the will of the divine Lord of the covenant, whose declaration in the Law dethroned all human autonomy, and compelled the individual striving after his own perfection to bow to the sovereign authority of a heavenly king who had no need of any human arguments designed to prove or to justify him (II, pp. 263-264).

Such a judgment is wholly beside the point of the sectarian proliferations; the sects arose precisely because it was NOT clear to men what God revealed and they differed sharply in their readings of his will.

Eichrodt then turns to some of the main Old Testament forms for describing man's personal relationship with God: fear of God, faith in God, and love for God. As in his accounts of the attributes of God, the modes of his relationship to the world, and the dimensions of man's nature, so here the types of piety are seen as aspects of a larger whole, shading off into one another and capable of reinforcing one another, although in the form of their combination in late postexilic Judaism they tend toward casuistry and "the lack of a unified religious attitude."

The section on Old Testament morality is articulated by categories drawn from ethics. Apparently Eichrodt saw this as the only feasible way to introduce a cross section into the welter of Old Testament moral judgments and admonitions. So he considers "the norms of moral conduct," "the goods of moral conduct," and "the motives of moral conduct." The basis of this division is not openly stated and the three subsections are among the most formless and repetitious in the book. The main note struck throughout is that Israel's notion of moral conduct derives from a constant pressure of the covenant faith upon notions of the good of which Israel was fully aware as part of mankind and members of the Semitic ethnic group in particular. Under "norms" he talks about those relatively independent imperatives which formed a part of popular morality and were raised to a new level by Yahwism and especially deepened and broadened by prophetism. Under "goods" he speaks of the tension between the natural goods of life which Yahwism accepted and the religious goods which it introduced. The interrelationship between the two—especially in times of natural and historical disturbances—was never satisfactorily worked out, so that "no proper comprehension of the dominant goal of all ethical action was ever attained" (II, p. 365). The "motives" recapitulate the way in which all the "oughts" known to Israel derived from "that *absolute Ought* which, *as* the will of the God of election, laid claim to regulate the whole of life" (II, p. 367). The prophets and D and P reestablished theonomy so that morality and piety were linked and motivated by the unconditional sovereign ought, but this unity was jeopardized by the later emphasis upon law-obedience as the prime or sole motive to moral conduct.

Sin is explicated under the headings of its nature, universality, origin, and consequences, as well as its removal through forgiveness. This section is highly reminiscent of the corresponding part of Otto Procksch's Old Testament theology.[5] Procksch was Eichrodt's teacher to whom the latter gives credit for providing him with the clue to a tripartite development of Old Testament theology. Eichrodt's treatment here is concerned with the relation between later more developed Jewish and Christian notions of sin and their roots in the Old Testament. As expected, he shows continuities while also excluding the presence in the Old Testament of dogmatic formulations such as the later doctrine of inherited original sin.

To his final chapter on immortality, Eichrodt gives the title, "The Indestructability of the Individual's Relationship with God." He sets the resurrection belief in its context both with respect to its religious motivation and its late eschatological form. All thought about life

---

[5] Otto Procksch, *Theologie des Alten Testaments* (Gütersloh: 1949), pp. 632-642.

beyond death in Israel is permeated by a common factor in that the conquest of death in the life of the individual *"is built on the gift of fellowship with God here and now"* (II, p. 525). Characteristically the New Testament proclamation of life in Christ is seen as the epitome and culmination of the varied strands of Old Testament hope.

A few comments about the structure of the theology are in order. It is advisable beforehand to get as clear a conception as possible of the kinds of criticism of Eichrodt's theology which are both possible and necessary. As I see it, there are three kinds of issues with which Eichrodt is dealing, and his accomplishment must be judged separately in the three cases. First, there is the question of the relation between the particular beliefs and practices of ancient Israel and the overall tendency or fundamental form of Israelite belief. Secondly, there is the question of how the various beliefs and practices seen in synopsis are to be set forth, i.e., in what order will ideas be taken up and which of their interconnections will be accented and developed? Thirdly, there is the question of the relation between our DESCRIBING Israel's ancient faith and our BELIEVING in it ourselves. The third order of question will be examined in the next two sections. The first two will be considered here.

What is the unity of conception and sentiment which unites the chaos of Israelite belief and practice over its many centuries of development? We have already seen Eichrodt's main answer to this question. It is a clear and forcibly stated answer: A free transcendent spiritual personal Being has created the world and entered into spiritual and moral communion with Israel with the aim of asserting his will over all aspects of Israel's life and eventually over all aspects of the world's life. Adjectively, Israel's faith is monotheistic, spiritual, personal, communal, historical, and eschatological. If one term is to be used as shorthand for the rest, COVENANTAL most adequately epitomizes the distinctive complex of Israel's faith.

Eichrodt never tires of stating and demonstrating the deep underlying unity amid all the details he ransacks and marshalls. The fact that he can do so on page after page, drawing upon diverse religious phenomena from all the centuries of Israel's existence, is indication enough that he has developed a very convincing ideal type of the general contours and inner dynamic of Yahwism. He does so chiefly in two ways. One method is to show the persistence of themes over long periods of time in which, despite important changes in circumstance and formulation of issues, the continuing concerns have to do with the way in which Yahweh is related to his people, what he expects of them, what he does for them, what they have or have not done in return, and what they must do if they are to respond to the present form of his demand. This approach is well illustrated in his cross sections based on historical panoramas of the covenant concept, of the law collections, of the course of prophetism, and of the relationship between community and individual.

The second method for showing the theological unity in the religious detail is to delineate a complex of concepts or practices and to show—in spite of significant differences in origin and in the aspects of religion referred to—that the totality of the concepts or practices is such as to point toward the one Yahweh and his one enduring will for his people. This approach emerges in Eichrodt's topical analysis of attributes of God, types of leaders, forms of God's relationship to his world, aspects of human nature, types of piety, and views of sin and forgiveness. We characterize these two methods as HISTORICAL CROSS SECTION and TOPICAL CROSS SECTION.

There are of course many demurrers that can be entered as to the adequacy of the model. We may ask if such a model was present to the consciousness of most Israelite believers or was rather restricted to certain leaders and writers of Old Testament books. We need only look at the difficulty Eichrodt has in incorporating the wisdom movement into his structure to realize that the model lies rather loosely upon considerable portions of the Old Testament. We may wonder whether the model has not become so dominating an ideal type that by its iteration Eichrodt tends to overlook the fact that it is only an approximation to reality, a construct which in its actual embodiments showed marked deviations in many directions from the theoretical form in which Eichrodt puts it. Of the model itself we may wonder how largely it partakes of the particular stance of Eichrodt in the Christian neoorthodox tradition against the background of western philosophical thought. Even with these provisos we may agree, nonetheless, that Eichrodt's model is an entirely feasible one and that he applies it with considerable flexibility and deftness and cites a very large body of historical evidence to support it. If his ideal type is abstract and all-encompassing, it at any rate has many connections with the history of Israel's religion and certainly more convincing connections than the previously regnant ideal types of religious dogmatism or of philosophical rationalism or idealism.

But now to the second order of critique. How has Eichrodt succeeded in explicating his view of Israelite faith? Does his arrangement of the materials reflect his view of the ideal type as a historical cross section? The results here are uneven and markedly arbitrary. In facing the procedural questions which have always harassed biblical theologians, Eichrodt takes an eclectic stance. Sometimes he surveys the material in historical sequence (the historical cross section). Sometimes he groups the material into topical units (the topical cross section). In both cases he sometimes merely lays out the data serially and at other times summarizes or synthesizes. Dissatisfaction with any single way of grouping the materials seems to have impelled him to shift about among several possible ways of arranging it. But the line from his conception of the religion to his particular arrangement is not always well-sustained and it is not difficult to see other ways of arranging the material which might have brought out his views of the whole even more strikingly and aptly. His choice of the eclectic approach has resulted in frequent surrender to verbosity, redundance, and tendentious argument. I think it no exaggeration to say that Eichrodt's work might be condensed by as much as one-third and not lose anything essential.

Let us be specific. Eichrodt begins commandingly with his leitmotif of the covenant, but what is there in his ideal type which requires that law should be the first subject he takes up? On the contrary, his belief that law is only one expression of the divine sovereignty suggests that he might more properly have moved directly into his treatment of the covenant God. If his model required the distinction between affirmations about the being of God and affirmations about the activity of God, should he not have defended the distinction with some admission of the implicit metaphysics by which he makes such a distinction, all the more so since he denies metaphysics to the Old Testament? At the same time there is no reason why he should not have transferred the majority of Part II on forms of God's self-manifestation, his cosmic powers, creation, and providence to the similar section on the nature of Yahweh in Part I. Much of Part II has to do with God's specific relation to Israel, and the enlargement of view he there describes is an extension of the powers of Israel's God. The expanded section on the covenant God might then have been followed by treatment of the covenant community, including its leaders and statutes, and a consideration of the relationship of the individual and the community, together with consolidated sections from Parts II and III on the nature of man and on the forms of human piety and morality. The problematic in the continuation of the covenant could have been treated by combining the individualistic coverage of sin and forgiveness and immortality from Part III with the covenant-breaking and judgment and the consummation of the covenant sections of Part I. This arrangement would better have highlighted Eichrodt's insistence that the individual in ancient Israel always remains a part of the historical covenant. In my opinion such an incorporation of Parts II and III into the revised structure of Part I would have allowed much more logical development of the generic and individual facets of the basic communal faith at those points where they were immediately relevant. It would have removed much repetition and thereby have reduced the schizophrenic demands on the reader constantly to refer to what was said hundreds of pages earlier in order to locate the argument to which Parts II and III are frequently merely appendages or elaborations.

Of course it would be gratuitous to believe that such a rearrangement and condensation would meet all objections and produce an unquestioned unity. In fact, the procedure I propose might well awaken Eichrodt's objection that it is a relapse to the rubrics of earlier dogmatic biblical theologies since it yields something like the suspect sequence: God, man, sin, salvation, eschatology. The reply to such an objection is that surely such a traditional topical sequence is in itself no more mistaken than the topical sequence Eichrodt employs in dealing with God and people, God and world, God and man. The critical point is not the specific order in which articles of theology are taken up but the sense of the dynamic interrelation of the parts and their rootage in history (or the lack of such sense) displayed in the specific articulation in question, whether it appears highly traditional or daringly novel.

In any event, since the Old Testament does not contain a systematic theology, some nonbiblical sequence is necessary. I do not believe that Eichrodt's is the best possible one to explicate the model he proposes, although it is undoubtedly better for that purpose than any proposed before his time. As a matter of fact, it is possible to imagine Eichrodt's cross-section method employed in an entirely different manner: for example, as the synoptic-synthetic conclusion to a detailed history of Israel's religion, either in a second half or at points in the history; or in some combination, such as synopses of periods (premonarchic, monarchic, exilic, etc.), and culminating in a synthesis of the whole. There are gains and losses in any method employed. It is my contention that Eichrodt's is not a consistently thought-through arrangement and certainly not one absolutely required by his model. It no more than explores some possibilities in a tentative and suggestive manner.

RELATIONSHIP BETWEEN FAITH AND HISTORY

Given Eichrodt's conception of Old Testament theology as a flowering of historical study, it is to be expected that the consequences of modern critical inquiry into the literature, history, and religion of ancient Israel should play a large part in his theology. The general stance of Eichrodt on historical reconstruction is moderately critical, not of course in the sense that he is only halfway critical, but in the sense that he sees the Old Testament materials as possessing a large measure of historical value for the task of reconstructing the life of ancient Israel. This is evident, for example, in the mediating position he occupies between those who begin the history of Israel's religion with the patriarchs and those who begin it with the occupation of Canaan. Eichrodt assumes that behind the quasi-historical traditions of the Pentateuch an actual historical figure can be discerned in the person of Moses as the founder of Yahwism. This judgment sharply separates him from von Rad who, in concert with Alt and Noth, regards it as impossible to treat Moses as anything more than a legendary construct.

On other matters, Eichrodt accepts the view that not all the Israelite tribes lived through the exodus and law-giving but that, through a process of tradition-extension, they all eventually came to adopt the traditions of Mosaic Yahwism as decisively their own. He accepts the thesis that there was an intense centuries-long struggle between Mosaic Yahwism and Canaanite naturalism. This battle was successfully won by Yahwism only with the help of the prophets and by the radical turn of events in the Babylonian exile which necessitated a total reconstruction of Israelite religion on a renewed Mosaic foundation. Eichrodt admits that Canaanite and other forms of ancient Near Eastern religion had some effect on Israel in the details of the cult and in mythological materials. But this effect is discounted; for the most part, he sees the influence chiefly as a challenge which forced Yahwism continually to define and consolidate itself over against foreign religions.

Postexilic Judaism is seen as a formal triumph for the religion of Moses and the prophets, but at the cost of a narrowing legalism which markedly shifted the center of gravity in the religion from gospellike freedom to lawlike bondage. Eichrodt's assessment of the spirit and shape of postexilic Judaism brings out sharply the disjunction between historical judgments based on sources and evaluative judgments based on other criteria imported by the interpreter. The texture of his historical evidence is more solidly woven for the monarchic period than for any other era. This is to be expected, since there are more extensive sources for that period than for any other. But in the earlier and later periods Eichrodt does not hesitate to draw very large generalizations on fairly meager data. These generalizations lead him to lavish praise for the early premonarchic faith of Israel and, in a fairly high-handed manner, to devaluate the postexilic faith. This tendency should at once be a signal for the reader to question how securely the historical data and Eichrodt's theological evaluations are in harmony.

Eichrodt's historical reconstruction is a fairly typical one in its broad features, reflecting something like a mid-twentieth century consensus of moderate critics. He has confidence that the Old Testament materials, although often fragmentary and largely shaped by interests not specifically historical as we understand the term, do offer the basis for reasonably probable historical judgments. Seldom is the actual sifting of the evidence carried on in the textual discussions. We are more likely to encounter summarizing sentences in which a whole history of discussion on debated points is condensed and a particular conclusion espoused. For example, a crucial judgment about the convenantal ground of Moses' religion is rested on two sentences:

It can be demonstrated that the covenant-union between Yahweh and Israel is an original element in all sources, despite their being in part in very fragmentary form. Indeed this is still true even of those passages where the word *berīt* has disappeared altogether (I, p. 36).

A footnote refers to Exodus 24:9-11 (J); 24:3-8 (E); 34:10, 27 (J2), and to Gressmann's analysis of the J1 passage. This again reflects the ambiguity in Eichrodt's use of "covenant," for he invokes the wider concept when the narrower one is not at hand. The assumption that the term *berith* was originally in pentateuchal contexts from which it has "disappeared altogether" is, to say the least, a gratuitous one. This extremely terse handling of the historical rootage of covenant in Moses is all the more surprising in the light of the large conclusions he draws about Moses' views on the subject (I, pp. 37-45), and the extended treatment of the "re-fashioning of the covenant concept" in which he traces the development of the notion through the JE narratives of Genesis, the eighth century prophets, D, P, the seventh and sixth century prophets, and postexilic psalms and Chronicler (I, pp. 49-69). In a later discussion of Moses as founder-mediator, he develops conclusions about the role of Moses in the covenant-making process which offer no more by way of historical support than to refer back to the sketchy judgments we have just cited (I, pp. 289-296).

If it was Eichrodt's intention to have the historical principle operating consistently within the theological, we should have to say that he has only partially succeeded in bringing them together. By his impulse to strike the cross section, to say what can be said of a summarizing nature about any period or concept, he tends to break short the historical analysis by passing quickly over it, and to assign important steps in the argument to terse or cryptic footnotes or to involuted dialectic-ridden sentences. By not feeling obliged to employ the historical principle in any great depth, except as he chooses, Eichrodt moves the reader along on the crest of his brilliantly modulated typological sketches. Only very specific and pointed questions about his historical base will uncover the fact that it is often skimpy and open to serious challenge. Because this work shows immense erudition and involved style, because the author obviously is well-acquainted with the historical literature and cites it so copiously in footnotes, the reader is tempted to overlook the skeletal historical structure which, in a less ample and more simply written book, would have been far more apparent. By comparison with many other Old Testament theologies, the historical considerations are relatively rich, but judged by Eichrodt's own intention to present Old Testament theology as the culmination of history of religion, the accomplishment is neither consistent nor adequate. To put it another way, historical data are not always marshaled and interpreted in such a manner that the religion being elucidated in the cross section is clear to the reader. In part, this weakness might have been corrected by better organization and ampler historical coverage. But the central factor in the inadequacy seems to be the way in which history and faith are related in Eichrodt's approach, and to that issue we need to devote particular attention.

In the excursus to the English translation of Volume I, entitled "The Problem of Old Testament Theology," the author discusses the relation between the history of Israel as critically reconstructed and "the theological expressions of Israel's historical tradition." The discussion is cast in the form of a debate with von Rad whose rival Old Testament theology Eichrodt rejects as incorrectly conceived. His first major objection is that von Rad cuts the connection between the facts of Israel's history and her theological assertions about history. We need not enter into the intricacies of the debate, but it is noteworthy that Eichrodt reiterates in many ways his fundamental point: Israel's claims about God's action refer to genuine historical events and must not be confined to kerygmatic consciousness. On that main point there is no real difference between the two theologians, for surely von Rad does not doubt that Israel believed God to be at work in history. The real issue that emerges in Eichrodt's exposition is this: How does the theological claim about the meaning of history relate to the history as we can best grasp it? Specifically, what is the direction of movement, from the history critically reconstructed toward the theological claims that arose in the course of the history? Or, from the theological claims regarded as normative toward the historical facts in such a manner that the theology can give us historical information useful in filling out, modifying, or displacing independently-reached historical conclusions?

While the announced intent of Eichrodt is to work from history to theology, his frequent mode of operation is to make theological assertions without textual support or on scant evidence and then to turn the assertions back upon unclear textual and historical situations in order to elucidate them. One disturbing habit of his is to present historical evidence in support of theological conclusions by initially ruling out the many alternative ways in which the historical data could be read. The argument simply becomes circular and unsupported. What are we to make, for example, of the conclusion that the distinctiveness of Israel in Canaan necessarily posits that Moses introduced a covenant with "factual revelation" and "clear divine will"? The undoubted distinctiveness of Israel shows only that a religious solidarity did appear among the people, "a people possessing unity in their situation as clients of a common God" (I, p. 40). Eichrodt has too blithely assumed that the admitted strong belief of Israel about the Mosaic covenant is tantamount to the historical assertion that Moses introduced the belief, and at the same time tantamount to the theological assertion that the way in which Israel understood the covenant must be regarded as the only valid way for the interpreter to view it. Any historian knows, however, that there are endless claims as to the meaning of events and that "descriptive" and "normative" are not one and the same.

There are many instances of Eichrodt arguing from a well-established point of Israel's faith, first to historical conclusions as to how it arose, and secondly to normative claims for the belief. He asserts that "only a Mosaic law-giving can explain the remarkable force and persistence of the true personality of Israel" (I, p. 84). The "only" in such a claim bears much unexamined weight. Similarly he insists that only if we accept the Decalogue and Book of the Covenant as Mosaic "can we get beyond the realm of mere possibilities and attractive suppositions" and that only such a view can explain "the strongly unified character of the Israelite view of the world . . . its robust affirmation of life" (I, pp. 38-39). The first part of the claim contends that unless we accept the tradition of Mosaic origin of certain of the laws we are left with hypothetical alternatives. If Eichrodt intends more than a truism, this must mean that, since certainty is better than uncertainty, it is best to accept tradition. Caricatured, this seems to say that believing will make it so! The second part of the claim purports to show that Israel's unified and robust view of the world could not have developed unless Moses originated the Decalogue and the

Covenant Code. That is a very strong claim and it is odd that Eichrodt leaves us in much doubt as to the sense in which he regards the Law as Mosaic. What does it mean to say that the law "ultimately" comes from Moses? Did Moses give impetus to later collections in the sense of ordering them to be made or rather in the sense of inspiring them indirectly, i.e., by his own emphases contributing a certain direction to them? For so pivotal a contention, these possible meanings should not be allowed to hang at loose ends.

As his work stands, the gradations and textures of historical argumentation are glossed over and telescoped into various statements which seem to be neither wholly historical nor wholly theological and whose bases, rules of evidence, and ramifications are obscure. Perhaps what Eichrodt is aiming at is to show that some historical experience must lie behind the theological developments in premonarchic Israel. This seems to be his meaning in the following: "In this sense the Old Testament tradition is absolutely right, when it says that Moses received the law on Sinai from God himself; for the contemplation of the divine Being must have exercised a decisive influence on its formation" (I, p. 76). But that in itself does not claim that the historical Moses was the contemplator; it merely claims that contemplation of the sort ascribed to Moses occurred in ancient Israel. Yet to move from that general historical position to endorsement of the traditions in their specific claims is to believe that the forcefulness with which a tradition is asserted or repeated is equivalent to demonstration of its historical accuracy. It appears that under the legitimate intention of arguing that certain views of divine reality lie behind the premonarchic traditions, Eichrodt has often taken the further step of validating the historicity of accounts on the basis of their attestation to Israel's faith or even on the basis of their attestation to the Christian faith as it employs aspects of Israel's faith. This style of argument is not always blatant but it is fairly widespread and not under sufficient critical control by the author.

Another aspect of Eichrodt's tendency to impose faith-judgments on history appears in his use of concepts such as "the faith" or "the divine will" as reifications conceived to be working in history in a manner as palpable as the working of human agents. He speaks of casuistic law as "seized upon by this out-and-out religious conception embodied in the apodeictic law" (I, p. 71), or he says, "In the legal tradition . . . is a force at work of a distinctive character" (I, p. 72). Many such statements can perhaps be viewed tolerantly as the writer's liberty to make generalizations by devices of personification or of hypostatization of forces or concepts. Taken in conjunction with his ideal type of personal theism, however, the cumulative result is to emphasize "Mosaic religion" or "covenant faith" as an entity given in finished form at the start and merely unfolding itself in history. His stress upon trends and movements of faith or of unfaith tends to push the historical Israelite believers into the background or to make them figures in a morality play. "This inner dynamic of the covenant concept" virtually replaces the human agents at times, for it "submits uncoordinated traditions" and "integrates them into a systematic sequence of events" (I, p. 50). In the process we are led to forget that it is men, in this case Israelite men, who had the insights and impulses which became dynamic in their history. The generalizing and norm-seeking impulses in Eichrodt frequently override the specifying and descriptive impulses.

We may further illustrate the confusions and contradictions in Eichrodt's view of faith and history by reference to his treatment of the covenant motif as the quintessence of ancient Israel's faith. He glorifies the covenant as an originally pure and virtually self-contained conception, only requiring amplification in changing historical circumstances. He begins to encounter difficulty, however, when he points out that the rise of legalism is an aberration of the covenant notion. How can he so argue, if Moses was both the originator of the covenant and the contributor of law to Israel? Does not the danger of legalism root in the very origins of the covenant? If it is an aberration, is it not a very ancient one, in fact intrinsic to the entire course of covenantal belief? Can legalism be opposed except by adopting some stance outside of the Old Testament faith itself?

Again, perhaps we are unfair to Eichrodt's perspective. It is true that many of his evaluative comments may be read as summaries of criticisms which arose within covenantal history itself, as in the prophets. He is even able to say of the prophets at one point, "the concept of the covenant never proved adequate to the outpouring of the riches of their vision of God" (I, p. 68). Observations of this type are the permissible work of taking the historical cross section, for certainly a proper cross section must show points of tension and opposition as well as points of concurrence in Old Testament religion. Allowing for this necessary work of internal criticism, Eichrodt still blurs the lines between what ancient Israelites thought of their faith and what he thinks about it as a Christian and as a modern intellectual. It is difficult to escape the impression that for Eichrodt covenant has become a cipher/symbol for all the "good" tendencies of Israelite faith, sometimes seen as consciously intended by Moses and sometimes conceived as the outlook reached at some point in Israel's or the church's later life. Thus, he can say that, with the monarchy, "henceforward the covenant also is no longer regarded as an inconceivable gift of grace" (I, p. 48). Does not "henceforward" here imply that there was a time when the covenant was clearly and dominantly seen as a gift of grace? Does this not ignore the waxing and waning of the grace element as a feature of the covenant in repeated problematic relationship to the legalism of the covenant? Is the history of Israel's religion really best seen as an effort to restore a pristine original, or is it more properly regarded as an ever-renewed effort at a contemporary basis for action, an effort which draws now on this and again on that aspect of the past?

Eichrodt has employed his ideal type of the covenant in far too embracing a fashion. Sometimes it is used historically to clarify the beliefs of specific Israelite circles. At other times it is used to sum up the whole course of the religious history. And further it is used to sketch a normative standard for all subsequent Jewish or Christian belief. These several usages are understandable but they are not separated sufficiently in his theologizing. It would be fatuous to imply that there is any simple solution to such confusion of genres; but Eichrodt's undertaking would have been much stronger had he more openly recognized the tension between descriptive and normative and not hidden it under the claim that, since Israel's God acts in history, a theology of the Old Testament must be historical. This failure of conception leaves the Eichrodt of this work (and we are not attempting to assess here his many other significant contributions to Old Testament study) an insufficiently precise historian and an insufficiently systematic thinker. While a great deal of historical material is canvassed and frequently treated with acumen, in the last analysis Eichrodt fails to draw the data together in their own terms or to offer a critique upon them from his own theological stance.

How could this unsatisfactory consequence follow from so brilliant and exhaustive an enterprise? This shortcoming has nothing to do with personal inadequacies of the author. The ambiguity in his attitude toward faith and history is no idiosyncrasy. In this regard Eichrodt epitomizes an entire theological milieu both in his brilliant evocativeness and in his ambiguous impressionism. The Achilles' heel of his work is well articulated in a remark he makes by way of summarizing his treatment of the names of God:

> We are dealing not with the symmetrical growth of a unified basic plan, but with a wealth of tensions, compelling an ever fresh and unique delineation of the knowledge of God. For the divine reality to which this refers is ultimately beyond reason and therefore only to be expressed in contradictory formulations (I, p. 205).

The divine reality beyond reason is Eichrodt's *deus ex machina* which proves useless, for how can there be either a history or a theology of a God who is unknowable? The cross section to which he has committed himself as a tool of inquiry must remain schizophrenically stretched between a historical summary and a theological pointer. In the terms of neo-orthodox theology, in which Eichrodt is broadly at home, there can be no resolution of the tension of faith and history but only an exhilarating zest and incohesiveness which teases and baffles both the historian and the believer.

RELATIONSHIP BETWEEN THE OLD TESTAMENT AND THE NEW TESTAMENT

A word must be said on this subject which is in actuality an extension of Eichrodt's view of the relationship of faith and history. The author positions himself clearly in distinction from orthodox Christian, Jewish, and secularist conceptions of Israel's religion in his manner of relating the two Testaments. In contrast to the orthodox Christian, he does not cite New Testament fulfillment of prophecies nor does he admit miracles as evidence to argue the unity of the Bible. He sees rather a consistent picture of the God-man relationship running through both Testaments,

> for it is these basic features [of the hope in the consummation of God's kingdom on earth], inseparably connected with the essence of the Old Testament picture of God, and not any other individual details, which must decide whether the Gospel of the New Testament has a right to be under-

stood as the real answer to the problem of Old Testament prediction (I, p. 507).

In contrast to the Jewish interpreter, he obviously does believe that the New Testament gospel is the consummation of the Mosaic gospel. At the same time he ignores the fact that postbiblical Judaism approaches the same Hebrew Bible from a very different angle than does he as a Christian. In contrast to the secularist, he argues that the fundamental theological beliefs of ancient Israel, shorn of their crudities, distortions, and time-bound limitations, carry on into the New Testament and form the basis of a valid contemporary view of God and man.

Eichrodt's case for the unity of the Bible is more an assumption than it is an argument. His comments on the subject are strewn through his work and are seldom developed systematically or at length. The result is that he makes random remarks on the theological appropriateness of Old Testament beliefs in a random manner. Often these remarks are introduced as though they are simply of one piece with his historical cross section of Israel's religion. Unlike von Rad, who concentrates his Christian assessment of Old Testament faith in the latter half of his second volume, Eichrodt largely decentralizes his treatment except for brief reflections in the opening pages on methodology and in the closing pages of his section on eschatology (to which may be added his excursus to Volume I).

Especially confusing is his treatment of postexilic Judaism. Sometimes he explicates its character with precision and sympathy, only to dismiss it as a departure from the mainstream of Israel's essential type (e.g., I, pp. 169, 177, 435). His sharp distinction between "good" preexilic cult and "bad" postexilic cult seems largely a function of Christian apologetics. His remark that only Christ brings an *"effective liberation from the need for sacrifice"* (I, p. 171)—not mysticism or legal observance—is hardly a judgment belonging to a culmination of historical study of the Old Testament. It is not a view expressed in the Old Testament nor does it explain the meaning of "effective" in the context, for that would require examination of the sense in which guilt and sacrifice can have contemporary meaning, as at least Bultmann from the side of the New Testament and von Rad from the side of the Old Testament try to do.

His stance as Christian theologian permits Eichrodt to speak with all-knowing condescension toward his subject matter, even though he speaks with benignity. That Jesus alone guards the personhood of God is flatly stated without argument. Eichrodt hands out degrees of reward and punishment to those who did and to those who did not uphold the true type of Israel's religion. Yahweh himself gets very good grades, for Eichrodt is able to praise his "wise self-limitation" (I, p. 213), but P is chided for his "impermissible methods of satisfying religious longings" (I, p. 218). In a highly dialectical analysis he shows how contrary views of nature in ancient Israel come together in a nonconceptual pragmatic harmonization which guards against dangers to the doctrine of God and at the same time reveals God's activity in the world. This carefully modulated harmonization looks less like a historical cross section of the Old Testament than like a broadly Barthian Christian critique of ancient religious belief and practice in Israelite dressing.

Eichrodt should be challenged for failing to identify his own contemporary religious position as highly influential on his method and results. He may further be challenged as to the adequacy of neo-orthodoxy as a basis for synthesizing Old Testament materials. His stance of personal theism assumes direct access to God in terms of New Testament Christianity, but the detailed implications of personal theism for the history of Israel's religion are either absent or blurred by the unknowability of the biblical God except in faith. An uneasy juxtaposition of faith and history, of Christian and Israelite, is the best that Eichrodt can do. The cross section is insufficiently ancient, in that it does not let the Israelite subject's understanding of his own religion stand in its own right; and the cross section is insufficiently modern, in that it does not explore the contemporary meaning of the God-concept for science-oriented, technologized, historicized, alienated man.

CRITIQUE

We have already set forth a critique of Eichrodt's Old Testament *Theology* on a number of counts. We have observed that his historical data are unevenly presented. We have shown his particular manner of articulating the details of Old Testament theology to have been reasonably adequate but in many respects arbitrary and redundant. We have contended that his view of the relation of faith and history is either that they are dualistically separated or naively fused. We have argued that his view of the relation of the Testaments is either undeveloped or arbitrary.

The critique may be extended and concluded by considering two additional points: Eichrodt's use of the ideal type as a normative conception, and his failure to see the intellectual significance of the type and its relationship to contemporary theological typology.

By the first objection, I have in mind Eichrodt's cliché-ridden dismissal of religious elements in ancient Israel which fall under the onus of "mysticism," "naturalism," or "metaphysics." There are abundant illustrations. He attacks mysticism in his discussion of prayer (I, p. 176). The best he can do with mystical aspects of Ezekiel is to speak of the prophet's "illness" (I, p. 341). Inconsistently, in his discussion of the amoral base of holiness Eichrodt defends it on just the grounds he has previously denigrated (I, p. 275). Yet, after a detailed exposition of a broadly "mystical" basis for holiness, he switches and summarizes altogether differently in terms of "the personal quality of God" (I, p. 276). It seems that religious features once absorbed into the dominant Israelite religious type thereby become acceptable and are to be defended apologetically, whereas the same features appearing outside the dominant type are said to be foreign intrusions or eductions. Of course the struggle over what was to be included and what was to be excluded from Israel's faith was a live one, but Eichrodt's way of approaching the problem comes close to simply giving approval in retrospect to those elements which made the grade in Yahwism and disapproval to those which didn't. The angle of approach is often apologetic when it ought to have been heuristic.

As a further instance, Eichrodt believes that ecstasy was never accepted by Yahwism as good in itself, but simply as a means. To judge so is not to enlighten us as to how ecstasy was regarded by individual Yahwists—as though ecstasy simply acquiesced in the face of interpretations put upon it by Yahwistic rationalists (I, pp. 305, 313-319). Aside from the very subjective criterion of "enjoying" or "cultivating" ecstasy in contrast to merely putting up with it, this approach ignores the difference between the universal phenomenon of ecstasy and the particular traditions in which it cloaks itself. Or, consider further that the constant depreciation of nature by Eichrodt is correct only insofar as it touches on one aspect of nature (i.e., the agricultural cults), but even the Exodus and law-giving are broadly "natural," i.e., events with wide-ranging psycho-social and geopolitical setting and significance, a fact which Eichrodt recognizes but does little with because it ill fits his typology.

Particularly heavy-handed are the jaundiced and impoverished views of metaphysical speculation as "bloodless and abstract." As with other pejoratively treated features, speculation which occurs within the covenant community as an aspect of its self-understanding is considered legitimate, but all other speculation is "un-historical" and "intellectualistic." Interestingly, at one point Eichrodt warns against systems of thought but this very warning occurs within the context of his own system (I, p. 389). He inveighs against a logical construction of God in ancient Israel. In the thirties this type of polemics doubtless had its place. Today such an argument looks merely quaint or even absurd, for who today is arguing that Israel had a logical construction of God in anything like the manner Eichrodt opposes? The real question for Eichrodt ought to have been: What was the intellectual/speculative component in Israel's lively concept of God? Eichrodt makes a considerable contribution toward answering that question by the material he marshals but, because he cannot formulate the question as a valid one, he does not even suggest the outlines of an answer.

We must also face the question of the validity of Eichrodt's ideal type of the sovereign free spiritual personhood of God *vis-à-vis* the human community of Israel. The strength of the type is that it does manage to embrace wide tracts of Israelite religious experience and to give them a meaningful pattern. The weakness of the type is that in Eichrodt's hands it tends to become statically normative and even a sacrosanct barrier to further inquiry. The actual result of his accomplishment is that Eichrodt impels us to move outside his framework and to ask how such a type developed and what human needs it served, as well as what needs it frustrated or could not serve. Finally, he goads us into the audacity of asking whether the type is still valid for Jews and Christians.

The point at which Eichrodt comes closest to breaking through his own typology and asking significant questions is in his exposition of prophecy. The section on prophecy is the most exciting in his work, for here he manages to evoke the prophetic view of God as a new reality transcending narrow personalism and nationalism, in fact as a powerful straining at the limitations of existing models of Yahweh and Israel. He says, for instance, "In a world which was racing to destruction, any attempt at representing God, at having God at one's disposal, as a means of escaping judgment and conflict, is, from such a standpoint, objectionable in itself" (I, p. 368). Or, "Men became accustomed to think of the *status quo* as the goal of the nation's history, a goal which no doubt needed improving in detail, but which on the whole was final" (I, pp. 382-383). This interpretation of the prophets might have become the basis for analyzing the intellectual dimension in the work of prophecy. Without the conceptual element in formulating a picture of human potentiality, the God of prophecy can hardly be taken seriously; in fact, prophetic seriousness becomes mere fanaticism. The intellectual work of prophecy is that of a higher order of conception in which older polarities are balanced, transcended, or broken through, and a claim is made about the conditions which must be observed for a good life in human community. But Eichrodt's distrust of metaphysics forces him to relegate the prophetic thirst for the new reality either experientially to their own moments in history or conceptually to modifications here and there in the existing ideal Israelite religious type. Even the prophets in their atypicality become at his hands hypostatized innovators, emasculated in their own historical contexts, or embroiderers of the traditional views of God.

The approach adopted by Eichrodt either closes or discourages inquiry into the ideal type itself, into its origins, functions, and potentialities for the present. The translator of the English edition puts the contemporary question succinctly when he asks: "Are we to go on believing in this kind of God, or not?" (J. Baker, II, p. 10). In the sixties the translator sees the issue rather more sharply than did the author in the thirties. Clearly both he and Eichrodt think that we are to go on believing within the confines of an ideal type not greatly changed since the time of Moses. Eichrodt's theology is a monumental expression of that type in its ancient Israelite form as well as an implicit celebration of its moral and spiritual relevancy for the present.

For many religiously oriented people today it is clearly inadequate to accept the Jewish-Christian traditional God-concept as finished and complete, to foreclose in short the kind of daring venture prophecy represented in its day. To rise to the whole challenge of the historical present and to act resolutely and venturously for the welfare of man requires of them that they rescrutinize the Jewish-Christian God-concept in the light of its psycho-social origins and functions. For them it is not enough to deliteralize and liberalize the concept while leaving its main outlines intact. For them the question now is: What can we believe, who stand in a tradition of belief in this kind of God, now that such belief has become patently dysfunctional and counter-productive? To what aspects of reality does the biblical concept of God point, and how can we decode it in terms that will contribute toward new models of reality as the basis for organizing thought and action?

As a piece of historical analysis and synthesis on a grand scale, Eichrodt is the stimulant of everyone who reflects on ancient Israel's faith. In the history of religious thought he shows one dominant view in the West of God rising and striking tenacious rootage. As a largely implicit defender of that view as valid for today, he raises many more problems than he treats. His way of looking at ancient Israel as the builder of a many-sided but centrally focused God-concept may be supplemented and revised by sociological and psychological analysis to provide the basis for new understandings of traditional theology which may help us to turn these historic concepts from burdens and idols, requiring uncomprehending homage, into tools and materials which are consonant with thought and action—as indeed the concepts once were for those who fashioned them.

SELECTED BIBLIOGRAPHY

Eichrodt, W., *Die Quellen der Genesis von neuem untersucht.* Giessen, 1916 BZAW 31).

————, *Man in the Old Testament.* Chicago, 1951. (Studies in Biblical Theology 4). Translation of *Das Menschenverständnis des Alten Testaments.* Zürich, 1947. (Abhandlungen zur Theologie des Alten und Neuen Testaments 4).

————, *Gottes Ruf im Alten Testament.* Zürich, 1951.

————, *Israel in der Weissagung des alten Testaments.* Zürich, 1951.

————, *Krisis der Gemeinschaft in Israel.* Basel, 1953. (Basler Universitäts-reden 33).

————, *Das Gottesbild des Alten Testaments*. Stuttgart, 1956. (Calwer Hefte 1).

————, *Theology of the Old Testament*. London, 1961-1967. Translation of *Theologie des Alten Testaments*. 5., neubearb. Aufl. Stuttgart, 1957-1961.

————, *Der Prophet Hesekiel*. 2 vols. Göttingen, 1959-66. (ATD 22).

————, *Der Heilige in Israel; Jesaja 1-12*. Stuttgart, 1960. (Die Botschaft des Alten Testaments 17:1).

————, *Der Herr der Geschichte; Jesaja 13-23 und 28-39*. Stuttgart, 1967. (Die Botschaft des Alten Testaments 17:2).

————, *Die soziale Botschaft des Alten Testaments für die Gegenwart*. Basel, n.d.

————, "Der Sabbat bei Hesekiel," in *Lex tua veritas*. Festschrift H. Junker. Trier, 1961, pp. 65-74.

————, "Das prophetische Wächteramt; zur Exegese von Hes 33," in *Tradition und Situation; Studien zur alttestamentlichen Prophetie*. Artur Weiser zum 70. Geburtstag. (E. Würthwein and O. Kaiser, eds.). Göttingen, 1963, pp. 31-41.

————, "Im Anfang; zur Erklärung des ersten Wortes der Bibel," *TZ* 20 (1964), pp. 161-171.

————, "Bund und Gesetz; Erwägungen zur neueren Diskussion," in *Gotteswort und Gottes Land*. H. W. Hertzberg zum 70. Geburtstag. (H. Graf Reventlow, ed.). Göttingen, 1965, pp. 30-49.

2
Gerhard von Rad
Old Testament Theology

by G. Henton Davies

Gerhard von Rad was born on October 21, 1901, at Nurnberg to evangelical parents, and was educated at the Universities of Erlangen and Tübingen. In 1930 he began as a privatdozent *at Leipzig, and subsequently served as a Professor in the Universities of Jena (1934-1945), Göttingen (1945-1949), and lastly (1949-present), at Heidelberg.*

GERHARD VON RAD HAS BEEN A REGULAR CONTRIBUTOR to Old Testament studies since 1929, although his main works were published between 1947 and 1960. His major writings include his studies on Deuteronomy; his commentary on Genesis; his two volumes of *The Theology of the Old Testament;* and a representative selection of his essays, extending from 1931-1964, which were translated and published as *The Problem of the Hexateuch and other Essays* in 1966, though the bulk of these were written in the late 1940's. The general outlines of von Rad's position have been widely known for a long time. His early essay on the Hexateuch, already mentioned, will be a convenient point with which to begin an appreciation and critique of one who undoubtedly belongs among the leading scholars in the world because of the originality of his contribution to Old Testament studies.

THE TRADITIONS-HISTORY FOUNDATION

In his essay on the Hexateuch von Rad seeks to depart from the admitted sterility of contemporary (1938) study, seen both in the end

65

of the usefulness of the source analysis of the documents of the Hexateuch and in the lack of study of the history and meaning of all the units of tradition of which the Hexateuch is composed. He finds it possible to break away from the stalemate by seeing the Hexateuch as "a history of redemption," basically "a creed." The study of the creedal passages in the Hexateuch in their constant feature (namely, of content), and in their variable feature (namely, the varying modes of their expression), became the starting point of his original contribution.

He considers first the short historical credos as they are illustrated in Deuteronomy 26:5b-10, the prayer for the presentation of the first fruits at the sanctuary; in Deuteronomy 6:20-24, a formula of the facts of Israel's redemption; and in Joshua 24:2b-13, Joshua's address to the gathered people at Shechem. Further examples of this basic literary type may also be found in poetic forms of the credo in such passages as Psalm 136, which goes back to the creation; in parts of the Red Sea Song, Exodus 15:4-5, 8-9, 10a, 12-16; with a wider scope and with more liberty from the traditional form in Psalm 105 (cf. vv. 8ff., 42); in Psalm 78; in the late Psalm 135; in the great prayer in Nehemiah 9:6ff., where for the first time the tradition concerning Sinai is interpolated into the "canonical story of redemption"; and lastly in Psalm 106, which ranges from the beginnings to the exile.

This review of the credos led von Rad to point out the omission of the events of Sinai and thus to suggest that the Sinaitic tradition had its own separate origin and transmission, and that only at a much later date was it combined with the other and canonical pattern.

Von Rad then turns to the investigation of the Sinai traditions, distinguishing the Kadesh narratives (Exodus 17–18; Numbers 10–14) and the Sinai cycle proper (Exodus 19–24, 32–34), of which only the former is closely connected with the story of the Exodus. The Kadesh and Sinai cycles of tradition are both concerned with a giving of the law (cf. Exodus 15:25; 18; with Exodus 19–24), and this duality presents an acute problem to the Old Testament interpreter.

The Exodus tradition is primarily one of redemption (Exodus 3:7ff. relating to the move from Egypt to Canaan), but the Sinai tradition is a unity of theophany and covenant (cf. Deuteronomy

33:2, 4; Judges 6:1; Habakkuk 3, where the theophany is the signal feature). To establish its character in this way leads to the consideration of the place of this tradition in the life and worship of ancient Israel. The constituent elements of the Sinai tradition presuppose a cultic situation; and these elements are: a hallowing, the trumpets, the theophany and divine requirements, and finally, sacrifices and covenant. In turn, these elements have led scholars like S. Mowinckel to suggest that the Sinai cycle is best explained in terms of the Jerusalem New Year Festival.

More important for von Rad than a solution in terms of the New Year Festival is the consideration of the Sinai narrative as a prototype for some cultic ceremony. The legend comes first, and that legend, comprising theophany and law, is further if indirectly illustrated in such passages as Psalms 50, 81 (cf. Psalms 15 and 24), as its occasion is suggested by such passages as Deuteronomy 31 and Nehemiah 8. Von Rad then further illustrates and confirms his thesis by a consideration of the liturgical form of Deuteronomy as a whole. Exodus 19–24 and Deuteronomy as a whole are parallel forms which belong to the same cultic situation in varying degrees of closeness. That cultic occasion associated with Exodus 19:1 was the Feast of Weeks, but the Feast of Tabernacles eventually has a stronger claim on the Sinai tradition (Deuteronomy 31:10; Nehemiah 8). A further analysis of the procedure at Shechem (Joshua 24) in comparison with the Sinai covenant shows that the Sinai tradition had its setting in the covenant ceremonies of the Israelite amphictyony at Shechem. Likewise the settlement tradition can be traced to the Feast of Weeks (Deuteronomy 26:5ff.; Exodus 23:16; cf. Leviticus 23:17) at the sanctuary of Gilgal.

Von Rad then shows how the tradition became literature. As the units of tradition were cut off from cultic contexts, they began to be reassembled in new literary and spiritual patterns. Such was the work of J and P. J interpolated the Sinai tradition into the settlement tradition, and the two traditions together illustrate Law and Gospel, which von Rad calls "two fundamental propositions of the whole message of the Bible." Then J added the various cycles of patriarchal and primeval legend to form the introductions to the enlarged settlement tradition, and thus united the history of creation with that of redemption, for which Genesis 12:1-3, with its threefold promise,[1] serves as a freely composed link passage. In this way J collected many of the units and cycles of the separate traditions and combined all the traditions to give us the so-called J work. The original traditions were thus removed from the cultic sphere into the service of that greater Israel of historical and political dimensions. Thus J illustrates a truly prophetic point of view whereby God is seen to be active in history, particularly in the events associated with the settlement in Canaan and with the rise of the Davidic dynasty.

On the basis of this reconstruction and transformation of Israel's traditions von Rad developed his study entitled *The Theology of the Old Testament*. In volume 1, following a brief outline of the history of Yahwism, he creates a theology of Israel's historical traditions embracing the Hexateuch and all its themes, together with the settlement. Further sections deal with Judges and the monarchy, the works of the Deuteronomist and the Chronicler. The fourth and final section of volume 1 of his *Theology* deals with Israel's response as seen in the Psalms and the wisdom literature.

The second volume of von Rad's *Theology* is concerned with general considerations relating to prophecy, then with an exposition of classical prophecy from Amos through Daniel. The final section of this second volume deals in an extraordinarily fruitful manner with the relation of the Old and New Testaments.

Such in main outline is the contribution of this great scholar to the understanding of the Old Testament, a contribution original in itself, comprehensive in its scope, relevant, and interesting, as well as professionally important for the scholar and the Christian.

The critical evaluation of so great a contribution is not easily accomplished within the space of a few pages. To deal adequately with the presuppositions and tendencies of the contribution would demand a treatment as detailed as the original. Inevitably then, the evaluation must be selective.

An obvious point from which to begin is von Rad's conception of the character and function of the credo in Israel's literature and religion. Von Rad tends to assume that the credos were intended as complete entities, but it is by no means certain that they were in-

---

[1] Cf. Ronald E. Clements, *Abraham and David: Genesis XV and Its Meaning for Israelite Tradition,* Studies in Biblical Theology, Second Series 5 (Chicago: Alec R. Allenson, Inc., 1967), pp. 15ff.

tended to be complete in their references. They were intended rather to be select summaries and not exhaustive agendas of the facts they record. Bright points out that the New Testament *kerygma*, for example, does not refer to the Last Supper.[2] Perhaps this is not a very happy example because the *kerygma* does refer to the death of Jesus, and so by implication refers to the associated complex of Cross traditions. Even so the *kerygma* does not refer to Caesarea Philippi (Mark 8:27-33), often recognized as the crisis and turning point in the gospel. The omission of Caesarea, and possibly the ensuing Transfiguration, from New Testament creedal passages does not support the conception of a credo as a complete summary of the events in question.[3]

A further striking illustration of incomplete credo is to be found in one of von Rad's own examples. Psalm 136 approaches the Egypt theme in vv. 10-16 through the creation of man. This is astonishing when the parallel between the psalm and Genesis 1 is recalled. The psalmist has used the tradition of Genesis 1 without reference to the climax of that tradition.[4]

The absence of reference to the Sinai traditions of which von Rad makes so much is essentially an *argumentum silentio,* and may not be pressed. Thus, if these credos were really prefaces to or parts of a liturgy for the renewal of the covenant (i.e., Sinai theme), then the absence of the main theme of the festival from the preface to that festival is intelligible. In other festivals, as for example, that of the First Fruits of Deuteronomy 26, the Sinai theme is not even relevant or useful.

There is, however, a further point which is of considerable importance in the assessment of von Rad's credo. He appears to assume that the statements of the credo mark the beginning or fountainhead of the streams of tradition. Accepting the credo as the beginning, the

[2] John Bright, *Early Israel in Recent History Writing,* Studies in Biblical Theology, Series 9 (Chicago: Alec R. Allenson, Inc., 1956), p. 105.

[3] In spite of the distance in time between Old Testament and New Testament creedal statements, the analogy is probably valid because of the character and content of the creedal sentences in both Testaments.

[4] Gerhard von Rad, *The Problem of the Hexateuch and Other Essays,* trans. E. W. Trueman Dicken (New York: McGraw-Hill Book Co., 1966), pp. 9-10.

various scholars following von Rad are then concerned to work out the principles that control the expansion of the credo into the themes, and then into streams, or strata, or documents, of the tradition.

This assumption that the credo is the beginning of the growth of tradition is probably the fundamental error. The credos are not points of inauguration; they are rather summaries of known tradition. Just as the *kerygma* in the mouth of Peter and the others in the early chapters of the book of the Acts of the Apostles is a hortatory summary of the experiences through which they passed and of which they had been the personal witnesses, so the Old Testament credos are summaries of already existing larger complexes of traditions.

Similarly von Rad's creedal summaries are not only the proleptically creative or magnetic points of an expanding tradition, they are also retrospective deductions from the traditions which afford an anticipatory analysis of what came to be its present content.

The creedal statements in the credos and the themes in the Pentateuch belong together, and so far as the credos go have always belonged together as the mnemonic or liturgical or catechetical recollections of widely known, widely accepted complexes of tradition.

R. E. Murphy in his review of the first volume of von Rad's *Theology* wisely remarks: "Thus there is reason to doubt that the presence or absence of a theme in the original confessional formula of [Deuteronomy 26:5ff.] can carry the weight which [von Rad] attaches to it." [5] Other writers have pointed out that von Rad's point of departure, namely, Israel's confessions of faith illustrated in the credo, does not permit the conclusions which he proceeds to draw.[6] B. Vawter rightly points out: "One might certainly hope for more exercise of the control of archeology which in the long run may have more to say about Hexateuchal history than the reconstruction of what lies behind cult-legends." [7] Israel attempts to write and preserve historical traditions not merely because of the needs of cultic occasions, but also because, as Vawter points out, her gift for etiology points to an embryonic historical sense, resulting from Israelite in-

[5] Roland E. Murphy, *CBQ*, 20 (1958), p. 259; cf. N. H. Snaith, *SJT*, 19 (1966), pp. 352-353; Walter Beyerlin, *Origins and History of the Oldest Sinaitic Traditions*, trans. S. Rudman (Oxford: Basil Blackwood, 1965).

[6] Bruce Vawter, *CBQ*, 21 (1959), pp. 221-223.

[7] *Ibid.*, p. 222.

dividuals who enjoyed the gift of narrative and others who enjoyed the listening, and also as consequence the Israelite sense of Yahweh's causality in history.

The assumption of these and other assessments of von Rad's separation of the Sinai traditions from those of the Exodus is that von Rad has made out his case that the Sinai traditions and the figure of Moses really are absent from the creedal confessions. In turn these scholars then proceed to justify the omission of the Sinai features, and to find compensation for that omission in other factors and considerations.[8] To pursue such considerations, and to discuss the credos as historical prologues to covenant and as the responses of the people in such contexts (Psalms 78, 105, 106, 135, 136), would be to be deflected into post-von Radian studies. Instead a prior consideration must be investigated.

Actually it is not even certain that Moses is absent from some of the credos. A comparison of the following passages at the points where Moses "ought" to appear is instructive.

No reference to Moses	*Reference to Moses*
Deuteronomy 26:8 And the LORD brought us out of Egypt with a mighty hand and an outstretched arm, . . . terror, . . . signs . . . wonders. . . .	**Joshua 24:5** And I sent Moses and Aaron, and I plagued Egypt with what I did in the midst of it.
Deuteronomy 6:21-22 . . . brought us out of Egypt with a mighty hand; and the LORD showed signs and wonders. . . .	**1 Samuel 12:8** . . . and the LORD sent Moses and Aaron, who brought forth your fathers out of Egypt. . . .
Psalm 136:11-12 . . . and brought Israel out from among them . . . with a strong hand and an outstretched arm. . . .	

[8] The reader may be referred to the very important article by Herbert B. Huffmon, "The Exodus, Sinai and the Credo," *CBQ*, 27 (1965), pp. 101-103, for a brief resumé of criticisms of von Rad's separation of the Exodus and Sinai themes, and for references to the relevant literature.

So also	So also
Psalm 78:11	Psalm 105:26
Miracles that he had shown them.	He sent Moses his servant, and Aaron whom he had chosen.
Psalm 78:12	
Marvels in the land of Egypt.	
Psalm 135:9	
Sent signs and wonders.	
Nehemiah 9:10	Nehemiah 9:14
Signs and wonders.	And a law by Moses thy servant.

With the exception of the Nehemiah passage, there appear to be two ways of describing events in the Exodus. In the left-hand column there is no reference to Moses, but there is a reference to a mighty hand or alternatively and in the later passages to miracles, marvels, signs, wonders; in the right-hand column Moses and Aaron appear, but there is no reference to a mighty hand and an outstretched arm. There seems therefore to be a *prima facie* case for supposing that "mighty hand' and "outstretched arm," may refer to Moses.

The narratives of the book of Exodus tend to confirm this. In 3:20, "So I will stretch out my hand and smite Egypt with all my wonders which I will do in it," is the preface to the story. In 7:4ff. there is a similar reference, "then I will lay my hand upon Egypt" (cf. 6:6). These references are general statements and in their context have naturally no immediate sequel or fulfillment. Within the plague stories themselves the threat of the DIVINE action is generally followed by a statement of its HUMAN fulfillment; for example, 7:17 reads, "Thus says the LORD, 'Behold, I will strike the water . . . with the rod that is in my hand.'" But in 7:19, "And the LORD said to Moses, 'Say to Aaron, "Take your rod and stretch out your hand over the waters of Egypt," ' " and in 7:20, "He lifted up the rod and struck the water."

What the Lord threatens Moses and Aaron fulfill; Exodus 7:25 thus concludes "after the LORD had struck the Nile." Compare 8:2 with vv. 5-6 (God threatens and Aaron only carries out the threat); and 8:16 with 17 (cf. v. 19). In the story of the flies (8:20-24), and the plague on the cattle (9:1-7), the Lord threatens and carries out his threat. In the plague of boils Moses and Aaron perform the act, following the divine instructions (9:8-12; compare also the darkness in 10:21-22, in which Moses only acts). Compare 9:18 with 12-13 (Moses only). Thus with the exception of the flies and the cattle plague, the threat of the Lord is actually carried out by Moses and Aaron, or by Aaron or Moses separately. Again, in the song of Moses, "Thou didst stretch out thy right hand, the earth swallowed them" (15:12) is the poetic description of "Then Moses stretched out his hand over the sea" (14:21, 26-27).

Thus it may be suggested that "a mighty hand and an outstretched arm" are the incognito of Moses. This is almost explicitly stated in the words, "all the miracles which I have put in your power" (Hebrew, "your hand," Exodus 4:21; cf. Deuteronomy 34:11-12). It is therefore by no means certain that von Rad's claim that Moses is not mentioned in the credos is sound. In the anonymous credos Deuteronomy 26 and 6, it is probable that Moses appears under the incognito "a mighty hand and an outstretched arm." It thus seems that in these phrases there is an overlay of meaning and actualizing of thought, so that the phrases themselves would suggest to the hearers or readers the fulfillment in the work of Moses and Aaron.

RELATIONSHIP BETWEEN FAITH AND HISTORY

Von Rad set out to write a theology of the Old Testament in what he claimed was the only way in which such a work could be attempted. Both his chosen method and the final outcome have incurred varying degrees of criticisms. The major question in the evaluation of von Rad's position is the methodology of his theology.

His new methodology was the recognition and relevance of traditions. So he set out to describe the Old Testament, and thus defines his method: "Re-telling [*Nacherzählung*] remains the most legitimate form of theological discourse on the Old Testament." (I, p. 121) [9]; as N. W. Porteous remarks: "The retelling is brilliantly done." [10] This descriptive retelling brought von Rad face to face with

[9] Gerhard von Rad, *Old Testament Theology* (New York: Harper & Row, Publishers, vol. 1, 1962; vol. 2, 1965). All citations to this book in the text are given in parentheses, roman numeral indicating the volume and arabic numeral the page.

[10] Norman Porteous, review of von Rad's *Theology* in *ET*, 74 (1962), p. 72.

what may be described as the intractible material of the Old Testament when only a critical-historical or a religious-theological method is employed. As long ago as 1787, J. Gabler tried to distinguish between what he called a biblical theology which was intended to be historical in design and purpose, and the more formal dogmatic theology. Successive scholars like Schultz, Sellin, Wheeler Robinson, and Procksch (to mention but a few), devoted either separate sections or even separate volumes to the history of Israel on the one hand, and to Old Testament theology on the other.

Inevitably then the material characteristic of the Old Testament forced upon von Rad the distinction between secular and sacred history—between *Historie* and *Heilsgeschichte;* and the proper treatment of the Old Testament requires adequate recognition of each type of material and the method of study appropriate for each. Inevitably any student or expositor will incline to one or other type of material. The exposition or retelling of the Old Testament will favor the divine strains of Scripture or be content with the more human story.

Now von Rad emphasizes the importance of *Historie* and, as H. Hummel observes, "does anything but minimize *in principle* the importance of history." [11] Nevertheless his starting point in the credos, his concern with "cultic memory and cultic celebration," his resultant preoccupation with *Heilsgeschichte,* and the fact that he "was the first to develop his theology around the credo or theme of 'the mighty acts of God' " [12] shows where his perhaps unconscious sympathies and certainly his eventual findings have their place. Inevitably criticism has been directed against his presuppositions and conclusions concerning the historical aspect of his study. Thus as J. Muilenburg points out: "No one has really grappled with the difficulties of a biblical theology so well as he, but it is precisely his historical formulations which make his work unsatisfactory to those who are more 'theologically' minded." [13] H. Hummel regrets that "von Rad often *does* depart unnecessarily from a literal reading of

[11] Horace Hummel, *Dialog,* 3 (1964), p. 76.
[12] G. Ernest Wright, "Old Testament Scholarship in Prospect," *JBR,* 28 (1960), pp. 182-193.
[13] James Muilenburg, "Old Testament Scholarship: Fifty Years in Retrospect," *JBR,* 28 (1960), p. 180.

the Old Testament." [14] Or, again: "We feel against von Rad that creative liturgies dare not take precedence over historical memory or tradition, however important the cult may have been (and probably was) in secondarily shaping the tradition for liturgical purposes." [15] Hummel thus rightly deplores von Rad's neglect of history and excessive scepticism, claiming that von Rad's position would have found confirmation and support if only he had been more sympathetic to the reliability of the traditions.

D. N. Freedman contributes one of the best brief reviews of von Rad's commentary on *Genesis* in which he makes the following observations. It is right to "question von Rad's reconstruction of the history of tradition in Israel, and its literary formulation." [16] Or again: "But we contend that the liturgy of any particular festival is derived and adapted from the great common body of tradition, already fixed in its general structure and content for all Israel, rather than the other way around. The narrative tradition of the Hexateuch is not the by-product of cultic recitation, but rather the source of it. Tradition is rooted finally in the chronological and historical experience of Israel and its ancestors, and not in the dramatic reality of cultic celebrations." [17] N. W. Porteous sums up the position thus: "Von Rad seems to avoid facing up to the problem of history." [18] And many, perhaps the majority, would agree with R. E. Murphy in his review of volume I of von Rad's *Theology*: "This reviewer is inclined to recognize more of objective history in the *Heilsgeschichte*." [19]

Recognizing this lack of historical sensitivity in von Rad's work, we may nevertheless say with B. W. Anderson that von Rad presents us with "a new methodological approach to the subject which puts this book in a class by itself" among recent theologies of the Old Testament.[20] However imperfectly von Rad seeks to grapple with both the human and divine aspects of the Old Testament, so often

[14] Hummel, *loc. cit.*
[15] *Ibid.*
[16] David Noel Freedman, review in *TT,* 20 (1963), p. 115. Reprinted with permission of *Theology Today.*
[17] *Ibid.*
[18] Porteous, *op. cit.*
[19] Murphy, *op. cit.*, p. 259.
[20] Bernhard W. Anderson, *Interpretation,* 19 (1965), p. 339.

the study of the Old Testament leads to an exclusive *Heilsgeschichte,* harbinger of a literal fundamentalism; or to a skeptical rejection, characteristic in varying degrees of so many scholars from Wellhausen to Bultmann; or to a typological or "spiritual" interpretation, recurrent at intervals in the history of ecclesiastical interpretation of the Bible. In seeking to avoid a too-easy acceptance, or a too-great rejection, or a spiritual bypass of the Old Testament traditions, von Rad seeks to pay due regard to both *Historie* and *Heilsgeschichte,* to history and confession, to fact and faith. He is largely in the position of a student of Christology. To study the Scriptures relating to the doctrine of Christ is to be confronted with divine and human elements which cannot be fully resolved by *Historie* or by *Heilsgeschichte* in isolation.

An example will perhaps help to illustrate the problem. Sooner or later the exegete is faced with the verse: "And the Word became flesh and dwelt among us" (John 1:14). The Greek may be given a minimal rendering "And the Word was—or happened—flesh," whereby the fact of the event is described. On the other hand the more customary rendering is: "And the Word became flesh," whereby, even at the cost of some over-exegesis, the process of the event is mentioned. Two further verses may be cited in partial explanation of each rendering. Peter's words in Acts 2:22 describe the fact or *Historie* of John 1:14; "Jesus of Nazareth, a man attested to you by God with mighty works and wonders and signs." But Paul's words in Colossians 1:19 attempt to describe the character and process of John 1:14, in brief the *Heilsgeschichte* of the passage: "For in him all the fullness of God was pleased to dwell." Thus any exegesis of John 1:14 must deal adequately with the human and divine valuation of Jesus Christ. When Archbishop Bernard's comment on the first verb of John 1:14 is recalled, then the difficulty of interpreting the verse is apparent: "To explain the exact significance of 'became' in this sentence is beyond the powers of any interpreter." [21] Precisely the same difficulty obtains in interpreting the advent, theophany, presence, revelatory, and redemptive components in the Old Testament. Neither a religious history nor a systematic theology is separately adequate to

[21] John Henry Bernard, *A Critical and Exegetical Commentary on the Gospel According to St. John,* vol. 1 (New York: Charles Scribner's Sons, 1929), p. 20.

a Christology or to the exposition or the retelling of the Old Testament.

To overemphasize the *Historie* is to incline to an Ebionitic view; to overemphasize the *Heilsgeschichte* is to incline to the Docetic view. In seeking to interpret the Old Testament or Christ, the interpreter is almost condemned to failure before he begins, for his task is to hold the divine and human in balance.

Inevitably various writers have denied that von Rad's *Theology* is properly so named. B. W. Anderson questions whether von Rad really satisfies the element of *logos* in his *Theology*.[22] R. C. Dentan considers the *Theology* (volume II) to be "a study in the history of traditions" which should be read for its incidental contributions, rather than a textbook in Old Testament theology.[23] The validity of the charge must be admitted, but how else could von Rad describe his *magnum opus?* The same difficulties have been felt in the discussion of the theology of Christ. Only here they have led to a new term, "Christology." If von Rad could have described his work as an Old "Testamentology," he could have avoided the charges that he had not dealt with the nature of the reality described in the traditions (R. C. Dentan), or that he had failed to define the framework or structure of Israel's faith (G. E. Wright), or its distinctiveness in the context of other religions. In spite of his title, then, and despite his presuppositions, and despite his neglect of history, von Rad has produced a new, original, and exciting approach to the context of the Old Testament which is descriptive, cultically based, yet which tries to see all sides of the Old Testament as a whole, which reflects the Old Testament concern with *Heilsgeschichte* rather than with *Historie.*

THE PROPHETIC TRADITIONS

In the second volume of his *Old Testament Theology* von Rad turns his attention to the theology of Israel's prophetic traditions.[24] The

---

[22] Anderson, *op. cit.,* pp. 340-341.

[23] Robert C. Dentan, *Preface to Old Testament Theology,* rev. ed. (New York: 1963), p. 79.

[24] Cf. e.g., G. Fohrer, "Tradition und Interpretation im Alten Testament," *ZAW,* 73 (1961), pp. 1-30; "Remarks on Modern Interpretations of the Prophets," *JBL* 80 (1961), pp. 309-319.

first part of this volume is devoted to questions familiar to those who have studied Old Testament prophecy. Those who seek von Rad's views on the rise of prophecy, the role of oral tradition in prophecy, and various theological concepts relating to prophets and prophecy, need to consult these seven general chapters. Of particular interest is von Rad's analysis of the "call visions" of the prophets. In discussing the office of the *nabis* in relation to the cult, he distinguishes clearly between the so-called cultic prophets and the so-called writing or canonical prophets, for the former are bitterly attacked by the latter. The independence and radical character of the major Old Testament prophets come mainly from the fact that their ministries were inaugurated by a definite "call." These prophets thus derived their commission from the circumstances and experiences of a particular occasion, and this tends to exclude the holding of a cultic office as such. The records of these "call visions" are numerous, extending indeed from Abram to the apostle Paul, and the comparison of the stories of how the prophets were called is interesting and rewarding.

Von Rad's analysis reveals the following factors: *(a)* God directly, and often abruptly, calls the prophets to their tasks. *(b)* The prophets are made responsible for certain tasks, some of which are lifelong. *(c)* The call of the prophets is generally associated with visions of impending events, externally motivated, and recorded in the first person singular, through which the prophet's discovery of the will of God is made known.

Under these themes von Rad discusses various topics and his discussion of ecstasy and of the psychological relation of Yahweh to the prophet are particularly noteworthy. His analysis of the narratives of the calls of Micaiah ben Imlah (1 Kings 22:19ff.), Isaiah (Isaiah 6) and Ezekiel (Ezekiel 1-3) vividly and constructively illustrate his methods of interpretation. Von Rad's chapter on the prophetic calls is one of the most interesting and valuable of this second volume. All serious students of the prophets must have made their own analysis. The present writer offers his own analysis by way of supplementation. For him the distinctive features are similar to and different from those of von Rad. These are:

1. The God who calls: God makes himself known as El Shaddai for Abram; the I AM for Moses; the intervener for Amos; the Holy One of Israel for Isaiah; the wakeful one for Jeremiah; the mobile

Yahweh for Ezekiel; the persecuted Jesus for Paul. A wealth of theology may be found in the different portrayals of that one and the same God who thus calls his servants to their tasks.

2. The man who is called: When the prophetic personalities are recalled, their different temperaments, their various vocations, and their different social positions, a range of human experience and knowledge is manifest. This theme also comprises all the psychological questions involved in a "call" and the reaction of the prophets as they face the divine confrontation.

3. The task that is assigned: Von Rad makes much of this and so prevents the conclusion that the prophets all had the same task. The task of each prophet needs to be separately ascertained in the context of the overall pattern of doom, or promise, or hope. Von Rad points the way but there is much more to be said than ever he says. This theme also comprises the social and historical circumstances of the prophets' own times.

4. The people to whom the prophet is sent: Again the answer appears to be just Israel, but if the question is pursued, then the con‑text of each particular Israel of each prophet is more keenly appreciated. Von Rad is scarcely concerned with this theme, but it is this theme which really shows the aim of the prophetic commissioning.

The prophet is called, summoned, sent, etc., to correct, condemn, comfort, deliver, and so on, the people of God. In a real sense the concern of God with the prophet is subordinate to God's larger concern for the people. God calls the prophets to serve his preoccupation with his people—wayward, sinful, lost, but nevertheless his people.

Several other minor features are also present, but enough has been said to show the value of this particular chapter by von Rad, and the interest, relevance, and worth of the question in general.

Part Two of von Rad's second volume of his *Theology* is concerned with classical prophecy and the individual messages of Israel's great prophets. The studies are uneven and this part is less valuable than other parts. While the reporting of the life and books of the prophets is objective and interesting, nevertheless von Rad does not seem to have caught or to have transmitted the moral passion which informs the point of view of these prophets. Older interpreters of the prophets like K. Budde, T. H. Robinson, and H. Wheeler Robinson (to mention those of whom the present writer has had personal experience) had themselves caught the inflection of the ethical emphases of the prophets. Von Rad mentions the property-owning class and the "little people" (Amos 5:11; 8:6) of Amos' day, but gives no sign that he is really aware of Amos' compassionate concern for his poverty-stricken and deprived people. Similarly chapters 1 and 3 of Hosea are for von Rad less biography than prophetic symbolism, and in this view the real heart of Hosea is hidden from von Rad. Perhaps von Rad's fundamental concern with the cultic ethos of the Old Testament has prevented him from entering fully into the ethical dimensions of Israel's faith and the records of the Old Testament itself, except as an observer and reporter.

His account of Isaiah of Jerusalem is a particularly interesting example of his exposition of the classical prophets. He rightly regards Isaiah's preaching as a high-water mark, theologically speaking, of the Old Testament. Yet moderation is the chief characteristic of the brilliant insights, of the sweep of ideas, and of the wealth of style which his writings exhibit. This restraint is the chief clue to his message. Israel's obduracy (Isaiah 6:8) which confronts Isaiah throughout his ministry (29:9-14; 30:5ff.) leads von Rad to a useful if inconclusive discussion concerning the hardening of Israel's heart.

Some claim that von Rad's work suffers from a lack of dialogue with other workers in the same field.[25] Such a complaint, if well-founded (and it is only partly so) is really a tribute to the originality and singularity of von Rad's contribution. More often than not originality in Old Testament scholarship is in inverse proportion to the quantity of footnotes and the wealth of quoted judgments, though there are of course honorable exceptions. The bibliography of von Rad's second volume is very brief, though the range of topics and minor themes in the text show how well he is versed in the contemporary studies of Old Testament prophecy.

Nevertheless he has not resolved the fundamental dilemma of Isaiah's mission, a dilemma which centers in the elucidation of the problem of Israel's hardening of heart.[26] For the solution of this

---

[25] Cf. e.g., the review by J. Barr in *JSS*, 4 (1959), pp. 286-288, in reference to vol. 1 of von Rad's *Theology*.

[26] Since von Rad refers by way of introduction to the hardening of Pharaoh's heart, the writer may be excused if he refers to his own treatment of this problem in his commentary on *Exodus* (London: Torch Commentaries, 1967).

problem reference to the two chapters on Isaiah in W. Robertson Smith's *The Prophets of Israel* is indispensable.[27] Von Rad does not mention this work in his bibliography, and his own chapter on Isaiah likewise shows no knowledge of Smith's penetrating studies. Indeed, Smith's work seems to be increasingly ignored, though in this writer's opinion no other scholar has ever explained more successfully than W. Robertson Smith the reasons why a hardened Israel, who was totally condemned, should yet in Isaiah's own days have escaped destruction. This problem is precisely the dilemma of Isaiah's mission and teaching, and von Rad's discussion of the problem failed to solve it.

The explanation of this failure is also illustrated by von Rad's inability to attach to the concept of the remnant the importance which Isaiah is generally regarded to attribute to it. For Isaiah the remnant was not only an idea but a reality which he himself had found that God had created out of his own life, the life of his family, and probably the life of some of his followers too.

On the other hand, von Rad excels in his discussion of the sacred traditions which Isaiah defended, namely the themes of Zion, of David, and of the Messiah. Likewise he places us all in his debt by his discussions of faith and of the concept of Yahweh's work, an illustration of Isaiah's own independent coinage.

A concluding chapter entitled "The New Element in Eighth Century Prophecy" shows von Rad at his best. His sympathetic understanding of the essential loneliness of these great Israelite figures, and his grasp of their revolutionary view of Israel's history, reveal von Rad's original insights and modes of expression. In the days of the prophets, Israel stood at the end of the old *Heilsgeschichte,* but the prophets also understood that a new salvation would follow on the wake of the judgment and thus pointed to a new future for Israel.

Von Rad's *Theology of the Old Testament* remains, as Barr says, "a very powerful and valuable contribution to the subject," [28] and in

---

[27] W. Robertson Smith, *The Prophets of Israel and Their Place in History to the Close of the Eighth Century* B.C. (London: Adam and Charles Black, 1902), pp. 235-316.

[28] J. Barr, *op. cit.,* p. 288. Barr's favorable remarks in this review should be borne in mind when his article on von Rad's *Theologie des Alten Testaments* in *ET, 73* (1962), pp. 142-146 is considered.

fact it ranks among the two or three best books in the field. Indeed the wise teacher will prescribe as basic reading the books by Eichrodt and von Rad as illustrating the systematic and the traditions-history approaches. Both writers and all readers gain from the comparison.

Within his presuppositions, then, von Rad contributes his study. He argues that the Hexateuch is full of the theme of the promise of the land, but that it was not Yahweh who originally promised it and it was not Israel to whom it was first promised. Likewise belonging to the days before Israel came into being, the events of Sinai, of the oasis of Kadesh, and of the Red Sea shine out of the prehistorical darkness (I, p. 8). But in fact Israel was born in Canaan, more exactly at Shechem (Joshua 24), and so land and people, covenant and cult, law and holy war, and in turn kings and capitals, took their rise and began their course in and from the period of the Judges.

Von Rad's commentaries on Genesis and Deuteronomy, and his volumes of essays entitled *Studies in Deuteronomy* and *The Problem of the Hexateuch and Other Essays* further illustrate the knowledge and themes which he has brought to the service of his *magnum opus*. In turn however, these suffer from the limitations imposed by his presuppositions. His third study in the volume of essays on Deuteronomy just mentioned is, "Deuteronomy's 'Name' Theology and the Priestly Document's 'Kabod' Theology." [29] For von Rad Deuteronomy is the middle point of the Old Testament, and its view of the communion between Yahweh and Israel is enshrined in the concept of the place in Israel where Yahweh causes his name to dwell. This Deuteronomic "name" theology is thus a theological correction of the old or crude idea of the presence of Yahweh in an earlier Israel when the presence was especially associated with the Ark.

On the other hand the Priestly Document offers an entirely different conception according to which the tent of meeting, the priestly tabernacle, is the meeting place or revelation point of the glory of Yahweh manifest in cloud and fire, as well as the place where Yahweh himself dwells (Exodus 29:45).

These two forms of the "presence" theology greatly differ from each other, and accordingly must have had widely differing origins.

---

[29] For what follows of von Rad's ideas see his *Studies in Deuteronomy*, Studies in Biblical Theology 9, trans. David Stalker (Chicago: Henry Regnery Co., 1953), pp. 37-44.

Though both forms are the purified reintroduction of old cultic traditions, von Rad finds the provenance of Deuteronomy's "name" theology in the liturgical occasions and institutions of the Israelite amphictyony at Shechem. On the other hand he searches in vain for the hinterland of the glory-mercy seat theology of the priestly writers and also of Ezekiel. Not only is the priestly theology of this theme complicated by the probably alien traditions of the tent, but the tent traditions of Exodus 33 :7ff.; Numbers 11 :24ff.; Deuteronomy 31 :14f. do not fit in with the dwelling conception of the priestly theology. Von Rad's essay is then given over to surmise and to various suggestions as to the possible provenance of these widespread, fascinating, and puzzling accounts of the theology of the presence of Yahweh in Israel.

His presuppositions concerning the Canaanite origin of Israel have of course blinded him to what is probably the true answer, and what may fairly be claimed to be the biblical answers. Behind both forms of the "presence" theology must lie the original discovery and experience of the idea, and for many this origin lies in the personal experience of Moses. Von Rad claims that the tradition shows that Deuteronomy was revealed to Moses and Israel on the mountain (e.g., Deuteronomy 4 :10), whereas the priestly traditions show that the "mercy seat of the Ark is now the most holy place, in which the mysterious meeting of Jahweh with Moses takes place, and out of which Jahweh speaks to Moses when he has appeared in the Kabod."[30] So either we have to assume that the figure of Moses is an extensive interpolation into two traditions of widely different origins, or else alternatively believe that the presence of Moses in both traditions is part of the tradition. Again the weight of the traditions seems to be more convincing than the reconstructions thus presented.

In this same volume of *Studies in Deuteronomy,* von Rad reverts in the fourth chapter[31] to one of his favorite themes, namely, the Holy War. In these pages he offers a brief outline of the features which are characteristic of the Holy War. As its name implies, the leading and indeed sole agent was Yahweh. He determined whether and how the people should go to war, how the course of the struggle

[30] *Ibid.,* p. 41.
[31] *Ibid.,* pp. 45-59.

should proceed, and how it should end. Yahweh gave the oracle, was present with the army, and finally dispatched that "numinous panic" which completed the enemies' discomfiture. For their part the people consulted Yahweh, relied on him, blew their trumpets, proclaimed the certainty of their victory, consecrated themselves, submitted themselves in confidence and if necessary in numerical weakness to Yahweh, and regarded all booty as "under the ban," that is, at Yahweh's disposal and not theirs to keep.

For von Rad the Holy War was not properly a desert institution, for it belonged essentially to the period of Israel's amphictyony in the days of the Judges. He even goes so far as to suggest: "Perhaps it was in the Holy War even more than the Covenant Festival at Shechem that ancient Israel really first entered into her grand form." [32] He is likewise inclined to the view that "the biblical demand for faith has its proper origin here in the Holy War of ancient Israel." [33]

As so often, von Rad's title and treatment of the theme are here also highly original and helpful. But as so often his presuppositions impose their limits; here it is immediately obvious that faith does not exclusively originate in the conditions of war.

Of course the ancient traditions of the Holy War persist in Israel's history and reappear in a quasi-codified form in the laws of Deuteronomy. But in Deuteronomy the "laws" of the Holy War have not merely been preserved and reissued, they have also been reinterpreted in the terms of the Deuteronomic theology and so made useful and applicable to the military conditions in the Southern Kingdom in the seventh century B.C.

This homiletical revision of old cultic material, including the preached law,[34] and the martial tone of so much of the book pose the problem and provide the solution of the provenance of Deuteronomy. These clues lead von Rad [35] to consider the events relative to the deposition of Athaliah and the coronation of Joash (2 Kings 11), to the reign and reforms of King Josiah (2 Kings 22f.), and especially to the part played by "the people of the land" in both incidents. Then

[32] *Ibid.*, p. 45.
[33] *Ibid.*, p. 48.
[34] *Ibid.*, p. 16.
[35] *Ibid.*, pp. 60-69.

he finally concludes that the provenance of Deuteronomy is to be found in the activity of the country Levites and in the new revival of military spirit among the free peasant population of the land. Von Rad is only able to achieve and defend this view by ignoring and indeed explicitly denying [36] any specific deposits from the prophets in this connection in the book. He of course does not deny the prophetic atmosphere of the book, but he attributes this to Deuteronomy's emergence in the prophetic centuries when the prophetic trend and influence could not have been avoided.

Valuable and compelling as is his thesis, it by no means takes account of all the contents of Deuteronomy. Take, for example, what may be conveniently described as the "crossing" theme of Deuteronomy and the principle ideas associated with that theme. Space does not permit a description of the varied terminology describing Israel's entry into Canaan. The forms, the ideas (explicit and implicit), and the dispersion of this varied terminology in the book reveal its prominence and importance but also lead, notably in Deuteronomy 8 and 10, to an evaluation of the settlement in Canaan in terms of Israel's theistic faith. These evaluations have the literary character of anticipatory warnings and promises; they are a prospect from Moab. In actual fact the evaluations are restrospective, and the prospective literary form conveys Israel's judgments on her experiences in Canaan. The promises and threats of the literary form thus present the approval and condemnation of a later Israel after several centuries of residence in the land.

Further, the evaluations or, as almost could be said, the philosophy, of the settlement in chapters 8 and 10 of Deuteronomy are reminiscent of the evaluations in Hosea, especially chapter 2 and significantly verse 8,[37] and again in Isaiah 28:25-29, and so could properly be described as originating in prophetic circles of thought. In spite of the scope of the second volume of his *Theology*, it may not unreasonably be claimed that von Rad has not plumbed the significance of prophecy in the Old Testament as deeply as its cultic ethos and con-

---

[36] *Ibid.*, p. 69.

[37] Von Rad quotes this very passage as illustrating Israel's courage in going out into the secular world for theological reasons. Rather the verse illustrates the prophetic demand to include the secular within the theistic, the sociological within the theological.

tribution. His treatment of Deuteronomy has failed to grapple with the sociological significance of the settlement, as distinct from its cultic and theological significance. This sociological significance, illustrated so clearly in Deuteronomy 8 and 10, is an important part of the prophetical deposit in Deuteronomy.

RELATIONSHIP BETWEEN THE
OLD TESTAMENT AND THE NEW TESTAMENT

Von Rad entitles part three of his second volume, and the concluding portion of his *Theology,* "The Old Testament and the New," and devotes the five chapters in this part to the question of the relation of the two Testaments. Again, our author places us all in his debt with a discussion which is notable and embryonic. The Old Testament reveals in its pages and parts an ever-widening expectation which is ever forward-looking. This is seen in the continuing adaptation of the traditions, and indeed their transformation, so that these become relevant to and interpretative of the situations in which Israel successively found herself. Along such avenues we may make the transition from the Old Testament to the New Testament. The two Testaments thus are not merely linked to each other, but belong to each other in terms of preparation and realization, of prediction and manifestation, and of promise and fulfillment.

Throughout the hundred pages devoted to these considerations von Rad employs various general terms to describe the link between, or the belongingness of, the two Testaments. The terms are given no systematic treatment but probably represent the emergence of images "on the boil" as he is caught up by the excitement of the climax of his work. Thus he speaks of what is virtually a broad correspondence between the two Testaments, and he bases this on the "list of theological themes taken from the Old Testament which Paul enumerates in Romans 9:4-5" (II, p. 337; cf. II, p. 358). Such a correspondence inevitably includes a continuation which itself involves an adaptation and an "enhancement" (II, p. 329). The likeness between the Testaments is thus compounded of an actualization and indeed an incorporation of the first in the second Testament, and not merely in the Old Testament supply of ideas or even "whole catenas of statements" (II, p. 352). The language, the living concepts, even the restless life of the first goes on into the second Testament.

Anyone who is interested in the Old Testament as part and parcel of Holy Writ, and not merely for anthropological or antiquarian reasons, cannot fail to be interested and excited by these pages. As we study the Old Testament "as a divine revelation which was the precursor of Christ's advent, and was full of pointers toward the coming of the Lord" (II, p. 329), the need and desire will be to go further along the way von Rad pointed out. Each interpreter will have his own predilections and will seek to make his own way. So among other things one may ask, for example: How far does A. R. Johnson's *The One and the Many in the Israelite Conception of God* take us towards the Christian doctrine of the Trinity?[38] Again, how far does Pedersen's account of Israelite blessing take us towards the content of the idea of the Incarnation?[39] Again, how far is it between the *panim* of Yahweh and the Person of Christ? Jesus was a Jew. Is this statement merely an ethnic comment or is there any meaning in the question: Was Israel the womb of Christ?

Others will ask other questions, but all will gladly acknowledge the stature, the influence, and the contribution of this very great scholar and interpreter of the Old Testament. For myself, I must add that I find his words and his thoughts yield an implication beyond themselves. There always appears to be an extra band of meaning in his paragraphs, an implicit dimension of extended meaning in his exposition, and an embryonic potential in his utterance. We are all indebted to him for this no less than for the words, the concepts, and the themes of his thought.

The foregoing essay is an attempt by a British student of the Old Testament to evaluate the theology of a great German expositor and scholar of the Old Testament for an American volume devoted to the Old Testament. These facts prompt some concluding generalized remarks, cautious in character and beneficial in intention.

Von Rad is no exception to what appears to be widely accepted in circles in the U.S.A. devoted to the study of the Old Testament—that it is nearly always German Old Testament scholarship which achieves new breakthroughs and opens up new prospects and avenues for the

[38] Aubrey R. Johnson, *The One and the Many in the Israelite Conception of God* (Cardiff: University of Wales Press, 1961).

[39] Johannes Pedersen, *Israel: Its Life and Culture,* vols. 1-2 (London: Oxford University Press, 1926), pp. 182-212.

pursuit of the study. British scholarship, with honorable exceptions in terms of men, movements, and ideas, has not as a rule generated new trends and dimensions in Old Testament study. Neither—and again with memorable exceptions—it may respectfully be pointed out, has American Old Testament scholarship done so. Very broadly speaking the role of German scholarship, now reinforced by Scandinavian scholars, has been discovery; British scholarship, discrimination; and American scholarship, dissemination. We are all grateful for German leads in Pentateuchal study, in Form Criticism, in the rediscovery of prophecy, and now more recently of cult. But true to Germanic form, these hypotheses have often led to extreme and unacceptable results. This consequence is the price of the union of discoveries with the light of new presuppositions. The assessment of new hypotheses, the withdrawal from extremes, and the evaluation of presuppositions has lain outside Germany and has been notably accomplished by British and Scandinavian scholars. In the vast multiplication of biblical students and scholars in the U.S.A., many have fallen victim to the glamor of the new in German scholarship and failed to appreciate the work of appraisal in other places. Many will challenge, and rightly, the full accuracy of the foregoing observations, but after forty years of studying, teaching, and especially of meditating on Old Testament scholarship, these are my impressions and I offer them for what they are worth. In the Germanic role of discovery and initiative, von Rad will ever have a deserved and lasting place. On that, general agreement is possible.

SELECTED BIBLIOGRAPHY

von Rad, G., *Das Gottesvolk im Deuteronomium*. Stuttgart, 1929 (BWANT 47).

————, *Das Geschichtsbild des chronistischen Werkes*. Stuttgart, 1930 (BWANT 55).

————, *Die Priesterschrift im Hexateuch*. Stuttgart, 1934 (BWANT 65).

————, *Das formgeschichtliche Problem des Hexateuch*. Stuttgart, 1938 (BWANT 78). Translated in *The Problem of the Hexateuch and Other Essays*. London, 1966, pp. 1-78.

————, *Mose*. Göttingen, 1940. Translated as *Moses*. London, 1960.

————, *Deuteronomium-Studien*. Zweite auf. Göttingen, 1948 (FRLANT 58). Translated as *Studies in Deuteronomy*. London, 1953 (Studies in Biblical Theology 9).

————, *Der Heilige Krieg im alten Israel*. Dritte auf. Göttingen, 1958.

—————, *Theologie des Alten Testaments*. Bd. I. Zweite auf. München, 1958. Bd. II. München, 1960. Translated as *Old Testament Theology*. vol. 1. New York, 1962. vol. 2. New York, 1965.

—————, *Gesammelte Studien zum Alten Testament*. München, 1958. Translated as *The Problem of the Hexateuch and Other Essays*. London, 1966.

—————, *Die Josephsgeschichte*. Dritte auf. Neukirchen, 1959.

—————, *Das erste Buch Mose. Genesis*. Zweite auf. Göttingen, 1956. Translated as *Genesis. A Commentary*. Philadelphia, 1961.

—————, "Das theologische Problem des alttestamentlichen Schöpfungsglaubens," in *Werden und Wesen des Alten Testaments* (P. Volz, F. Stummer, J. Hempel, eds.). Berlin, 1936 (BZAW 66), pp. 138-147.

—————, "Vom Menschenbild des Alten Testaments," in *Der alte und der neue Mensch*. München, 1942 (BEvTh 8), pp. 5-23.

—————, "Typologische Auslegung des Alten Testaments," *EvTh* 12 (1952-53), pp. 17-33. Translated in *Essays on Old Testament Interpretation* (C. Westermann, ed.), pp. 17-39.

—————, "Hiob 38 und die altägyptische Weisheit," *VT* Supplement 3 (1955), pp. 293-301. Translated in *The Problem of the Hexateuch*, pp. 281-291.

—————, "Es ist noch eine Ruhe vorhanden dem Volk Gottes," *ZZ* 11 (1932-33), pp. 104-111. Translated in *The Problem of the Hexateuch*, pp. 94-102.

—————, "Zur prophetischen Verkündigung Deuterojesajas," *VF* (1940), pp. 58-65.

—————, "Grundprobleme einer biblischen Theologie des Alten Testaments," *ThLZ* 68 (1943), cols. 225-234.

—————, "Verheissenes Land und Jahwes Land im Hexateuch," *ZDPV* 66 (1943), pp. 191-204. Translated in *The Problem of the Hexateuch*, pp. 79-93.

—————, "Das hermeneutische Problem im Buche Genesis," *VF* (1942-46), pp. 43-51.

—————, "Herkunft und Absicht des Deuteronomiums," *ThLZ* 72 (1947), cols. 151-158.

—————, "Theologische Geschichtsschreibung im Alten Testament," *TZ* 4 (1948), pp. 161-174.

—————, "Das Zeugnis der biblischen Erzvätergeschichten," *DtPfrBl* 49 (1949), pp. 105-107.

—————, "Die Anrechnung des Glaubens zur Gerechtigkeit," *ThLZ* 76 (1951), cols. 129-132. Translated in *The Problem of the Hexateuch*, pp. 125-130.

—————, "The Origin of the Concept of the Day of Yahweh," *JSS* 4 (1959), pp. 97-108.

—————, "Das Alte Testament ist ein Geschichtsbuch," in *Probleme alttestamentlicher Hermeneutik* (C. Westermann, ed.). München, 1960, pp. 11-17.

—————, "Ancient Word and Living Word. The Preaching of Deuteronomy and Our Preaching," *Interpretation* 15 (1961), pp. 3-13.

For a complete bibliography up to 1961, cf. R. Rendtorff and K. Koch (eds.), *Studien zur Theologie der alttestamentlichen Überlieferungen*. Neukirchen, 1961, pp. 163-174.

3
Otto Procksch
Theology of the Old Testament

by John N. Schofield

Otto Procksch was born in Eisenberg, Germany, in 1874. In 1906 he became an ausserordentlicher *professor at Greifswald, and in 1909 was promoted to* ordentlicher *professor. He held this position until 1925, when he moved to a similar chair at Erlangen. He died in 1947.*

Otto Procksch was a scholar with wide-ranging interests. He wrote on blood revenge among pre-Islamic Arabs, historical tradition in the preexilic prophets, the history of the Septuagint, the sagas in the Elohist tradition, and commentaries on various Old Testament books. But the harvest of his lifework is gathered into his *magnum opus* on Old Testament theology. Anyone reading the book in the light of modern developments in Old Testament studies is amazed by his seminal mind and his influence—particularly on his pupils. A. Alt and G. von Rad edited the book, assisted by O. Grether and V. Ebeling; W. Eichrodt, another of his pupils, used his arrangement of material for Old Testament theology. As the work is not translated, much of this essay is devoted to a summary of his theology.

ARRANGEMENT OF OLD TESTAMENT THEOLOGY

Procksch's great work on theology was published posthumously in 1950.[1] It is a massive book of 787 pages. After an introduction (pp. 1-47), Procksch first traces the history of Israel's religion

[1] Otto Procksch, *Theologie des Alten Testaments* (Gütersloh: 1949).

chronologically from the patriarchal to the apocalyptic period (pp. 48-419), and then deals at length with systematic theology (pp. 420-715). The fact that he continually bases his writing on the text is shown by the extensive index of biblical references that concludes the work (pp. 715-756).

Procksch's aim in the separate treatments of the history of Israel's religion and of its theology is to present longitudinal and transverse sections. In the former treatment we watch Israel's faith springing up in individuals and through events at such crucial points as the old prophetic period, the monarchy, and the time of the church-state, and we trace its development toward a goal. There are in this section many new and penetrating insights into Old Testament religion which would repay research, but which cannot be dealt with in this essay. In the latter treatment we watch the spread and interaction of the great theological themes on different planes, such as prophetic thought, the cult, attitude to the world and history. But throughout the Old Testament the central thought is the relation of history to God. So by moving onward from God's relation with the universe to his relation with Israel and finally with individual Israelites, we obtain three great thought circles: God and the world, God and the people, God and man.

RELATIONSHIP BETWEEN FAITH AND HISTORY

The formative period of Procksch's life was dominated by the approach popularized by Wellhausen. In general outline he accepted the documentary hypothesis put forth by Wellhausen, but not his dating, either of the sources or of the decalogue; nor does he accept his evolutionary view of progressive revelation. Procksch believed that the Bible requires a theology of history which is teleological and eschatological. But his own independent attitude stressed the necessity of personal religious experience and relationship to Jesus Christ. Whatever the outcome of modern research, to him it is clear that the Old Testament writers treated the great figures of the story as historical, and an Old Testament theology should not waste time discussing the problem. Of Abraham, Procksch says that though his figure is veiled by saga it is quite distinct from myth; his story has a valuable historical kernel and a spiritual impress has been preserved in the tradition.

Procksch cannot agree with the historian who, writing a history of Old Testament religion, treats it "objectively" as part of a series of histories of religions, without asking questions about the Originator and the personal elements of the biblical world-faith. The biblical theologian must recognize the fact of direct revelation to the prophet in word or vision as distinct from manifestations in natural and historical events, or through the prophet to men. The historian of religion deals only with manifestation and so sees only a difference in value and not a real difference between biblical and nonbiblical religions. Procksch illustrates the meaning of the two words by reference to Romans 1:17 and 3:21. In the gospel the righteousness of God is revealed through faith for faith (1:17). But now the righteousness of God has been manifested apart from the law, although the law and the prophets bear witness to it; it is manifested through faith in Jesus Christ (as indirect; 3:21). Like Paul, Procksch stresses the importance of faith in the apprehension of this manifestation and also the share which the theologian's own faith has in the form which faith has taken in history. Procksch knew that his own faith had been shaped by the figures and events of the faith-history—especially Christ, but also Abraham, Paul, Luther—each made his own characteristic contribution; if Abraham or Moses had to be given up as a historical figure, his own Christianity would not be destroyed but would be modified in a decisive point; and in the same way contact with a new figure of faith could enrich his own faith. Despite the references in Dentan,[2] in this work it certainly does not appear that Procksch regards "faith" as a separate organ of perception. He believes rather, that for the Christian the only approach to any problem must be from the standpoint of his faith. Similarly he does not suggest that only a sectarian, not a general Christian, theology of the Old Testament is possible, but only that every approach is inevitably conditioned by the theologian's church allegiance and environment in which he has found his relationship with Christ.

CONTENTS OF OLD TESTAMENT THEOLOGY

Procksch's twofold arrangement of his material—religious and theological—causes much repetition but in effect this is a good fault,

[2] Robert Dentan, *Preface to Old Testament Theology*, rev. ed. (New York: The Seabury Press, 1963), pp. 73-74.

because theological ideas are seen in different lights. Both sections are really complementary. Though the movement of history can be traced, there can be no development in God's revelation or manifestation, only what is now called *Lichtungsgeschichte*—a similar pattern at various successive crises in the history of Israel's religion. Although his vocabulary is (fortunately!) not the same as is used in many more modern Old Testament studies, his ideas provide the point of departure for later studies.

GOD AND THE WORLD

In the first section of his work Procksch discusses revelation, creation, and world-picture. Believing that the whole Old Testament is theocratic, he begins with God's REVELATION of himself, through angel or messenger, through the peculiar Hebrew thought of his Glory, through all life, and finally through his Name. That the angel has a human form is important, because this excludes the demonism of Egyptian animal representation and allows the thought of an invisible God taking the form of a man, so giving a clear mental picture of God. Yet there is often no distinction between God and angel in these visitations, but because the angel is regarded as a vision, there is no danger of a material representation of God. Balaam's eyes have to be opened to perceive the angel (Numbers 22:31). Revelation through angels enabled the Hebrews to think of the presence of God away from cult places—Yahweh may dwell in holy places or on Mount Sinai, but the angel can appear to guide men far from any cult center. In general, the humanity of the angel emphasizes the friendly, merciful character of God.

The Sinai theophany revealed a more grandiose and majestic picture of God—his glory—as free light seen through clouds, formless, invisible, immanent and omnipresent, filling all the earth. The God of Isaiah's revelation (Isaiah 6) is particularly linked with the sanctuary and probably with the Ark, but is throned above the heavens and outside space. The glory of God is not an abstraction but a revelatory appearance, and Ezekiel can ascribe to it a human form.

The paradox of Hebrew thought is that God is revealed in everything, working in time and space yet not limited to either. Both Amos (9:2ff) and Psalm 139 stress his omnipresence. He is also known as God of Eternity *(El 'ōlām,* Genesis 21:33), a name which appears in the cult at Beersheba and must be regarded as a historical element in the Abraham saga and which is the kernel of the patriarchal faith. This name asserts that God is not bound to time or space but IS. He is hidden and without beginning or end. Both meanings are found in Second Isaiah, and are fundamental to Old Testament theology. For Procksch the basic element in *El,* as in our word "religion," is "binding," duty being at the heart of religion.

God became more comprehensible to Israel through his self-revelation of his personal name, Yahweh. Procksch begins from the statement (Exodus 3:6) that Yahweh was the God of Moses' father, and thinks that he was known by this name to Levi and Judah of the Leah-Israel tribes, and possibly worshiped by the Israel amphictyony at Shechem. Moses made Yahweh known as God to the Rachel-Jacob tribes coming out of Egypt, and introduced the name as a palladium for all Israel. Yahweh became known as God of Israel rather than of Jacob, probably because Moses himself belonged to the Leah-Israel group. This personal name expressed the essence of his divinity as "being," as "existing"; it guaranteed monotheism, avoided abstractions, and united under one name the God worshiped at Shechem by the Leah-Israel group from which Moses derived, and the God of the Rachel-Jacob group at Beersheba. This one and the same God met Moses in the wilderness away from cult and tribal links; though the God of the Levites at Kadesh, he remained free from limitations of cult and tribe, and he became the warlike God accompanying and fighting for his people. It is significant, however, that God's solemn proclamation prefaced by the repetition of his name (Exodus 34:6-7) retains the early, friendly concept of mercy and the choice of Israel. When "made to dwell" in cult place or ark, the name expressed a more spiritual presence of the deity than any bodily form, and by the use of this phrase the tension between prophet and priest could be resolved.

CREATION is considered as "wonder." God and the world are distinct from each other, and the story of creation refutes myths of a god and world derived one from the other; God and world are different regions of being. The Hebrew verb "create" as used in Genesis and by Second Isaiah always emphasizes the miraculous wonder of God's actions. Wonderful creations emerge in human history as ordinary events though beyond man's understanding; heaven and earth, life, man, Israel, and the new age of Cyrus are all wonderful creations. That they exist at all is wonderful. The Old Testament knows nothing of natural laws or law of history, but only of portents and signs proclaiming absolute divine freedom.

"Spirit," "word," "wisdom" are all used to express divine elements present at creation. "Spirit" expresses the principle of divine life working invisibly, irresistibly, like the wind, omnipresent. Because control by the Spirit could give rise to enthusiasm and fanaticism, the growth of Law tended to suppress spirit-control. Many of the great writing prophets derived their mission from inspiration by the Word, rather than the Spirit, of God, but Word and Spirit continued to be used for the living presence of God, an inner driving force binding his people to him in a spiritual rather than a cultic fellowship.

"Word" is the intelligible element in creation. Every word has meaning and power. God's Word is revelation in both law and the prophets, who give form to the divine voice. "Wisdom" was originally a worldly idea, but by the time of Solomon (in J) it had moral content and thus was linked with the divine world. It is a gift of God to man, in whom it appears as piety—the fear of the Lord. In Job and Proverbs there is a tendency to regard Wisdom as an independent being who teaches the worldly man, warns fools, and gives to man abundance of life. The first of God's creation, she is the mediator between God and creation.

In the Hebrew WORLD-PICTURE are heaven, earth, and underworld. "Heaven" may be thought of as an inverted bowl cut off by the horizon, or as a stretched-out tent; and God, thought of as dwelling inside the bowl but above the earth, comes down to Sinai. We might say, "He stretches out the North Pole above the waste places, hanging the earth in space" (Job 26:7). God's distance is exalted by the idea of the heaven of heavens—the invisible heaven above the visible one.

"Earth" consists of nature and man, both having meaning only in God. Procksch thinks that in Genesis 1 there are two parallel groups of three days, with light on the first and fourth; water, firmament, and their creatures on the second and fifth; dry land and its creatures on the third and sixth. The creation of the sabbath comes in later, from the Decalogue. The Hebrew idea of the origin of man goes back to a common Semitic tradition of man's early home in either the mountain of God in the far north, or Eden in the Syrian waste of the northeast. In Genesis 2 there is a clear distinction between man's relationship with beasts and his intimate companionship with woman. The origin of evil is ascribed to demonic power, rebelling against God, and persuading man to barter his innocence for the divine knowledge of good and evil, to reject the lordship of God and to grasp at the mystical, sensuous gratification of union with God. This sin breaks the relationship between man and God through its separating power, and here begins the heritage of guilt which is one of the great Old Testament truths about man. The thought in P of the *Imago Dei* is as important theologically as the story of the fall. "Our image" (Genesis 1:26) refers to the divine nature shared by all the heavenly beings. This nature makes man's life inviolable (9:6); it enables man to comprehend the person of God, receive him, and be his living mirror; but because of man's heritage of guilt, only Christ is the full man of God (2 Corinthians 4:4).

The Babylonian threefold division of "heaven," "earth," and "underworld," as contrasted with the Hebrew twofold division of heaven and earth (Genesis 1:1), entered later, probably in Solomon's time from Phoenicia. Also from outside, perhaps, come the concept and name of Sheol, distinct from the grave but linked with death; in Sheol there is only existence, not real life, because no fellowship with God is possible—even the pious cannot praise him. But their anguish gives rise to the first approach to a faith in resurrection (Job 19:25-29).

GOD AND PEOPLE

This section of Procksch's work is subdivided into presentations of mercy-choice, cult, law, and messianic hope.

Under the topic of MERCY-CHOICE Procksch considers "God's family" and "God's covenant." In both J and P all peoples are one great family derived from Noah, and there are no "barbarians," but God has different relationships with different groups of people. He created all peoples, but in a special sense he is God of Abraham and his chosen people Israel. The father-son relationship is seen in the father's compassion for his lost son, and springs from his mercy-choice, not from nature. Emphasis on Israel as son is early (Exodus 4:22,

E) and is a legal relationship of adoption, but the deep look into the nature of God (Hosea 11 :1 ; Jeremiah 31 :20) shows that the essence of this relationship is love. As son, Israel has the rights of a firstborn and inherits Canaan—an idea introduced by Deuteronomy where, however, sonship is not emphasized. This promised heritage and the unity of God, people, and land gave hope to Israel in the exile, although the promise was never unconditional. The word "choice" in reference to Israel is late, but the consciousness of God's mercy-choice is old. It is taken up by Second Isaiah and under his deep influence passes into the Psalter.

"God's covenant" with Israel is treated under two aspects—idea and history. The covenant concept expresses choice more clearly than the idea of natural or adopted sonship. It became dominant through Moses and is central to both Old and New Testaments. Basic to it was probably a common meal and an oath involving curses. In the Sinai covenant God is a contracting party, but he is absolute and even has to give Israel power to contract. So the covenant is not a bargain but was established by God, and Israel must carry out its conditions. The necessity for reconciliation is seen in the offering of the meal in which God shares, and this offering need not be repeated because reconciliation has taken place. The decalogue belongs to the original basic document of the Sinai covenant. The "Thou" in which it is expressed signifies that Israel is treated as a person and a unity in which every Israelite shares. The first five commandments concern piety of relationship to God and parents, both parents being equally mentioned; from this piety comes the charity—moral not legal—of the second five commandments. The covenant is thinkable only if meditated by a prophet who declares God's will to his people.

The history of covenant thought begins with J's account of the covenant which God made with Abraham (Genesis 15) directed to an heir and the future and concluded by the smoking oven, symbolic of the rock at Sinai. The covenant in E (Exodus 24, Joshua 24) comes after Sinai and includes all twelve tribes after the settlement. Deuteronomy knows the covenant with the patriarchs about the land of Canaan; and a redactor after 586 B.C. adds a covenant in Moab, not referred to elsewhere. In P the covenant is a one-sided ordinance whose contents are decided by God alone. It is made first with Noah, father of historical humanity, and then with Abraham in a new revelation of God's name in which not people and land, but God himself, is the promised blessing. To Moses there was no new covenant, but another new revelation. There are thus two stages of revelation in one covenant, the first a cultless relationship with one man, the second with a whole people and including cult. The covenant concept in P became the backbone of the concept of history in the Old Testament, passing thence to the New Testament.

There is no reference to the covenant in the predeuteronomic Judean prophets, Amos, Isaiah, Micah, and Zephaniah, possibly because the Mosaic covenant was made with Rachel tribes coming out of Egypt, while the Leah tribes, including Judah, entered the covenant through Joshua. The mercy-choice was expressed in the imagery of marriage and father-son relationship, in which love goes beyond the law of the covenant. Isaiah expresses the idea of mercy-choice in terms of the messianic king and Zion the chosen city. Hosea, however, in the north uses the thought of covenant and law as well as marriage and adoption. Jeremiah, too, also a son of Rachel, knows the Sinai covenant and the decalogue, but he believes that covenant was broken and will be replaced by a new, whose law will be fulfilled by an inner compulsion, for it will rest not on tradition but on experience of God. Ezekiel and Second Isaiah both proclaim a new unbreakable covenant of peace. For the fulfillment of the covenant with David, Ezekiel thinks of him as rising from the dead, but Second Isaiah regards the whole people as his heirs. The Davidic covenant becomes the messianic focal point, God's mercy-covenant personalized in the Davidic prince. The height of covenant relationship is seen in the Servant of Second Isaiah, who mediates the covenant to the people, reconciling them to God and becoming the origin of a new race of covenant people (Isaiah 53:10). In Malachi the Levitical priests are taken up into the covenant with king, prophet, and people. In the final stage in Daniel (11:22) the high priest is spoken of as prince of the covenant.

In the relationship between God and people, CULT is the normal form of the worship of God and is necessary. It rests on the covenant, and cultic forms are valid for the individual only as he is a member of the community. It implies holy place, holy time, and holy act, its basis being the idea of the holy. There are five subheadings in this section (put in quotation marks below). After Moses, the noun "holiness" is generally used of material things, though it is applied to Israel (Jeremiah 2:3; Exodus 22:31). A dangerous, magical, archaic element, from a lower layer of thought, is retained within the concept of holiness by the priests, but rejected by the prophets. The adjective "holy" on the other hand stresses the personal element, particularly as used by Hosea and First and Second Isaiah. In Hosea it expresses the contrast between man and the holy God who comes in love to heal, not destroy. To Isaiah it is the central epithet for God, denoting judgment, which brings life only to the reconciled. Second Isaiah brings the new emphasis of redemption after judgment. These prophets freed holiness from the cult. Elisha as a prophet, not a priest, is a holy man of God (2 Kings 4:9), and the whole people of God is holy (Exodus 19:6; Deuteronomy 7:6). Yahweh himself makes them holy as a moral rather than as a cultic community (Leviticus 20:8). After the exile—after Ezra—there is renewed stress on the holiness of material objects, but it is of interest that even then the Old Testament is not called Holy Writings, because it is linked less with the cult than with the prophets.

The "Holy Place" is the meeting place of man with the God who has revealed himself. There man can "see God's face" (Genesis 32:30; Isaiah 6:1) or enter his invisible presence—the ark is not God's throne but his dwelling. The tent of meeting and the tabernacle were forerunners of the royal temple of Solomon, which was at first also the national shrine for the twelve tribes. After the division of the kingdom there were royal and tribal holy places in the north. Deuteronomy blazed the trail toward a single holy place in Jerusalem, but even after the exile Jerusalem had to compete with holy places at Gerizim and Yeb (Elephantine). However, only the temple at Jerusalem was legitimate. There national piety concentrated, and there the great battle for imageless religion, which gave Israelite religion its superiority, was won by the prophets, often against the priests. Older than the house of God as a holy place was the altar, perhaps at first linked with a stone pillar as at Bethel. However, at a very early stage the two were separated, and the pillar became a memorial. The altar was the place of slaughter; at first there was one altar to each holy place, but later there was an incense altar (1 Kings 7:48) as well as an altar for burnt offering.

"Feasts" are holy times determined by the sun and moon. There was a tribal festival at the new moon in the time of David (1 Samuel 20:5-8), and the full moon, or a monthly sabbath, as a remembrance day may have been known to pre-Mosaic Israel. The seven-day week was known to J, but in preexilic times the sabbath was not a day of absolute rest (2 Kings 4:23). It gained its importance in the exile, when feasts were not possible, and in postexilic periods. The Passover existed before Sinai, being a wilderness shepherds' feast celebrated in the family by night at the spring full moon. God had no share in the slaughtered animal, whose blood on tent and doorpost ransomed the firstborn from Yahweh's claim. The historicizing of the feast by linking it with the ransom from Egypt is first seen in Deuteronomy, where the feast loses its domestic character and must be celebrated at the temple when the barley is in ear (Exodus 9:31); but after the exile, Passover is again a family festival with its character of sin-offering and solemn remembrance.

The three agricultural feasts—of unleavened bread, weeks, and booths—cannot be traced back to the time before Moses, but after the settlement they formed the basis of the calendar. The first, when the sickle was put into the ripe barley, followed closely on Passover, but after the people had returned home (Deuteronomy 16:7); its date would depend on the ripening of the grain—Ezekiel (45:21) is the first to date the calendar. The feast of weeks (Whitsun) was celebrated with great joy: Ezekiel omits this feast, though he usually follows H, which accepts it (Leviticus 23:12ff.); the observance returns, however, after the exile (Numbers 28:26), but without its former importance. The feast of booths or tabernacles, first mentioned by this name in Deuteronomy (16:13), is more elaborate. It was the old Hebrew New Year feast celebrated in autumn when the fruits of the year were gathered, at the first new moon of the new year when sun year and moon year were level. At Shiloh and later at Jerusalem it became the feast where the covenant was remembered. Unlike Passover, it was called a *hag*—a word that seems to denote joyful ritual dancing. Other feasts were each called a *mo'edh,* a meeting of God and people.

"Offerings" ordained by God as a means of atonement made it possible for profane man to enter the sphere of the holy, and to have fellowship with God and also with the fellow members of the cult community. Culture and cult were inseparable, and only pure domestic animals and cultivated field plants could be offered. Offerings implied surrender by the offerer, and their value was relative to their value to the one making the offering. Burnt offering and the presentation of food were linked with atonement early for individuals and single deeds, later for the people and their common state. Daily offerings were public, and private offerings expressed the individual's share in the cult, just as his hands, placed on the victim's head, were a pledge that he shared in atonement. As early as J the smoke of the burnt offering also had value for atonement (Genesis 8:21), as had the good smell of the burning of the food-present mixed with oil. The evening bread-and-fruit offering was an invitation to Yahweh to be present at the meal, and the shewbread as the bread of "face" was accepted by him with favor.

The "slaughter-offering-for-a-meal" *(zébaḥ šelāmîm)* was probably made at the great feasts, when one whole animal was used as a burnt offering, and another animal was shared with God, who received the fat, priests, who received the right breast and foreleg, and the offerer's family in a communal meal of joy, praise, and song. To the prophet the implicit danger was that this offering might be regarded as a means of guaranteeing God's favor.

Other burnt offerings were for sin and guilt, and the offerer had no share in eating them; their aim was atonement, the purification of priest and people. The oldest form of atonement offering is found in the Passover, with its sprinkling of blood and eating of flesh. After Ezra the great day of atonement was instituted on the tenth day of the seventh month; and from that time the sin-offering, for ritual or unwitting offences, was differentiated from the guilt-offering, made not only for ritual but also for grosser offences.

"Expiation" is theologically the most important element in offering. The Hebrew word means "covering," [3] and applies to the value of the substitute by which the guilt is "covered." All men are involved in original guilt (Genesis 6) which only death can expiate. Expiation is possible only by a ransom ordained and accepted by God as a valid substitute. For man's guilt God alone can ordain the "covering"; there is no priestly magic. God has ordained that, as life resides in the blood, he will accept blood on the altar to make expiation. Thus,

[3] But cf. the meaning "wipe clean," in John Noel Schofield, *Law, Prophets and Writings* (London: 1969), p. 56, n. 5.

the lifeblood of the dying animal makes expiation as one life for another. The writer of Isaiah 53 was the one prophet to realize that a fully valid substitute for guilty mankind could be provided by the perfection of a guiltless human being, and could create a people reconciled with God.

God alone is lawgiver in Israel, and LAW and covenant come from divine initiative. The law was mediated by prophet and priest (Deuteronomy 33:4, 10), servant and wise man. Law is God's personal address to man, as a father addresses a son (Proverbs 6:20). This understanding of the law explains the love for law expressed in the Psalter, and also explains why, in the Old Testament, law is regarded not as a burden but as a blessing from God to his people. The law is also called God's command, his witness, and reference is made to listening to his ordinances and statutes. The law includes justice, springing from custom or unwritten law; and sacral and civil law are not easily distinguishable in the Old Testament. P (Leviticus 7:1) calls cultic sayings "law," and in Ezra, Nehemiah, and some psalms the word "law" denotes the whole Pentateuch.

The Hebrew verbal root for righteousness is intransitive, and so refers to a quality or relationship; its meaning is not legal but moral (piety). The righteousness of God includes mercy and rescue; for example, he does not have to destroy the wicked at Sodom, but can save the whole city for the sake of a few righteous. This meaning is denied by Ezekiel, who regards righteousness as a personal possession which cannot be transferred to others, in contrast to Isaiah 53 in which God's servant makes many righteous. Second Isaiah thinks of righteousness as God's moral ordering of the world, sometimes synonymous with victory, though the Holy War element in it is rare. Second Isaiah is the father of the theological ideas in the Psalter, where his idea of righteousness is seen. In both Second Isaiah and The Psalms, God's righteous judgment is valid for all people and saves them. In Psalm 88:11 the underworld is dreadful because God's righteousness is not declared there. For Jeremiah, God's righteousness raised a theological problem which was to be of great importance after the exile: Why do the wicked prosper and the righteous suffer? God's answer is that further suffering will come, but with the promise of final victory. Thus, the suffering of the righteous becomes part of the divine righteous plan, the moral ordering of the world, and therefore it is a sin to refuse martyrdom. Jeremiah's struggle over theodicy was epoch-making, and Job, to whom this theme of suffering was central, often shows acquaintance with Jeremiah's agony. Both Jeremiah and Job are righteous, not sinless, and the theophany to Job makes clear that God's world-plan is beyond human knowledge. But God's pious ones, to whom he reveals himself, know him to be righteous; hence, his ordering of the world only has meaning from the theocentric standpoint. Finally, the difference between the righteous and the godless will be discernible when the sun of righteousness arises (Malachi 3:18) in the messianic age. That the distinction between the righteous and the godless is based on different, moral conduct is clear in Ezekiel, Proverbs, and Psalms, although the last is not always free from tendencies to self-righteousness, which is corrected in Psalm 143:2. In the Davidic prince and the messianic age righteousness will be exalted and all unrighteousness perish.

"Judgment" involves retribution, without which righteousness is unthinkable. This thought rings through all prophecy. God's wrath, a violent expression of his zeal, is sometimes inexplicable; but for the prophets, beginning with Amos, wrath breaks out in judgment on God's people when they have broken his covenant. Divine judgment will be fully revealed on the Day of Yahweh—the final eschatological act of history, involving destruction of the world. The Last Day is an integral part of Judaism, Christianity, and Islam. Israel, too, the chosen people, and her successor the Judean church-state will be punished, but there is also a second theme of a rescued remnant. From the time of Elijah, the faithful are distinguished from sinners within the nation, and this thought dominates Old Testament religious life. To Zephaniah the faithful are the quiet in the land who dwell in the midst of the people—they will be the saved remnant.

Israel's national hopes, including the MESSIANIC HOPE, were rooted in the mercy-choice by God; even as he had no end, so they, whatever the final judgment, would be saved. A passage (2 Samuel 23:1-7), whose importance and genuineness is stressed by Procksch, contains David's clear statement of God's messianic promise to himself and his son the prince, and shows that he was placed in a messianic light, probably in his own lifetime and certainly in Solomon's age. In Isaiah is seen the full brightness of messianic light. Judah will be divided into the lost under Ahaz and the saved under Immanuel.

After judgment and want the latter group will grow into the spiritual messianic kingdom. The child to be born is not called king nor Davidic, but his names disclose his nature; he is a son of Jesse and sits on David's throne. Isaiah's picture is repeated by Micah at the beginning of the Deuteronomic age, and by Jeremiah's "righteous branch" at the close of the same period. In Ezekiel also the Messiah appears against a background of judgment as a twig from a tree which will grow in Palestine after the exile; with Ezekiel begins the apocalyptic distinction between the kingdom before and after judgment.

The messianic prince is a constant figure in the prophets, though presented differently in various passages. Beside him stands the Mosaic figure of the prophet foretold (Deuteronomy 18:15-22) as the final God-send figure for the future. Malachi (4:5) speaks of Elijah as the final prophet who will return as preacher of repentance and prepare for the Messiah. But it is the Servant of Second Isaiah who in the five songs (Procksch includes 61:1-3, as a Servant song) presents the clearest picture of the prophetic Messiah. Jeremiah is the model, but is not identical with the Servant who is a perfect figure anointed by God and filled with his spirit. There are kingly features, but he is a prophet who announces the word of God. He is downcast by the failure of his preaching, is imprisoned and killed, but rises to give freedom to the bound. Without the personality of the Servant, the covenant is no longer thinkable; he embodies it in himself, and is also the light of the heathen outside the covenant.

"The kingdom of God" expresses the eschatological idea of the completion of God's world-plan. Linked with the coming Messiah, it bursts national and historical limits. In Second Isaiah Yahweh, not David, is king, and the prophet stands at the point of time when the new kingdom, to which other nations as well as Israel belong, is breaking into history. This great height is never reached again, but the universalism remained valid for all time. Procksch does not accept the theory that would limit Yahweh's enthronement-announcement to an annual New Year festival. Later the high priest becomes the type of the Messiah as the Branch (Jeremiah 23:5; Zechariah 3:8). In Malachi it is the heavenly being, angel of the covenant, who prepares for God's advent. Various pictures of the messianic hope appear in the Psalter: Suprahistorical hopes are associated with the historic

Judean ruler (72:8); the warlike priest-king (110; cf. Genesis 14:20) is regarded not as teaching the law, but as making eternal atonement; the Messiah goes far beyond history in Psalm 2:6-7, sitting as king on Zion, begotten of God, not adopted like David. The (earthly) kingdom is not an eschatological, but a theological, picture of the world ruled by God, as limitless as God himself. In the apocalypse of Isaiah (24–27) there is no Messiah, and after judgment God will appear as king on Zion, destroy death forever, and all people will share his revelation. After the time of Alexander the Great, Daniel gives a new form to Isaiah's conflict between the kingdom of God and the world, and there appears the Son of Man and the people of the Most High (Daniel 7:13, 27), who are heavenly beings. This conception stands between that of Ezekiel (1:26) and Jesus. In Ezekiel the human figure is an image of God and is the son of God. Jesus uses the title Son of Man to conceal the title Son of God which means much more than the Davidic Messiah.

GOD AND MAN

This part of Procksch's work is subdivided into sections on faith, atonement, and fellowship with God.

The ORIGIN OF FAITH to the prophets is a call, vision, or audition which suddenly gives them a direct revelation, to which the prophets alone lay claim. Only faith recognizes God's self-revelation without which there is no communion with God. For the Old Testament prophets this basic experience of meeting with God is creative and direct; in Christian experience the encounter with God comes from the life of faith of Christianity, derived from the prophets' experience.

From the prophetic contact is developed the word of revelation which can be passed on more easily than vision. Over man's eye or ear is a covering, which God must remove before the man can receive revelation. Revelation results from faith, expressed by words formed from the *'mn* root, basically meaning truth, reliance, or loyalty, and applying originally more to persons than to things. The fundamental truth of prophetic faith was monotheism, which became the faith of the people after the exile. The only God has proved himself in history to be God of the world, and to be holy, by judging his own people. He is true, trustworthy, loyal, and can always be relied upon.

Faith, first attributed to Abraham, is an inner attitude of acceptance of God's moral ordering of the world, and is reliance on God; it is not a relationship, but a state of loyalty. From this loyalty comes the element of certainty which allows a man to stand before God.

The "sphere of faith" involves, first, the fear of God. Prophetic faith gives to Old Testament religion its specific character as a relationship between two persons, each retaining personality. The relationship begins with God's self-revelation to man, and its goal is threefold—fear, knowledge, and love of God. No religion is possible without the fear of God, which in the Old Testament loses its vagueness as God reveals himself as wholly Other over against man, and yet as partially secret (Genesis 32:24-32). Here arises the paradox of desire both for flight and nearness, smallness before God yet greatness above the animal creation (Psalm 8). The "fear of God" could be translated as "religion." It expresses the basic attitude in the patriarchal and the Mosaic age. It is the condition of man's receiving revelation and keeps him from sin. In the wisdom writings fear is the beginning of wisdom, and the principle of moral life.

The knowledge of God is the second sphere of faith. It is not theoretical or contemplative, but is a very personal relationship involving the whole person, emotions as well as intellect. Hosea and Jeremiah express clearly the moral character of the knowledge of God. It includes truth and mercy, and the care of the poor and needy. Hosea contrasts it with the cult, but regards the priest as responsible for it because he is in charge of the Torah. Wisdom writers also stress its moral character. Ezekiel, Second Isaiah, and the Psalter link it with monotheism, the knowledge of the sole godhead of Yahweh.

The love of God is the third sphere of faith. Because God reveals himself as loving, man can love him in return. Hosea boldly introduced the image of marriage to illustrate the relation of God and man. Love is its basis, a love for the lost still persisting even when all legal claims have lost their validity. This love is based on God's choice. Hosea is followed by Jeremiah and Deuteronomy. Human love must respond to the divine; love of God as the great commandment appears only in Deuteronomy where, too, love is linked with godly fear, and includes cult, morality, and law. In Amos (5:14) love of the good goes together with love of God, and in the Psalter (31:23) love is enjoined on the pious as right feeling.

The "proof of faith" comes, first, by endurance. Isaiah demanded faith from Ahaz in a historical crisis, as a personal attitude which would have enabled him to hold out till God rescued him. Faith creates certainty in God, which gives man the power to endure. Isaiah (30:15) analyzes the idea of faith as return, rest, quietness, reliance—all active attitudes. In the psalms and even in the proverbs faith is pure trust in God and guarantees rescue. To Isaiah, faith is surrender to God, renouncing all worldly powers and relying on the power that overcomes the world (cf. 1 John 5:4). Faith waits and hopes against all appearances.

A second proof of faith is through prayer. Faith is unthinkable without prayer, which like fear is basic to religion. In the Old Testament, prayer is never a mystical merging with God, but is a sense of tension until man accepts God's will made known in revelation. The oldest form of prayer, and the prelude to true prayer, is calling on the name of God, a personal call for divine help. From this comes the symbol of struggle for blessing, thanksgiving, and the humble plea for deliverance. Jeremiah is the father of true prayer. Faith is also shown in petitions and intercessions, led by prophet, not by priest. In the prophets, petition is never *opus operatum* but depends on the piety of the petitioner, and intercession for the unrighteous is unavailing if there is no repentance, though the sinless Servant can make "many" righteous because he prays for evildoers.

Finally, confession is the open acknowledgment of God's will for men, and can be seen in the praise of God in which the heathen must join (Psalm 67:5), as well as in the prophetic struggle against the wicked. In Hosea and Jeremiah is seen the suffering that lies in confession, and in the Servant this becomes martyrdom. The whole history of Israel and the Old Testament itself is a great confession to the truth of God.

Under ATONEMENT Procksch includes sin, wrath, and ransom. Man is conscious will, appointed for fellowship with God, and so must be pure and holy. But in historical activity man oversteps the limits of God's "Thou shalt not," and becomes guilty. The fall to "sin" (Genesis 3) is presupposed throughout the Bible. For the writer of the story, the desire to attain likeness to God, to overstep the limits inherent in innocence and to penetrate the secrets of God, has a demonic origin in the serpent which is neither divine nor human. Sin is always against God and is not simply immorality. It belongs to the realm of faith, not law, causing doubts about God's truth and making man untrustworthy. Sin is an activity that misses God, the true aim of man, and produces the state of guilt which can be removed only by substitution, a guilt- or sin-offering.

Another concept of sin means rebellion (RSV, transgression). We must speak of original guilt because, though every man is created innocent, each falls by the same temptation into the same sin. Jeremiah (17:14) speaks of sin as sickness. There is in Old Testament thought not only the moral contrast between good and bad, but also the contrast between healthy and unhealthy, applied to the whole community as well as to the individual.

The "wrath of God" is his reaction to sin which is directed against him personally, not against his laws or his work. Wrath springs from God's holiness. The Old Testament thinks of God as meeting bad with good in divine suffering. His power lies in his pathos, and especially after the exile God is spoken of as longsuffering (Exodus 34:1). The wrath of God brings curse, suffering, and death.

First of all, the divine curse must be distinguished from the human, which is often linked with magic and is not theological. God's curse excludes those whom he curses from fellowship with him. Not Adam but the ground was cursed because of sin, and this curse was removed for Noah. God alone holds the power to curse (Numbers 23:8).

Next, suffering was primitively ascribed to God's wrath at sin, but the suffering of the righteous suggested that sin and suffering did not always coincide. To Jeremiah the cause of suffering was hidden, but its aim was the evocation of confession and repentance. In Job, Satan, a demonic power, causes suffering, which God allows in order to show the disinterestedness of Job's faith. In the Psalter, too, suffering, though often the result of sin, is not punishment for it but leads to discipline and rejection of the temptation to fall away from God (Psalm 73:21-24).

Finally death, not natural but spiritual death which is exclusion from the presence of God, took its beginning on the day of sin (Genesis 3). Death as being gathered to the fathers is peace, not punishment; but to the individual death means the anguish of separation from the community, and this is seen as separation from God. Theologically, the dead exist but do not live, because human life comes only from God, who is not present in the underworld where man is torn from fellowship with God.

Procksch next deals with "ransom" as a part of atonement including conscience, conversion, and forgiveness. "Conscience" is the last remnant of the knowledge of God in the natural man. It leads him towards realization of his own fallen position over against the divine and moral world, and so toward choosing good and rejecting evil. It also gives him a knowledge of guilt which no sin-offering can remove. The religious element present in conscience is man's responsibility to God; it is the sign of the divine and exists outside the moral community. The offering expresses clearly the necessity of reconciliation with God and the attempt to get redemption. The prophets opposed offering as *opus operatum;* they saw it as a confession, and it remained so till the end of the Old Testament. In the cultless exilic period cultic songs replaced cultic acts, and the psalms of repentance reveal the fineness of conscience, emphasizing the necessity of confession to bridge the gap between God and man, and to obtain mercy and wholeness.

"Conversion," or returning, is very important in Old Testament theology. It involves decision, an act of the will. The initiative lies always with God, who causes the returning, which however is impossible without the personal will of man on whom responsibility rests. When conversion happens it is a mutual act of God and man, and the convert has power to move others to return. There is an eschatological idea of the great, final turning and salvation, but the older idea is of God's restoring man's fortune (turn the turning); his restoration will make Israel feel shame and turn with loathing from his sin (Ezekiel 16:53-58).

Three main metaphors are used for "forgiveness." *(a)* Covering, an image from civil law, is applied to sacral law. In Isaiah 6:7 it is obtained by the glowing stone from the altar without sacrifice or sin-offering, although the imagery is cultic. *(b)* Redeeming by the next of kin is linked with family law and the honor of the family. This is not a cult word. God as next of kin has bound himself to man and draws him into his community. *(c)* Ransoming comes neither from cult nor family life. It speaks of freeing from outside foreign control. In Deuteronomy it emphasizes God's free choice and grace to those without any legal claim upon God. There is no reference to price paid; God acts as sovereign lord. The distinction between redeeming and ransoming became weakened; originally both referred to saving from evil and misfortune, and the New Testament concept of redemption from sin is scarcely reached in the Old Testament. There are other metaphors of forgiveness, of which washing and purification are of cultic origin; "lifting" guilt may come from receiving a sin-offering. Jeremiah rejects offerings as a means of forgiveness and recognizes only grace. The final motive is the free love of God, and his power can heal and create life anew; the picture of bridal love is later replaced by that of the father's love, calling back lost sons. In the Servant-songs substitution, with its roots in the offering-cult, is introduced. The life of the guiltless one is offered as atonement for sinners, and his wounds heal "many." This prophetic vision is applied in the Psalter only to single men, not to the "many" until the time of Jesus.

The "state of grace" is the first aspect of FELLOWSHIP WITH GOD. The metaphor expressing in Semitic thought the relation between God and man is that of servant and lord, but there are two elements in tension—the servant as slave, included in the household but without legal rights, completely at the lord's mercy, and the servant as trusted retainer, serving his lord with loyalty. In both senses of the word the prophets, the people, and the pious are God's servants, dependent on his powerful moral, not legal mercy. God's mercy *(ḥesedh)* to man expresses an attitude of graciousness, compassion, sympathy; it is always extraordinary. There is tension, too, in a theophany between the fear of death and joy at seeing God in vision —a joy sometimes at its height in the cultic festival (Psalm 63:2). Reconciled man can see God because the barriers of sin have gone, so that in love he knows the complete joy of fellowship with God.

"Morality" is the next aspect of fellowship. Faith and morality are inseparable in both Old and New Testament theology. God's relation to a man does not isolate him, but makes him part of God's people. The moral motive includes: *(a)* The command or word of God, implied in the whole law, prophets and writings; in the Pentateuch not only the legal but also the historical sections were binding as patterns for behavior. Similarly in superscriptions to psalms, David's situation was described as an analogy for the life of the pious. The mainspring of keeping the law lies in the primitive phenomenon of fear, essential to morality, and love, a specifically Israelite contribution. *(b)* Community or human groupings, part of God's plan, provide a strong moral motive. In the Old Testament marriage is the oldest bond for such a group. Monogamy is known in J and P, polygamy is foreign to the prophetic spirit and causes the downfall of morality. From marriage springs the family group, the basis of the blood tie expressed in honoring parents, brotherhood, and guardianship of sisters. This bond forms a contemporaneous moral group extending to people, tribe, and race. Friendship and neighborliness supply another moral motive, as also does the protected guest, Israelite or foreigner, and the foreigner himself as part of God's creation. *(c)* The call of man gives him a moral task which, like the prophetic call, puts him beyond his human group and under God's compulsion. Despite his struggle against it, the power of God makes a man a servant of the divine plan. This is true of kings, judges, and of the ordinary man whose duties grow out of his association with human groups (cf. Micah 6:8).

The moral goal is: *(a)* The people of God. God and Good are inseparable, and the way to God leads to the Good, which is the moral goal. In the Psalter righteousness is the moral aim, and its essence includes peace, love, loyalty. Eschatology shows the moral aim in its pure form after evil has been rooted out. But in the historical present of the Old Testament, Israel as the chosen people must be holy with an exclusive relationship to God, in which righteousness includes piety and morality and is linked with truth and friendliness *(ḥesedh)*. The relationship with God is a model for the relationship among men. Friendliness to the weak is basic to Old Testament morality. Even love of enemies, seeking to overcome evil with good, is a moral aim for the people in the Old Testament as in the New.

(b) Moral character in the man of God, not simply in the people of God, is essential to the moral goal. Such character results from the development of all man's powers, so that he is continually becoming. The Greek concept of self-reliant superman or hero is not the Hebrew ideal, whose highest expression is the prophet who relies on God while he is struggling alone and willing to suffer. In Old Testament morality there is also the type of the wise man, contemplative rather than combative. Wisdom is a divine charisma, which in the Old Testament comes from God but has analogies among all

oriental peoples. It is mixed with worldly cleverness and experience of life. In later writings wisdom is linked with righteousness, and the education of youth in morality becomes the task of the wise— dealing with such matters as purity of marriage, family life, value of property and boundaries, true weights and measures, kindness to the needy. The ideal moral character is seen most clearly in Job where, despite the two different pictures in the dialogue and the prologue, suffering has a significant place in the picture of Old Testament morality.

The last aspect of fellowship with God is "eternal life." Old Testament faith takes death seriously; man has no power to bridge death, for it is grounded in the contrast between the living God and his creature man. Faith is grounded in this life, not in fantastic speculation about the afterlife; hope of eternal life was the fruit, not the root, of faith.

Old Testament eschatology replaces myth and has its roots in the historic revelation of God. It shows that life, not death, is the goal of God's activity even though man lost eternal life through guilt. But stories, showing that life with God is possible without death, kept alive faith in a beyond which possibly was within man's reach. There is a change in Ezekiel who in his thought of the messianic age comes to terms with death and speaks of the resurrection of David and Israel (34; 37). The resurrection is also thought of in Isaiah 24–27; 52–53; and in Daniel, where it is limited to the very good and the very bad—there is no general resurrection even for Israel. There is no need to assume foreign influences on the belief in resurrection, for both Elijah and the Messiah are Old Testament figures, but it is possible that Persian eschatology gave form and color to Israel's thought.

Eternal life also involves seeing God. Eternal life had its home in heaven to which Elijah and Enoch were taken, but it will appear on earth in the messianic kingdom after sin has been destroyed. In Old Testament thought, eternal life can be experienced on earth through "the sight of God," in which lies the possibility of death as well as of life. Where God let himself be seen, there was life and highest mercy, and a cult place was founded where an atoning offering protected man. The prophetic call was detached from the cult place and became an experience of eternal life within time. Isaiah's "to us"

(9:6) shows that he hoped to share in the messianic age, and Job, too, (42:5) speaks of seeing God before death. Ezekiel (18) suggests that the righteous survive the judgment. In the Psalter the thought of resurrection must be recognized. The highest point of Old Testament theology is reached by the anonymous poet of Psalm 73 with his faith that he remains with God who opens the way to glory.

The theology of the Old Testament represents a thousand years of writing which reflected the many changes that took place during that period, but the faith remained centered on the one eternal God, without beginning or end, who created with an ultimate purpose that will be achieved. Judaism, Christianity, and Islam depend on this God. In the Old Testament he is the revealed God, whose revelation is, in general, carried not by priest, nor by poet, but by prophet. Man must subject himself to this God in order to know him. Although he will presently see God as though veiled, one day man will see God as he is.

RELATIONSHIP BETWEEN OLD TESTAMENT AND NEW TESTAMENT

To Procksch all theology is Christology as the fullest revelation of God, and the goal of the Old Testament is Christ. He begins with an account of his own Christology, describing the relation between Christ and the world, church, and individual Christian in much the same terms as he uses later of God and the world, Israel, and man. Though the pre-Christian spiritual world has been superseded by the New Testament and Christ, and the Old Testament cannot be understood without Christ, yet it is also true that Christ is not understandable without his roots in the Old Testament. It gives his figure color, it was his Bible, and he regards himself as its fulfillment. God's choice and mercy, and his absolute will in calling a people into life, are basic to both Testaments, and in both, belief in God is the condition of right relation between man and God. Thus the apostolic confession, "Jesus is Christ," perfectly links the Old Testament with the New Testament.

CRITIQUE

Procksch was in the front rank of exegetes, exact in his philology, reared in the traditions of Delitzsch and Dillmann, and considerably influenced by Dalman at Jerusalem. But the basic aim of his life was to work out a theology of history, a tremendous synthesis. Interest in history is seen in all his work, particularly in his study of the preexilic prophets, and of the source E, where he wrote that we must get the "gold of history" from behind the world of saga. He had a great respect for sound literary scholarship and for the scholarship of others. Views as to the relationship between history of religion and theology expressed in Procksch's *Theologie* were the fruit of practical experience at Griefswald. His great commentaries were written on Genesis and Isaiah; here he affirms the necessity for full understanding of the Scriptures, for penetration and sympathetic imagination *(Einfühlung),* but also for "the supraworldly organ of faith" which alone makes contact with the life-nerve of the writing.[4] Especially characteristic of this view is his article on Christ in the Old Testament.[5] He went far to bring the Old Testament back within theology from which it had been estranged.

Otto Procksch had a profound influence on German Old Testament scholarship, and made a tremendous contribution to our understanding of Old Testament religion by pointing out the value of the patriarchal sagas, the traditions of Sinai and of Jerusalem, and especially by his emphasis on the importance of the covenant concept. His direct influence on English and American scholars would have been greater had his works been translated, but his indirect influence has been immeasurable. Eichrodt, in the fifth English edition of his *Theology of the Old Testament,* added a footnote (vol. I, p. 33, n. 1) acknowledging his indebtedness to his great teacher after Procksch himself had pointed out the fact in his *Theologie* (p. 421, n. 1). All of us reproduce the ideas of our beloved masters unconsciously, and Procksch's pupils were no exception.

His supreme interest was in the Old Testament as revelation, something that only faith—"existential involvement in the faith"—can apprehend. As we have said, for Procksch the revelation of the Old Testament culminates in Jesus Christ. However, his dogmatic stress

---

[4] It should, however, be noted that the phrase "organ of faith" mentioned here and quoted by Eissfeldt, *ZAW,* 44 (1926), p. 4, is avoided by Procksch in the *Theologie,* where the stress is, as always, on God-given faith. See also R. C. Dentan, *Preface to Old Testament Theology,* rev. ed., pp. 63f.

[5] "Christus im Alten Testament," *NKZ,* 44 (1933), pp. 57-83.

on the necessity for faith and the culmination of revelation in Christ probably limits the value of his contribution to modern Old Testament thought. His own background was Protestant and Lutheran, and continually he shows that it was easier for him to appreciate the prophetic than the priestly element in the Old Testament. To him the prophet, not the priest, is the bearer of revelation. Faith as seen in the Abraham saga and the teaching of First Isaiah dominates his Old Testament theology. The basis of Yahweh religion to him lies in the prophetic, apodictic sayings in the Decalogue, which, unlike Wellhausen, he regarded as possibly Mosaic. To him the Decalogue is clearly prophetic religion in its call for no images, no profaning of the Lord's name, keeping the sabbath and the moral commandments, but no mention of sacrifice.

In his attempt to formulate a theology of sacrifice, Procksch argues that the aim of the cult is communion with the Divine, and the root of the cult is in human community. This community is based on blood relationship, hence blood is very important in the primitive Semitic cultus. The blood tie has to establish connection with God just as it connects humans within the community. The death of the sacrifice sets the blood free for its cultic purpose of expiation and reconciliation. The basic Semitic contrast between God as holy and man as unholy makes man aware of his guilt and the need for reconciliation. So the center of the cult is the guilt-offering, which in its gloomiest and most burdensome form had been human sacrifice, an original part of Semitic religion rejected in the Abraham saga. For Procksch the aim of all bloody sacrifice was expiation, not communion, and there is no idea of magic or of gift.[6] In nonbloody sacrifice there was an idea of gift as a sign of self-surrender, and there expiation was overshadowed. But in human sacrifice, in the form of the son, man surrenders himself in order that expiation may be realized. So we must understand the death of Jesus which retained something of the depth and terror experienced in primitive Semitic religion.

This concept of sacrifice illustrates the importance of Procksch's statement that all theology is Christology, a statement that does not admit an intrinsic theology of the Old Testament apart from the

[6] Cf. Walther Eichrodt, *Theology of the Old Testament*, vol. 1, trans. J. A. Baker (Philadelphia: The Westminster Press, 1961), pp. 144ff.

New. Although he does not admit the value of a God-centered theology of the Old Testament apart from the Christ-centered theology of the New, it seems clear today that an element which is bringing the Old Testament back into importance is the recognition that its center is not the word nor wisdom nor the Anointed One, but God as Creator and Savior of the world. One cannot understand the Old Testament without recognizing the unity of prophet, priest, and wise man; and in the same way the unity of the whole Bible demands that Christology be seen in the setting of theology, in the God-centeredness of the Old Testament. Procksch certainly sees that God is at the center of the Old Testament, but he demands that the Old Testament be seen through Christology.

Two other beliefs of Procksch are important to recognize: the centrality of the covenant, and the People of God concept. In Semitic thought every covenant was witnessed by God and thus was a religious act, but the new element in the Sinai covenant was that God was not a witness and guardian but one of the contracting parties. Procksch does not talk of suzerain and vassal, but stresses that covenant is vertical and not horizontal. It is established by God and is not a bargain made by man with God. All the power is on God's side. The covenant springs from his mercy-choice, and even Israel's power to accept it comes from God. It was as a prophet, not as a priest, that Moses was mediator of the covenant, but the covenant itself was made not with the prophet alone but with the People of Israel. The Sinai covenant was concluded with a sacrificial meal and sealed with the blood of the sacrifice for expiation. With the sacrifice on Sinai God's covenant was perfect, there was no need for it to be repeated. It was made once for all, though possibly there was an annual remembrance feast for the renewal of the covenant.

The covenant was made with Israel as a people or nation. Procksch stresses that the covenant was not made with a responsive group within Israel or with a holy community gathered out of Israel, but with the whole people. The building up of this People of God can come only through the moral cooperation of the individual members. No king, no priest, no political nor cultic figure is adequate. The unique originality of this nation of Israel is that she can realize herself only in the figure of faith that is recognized more and more in the prophetic history.

SELECTED BIBLIOGRAPHY

O. Procksch, *Über die blutrache bei den vorislamischen Arabern und Mohammeds Stellung zu ihr.* Leipzig, 1899.

————, *Geschichtsbetrachtung und geschichtliche Überlieferung bei den vorexilischen Propheten.* Leipzig, 1902.

————, *Das nordhebräische Sagenbuch. Die Elohimquelle.* Leipzig, 1906.

————, *Studien zur Geschichte der Septuaginta. Die Propheten.* Leipzig, 1910.

————, *Die kleinen prophetischen Schriften.* Leipzig, 1910 (vol. I), 1929 (vol. I; 2nd ed.).

————, *Die Völker Altpalästinas.* Leipzig, 1914.

————, *Altes Testament und Judentum.* Leipzig, 1921.

————, *König und Prophet in Israel.* Greifswald, 1924 (Greifswald Univ. Reden 11).

————, *Die Genesis.* Third ed. Leipzig, 1924.

————, *Jesaia I.* Leipzig, 1930 (KAT).

————, *Das Bekenntnis im Alten Testament.* Leipzig, 1936.

————, *Theologie des Alten Testaments.* Gutersloh, 1950.

————, "Die Berufungsvision Hesekiels," *Beiträge zur alttestamentlichen Wissenschaft* (K. Marti, ed.). Giessen, 1920, pp. 141-149 (BZAW 34).

————, "Geschichte als Glaubensinhalt," *NKZ* 36 (1925), pp. 485-499.

————, "Ziele und Grenzen der Exegese," *NKZ* 36 (1925), pp. 715-730.

————, "Die kirchliche Bedeutung des Alten Testaments," *NKZ* 42 (1931), pp. 295-306.

————, "Christus im Alten Testament," *NKZ* 44 (1933), pp. 57-83.

————, "Fürst und Priester bei Hesekiel," *ZAW* 17 (1940-41), pp. 99-133.

4
Theodorus C. Vriezen
An Outline
of Old Testament Theology

by Ronald E. Clements

Theodorus C. Vriezen was born at Dinxperlo, Netherlands, in 1899. His studies were undertaken at the Universities of Utrecht, Leiden, and Groningen. After serving as minister of the Dutch Reformed Church at Tubbergen en Sittard from 1925-1929, he was professor at The Hague from 1929-1941, professor at the University of Groningen (1941-1957), and presently is professor at the University of Utrecht. In 1965 he was the Director of the Near East School of Theology, Beirut, Lebanon.

THEODORUS C. VRIEZEN'S STUDY of Old Testament theology was first published in Dutch in 1949, and a much revised second edition appeared in 1954. A third edition, with further extensive revisions and some rearrangement, was published in 1966. German and English translations of the second Dutch edition, with some variations in detail and in the bibliographical references, were published in 1956 and 1958 respectively. Although there are significant changes in the ordering and detail of the material throughout these editions, the basic method and approach to the subject have remained unchanged. As a useful companion to this major work Vriezen has published an extended critique of recent writing on Old Testament theology, particularly that which owes its stimulus to the work of G. von Rad, under the title "Geloof, openbaring en geschiedenis in de nieuwste Oud-Testamentische theologie." This contains a valuable criticism of attempts to write Old Testament theology as a theology of history, and serves in some measure as a defense of Vriezen's own position. There is also a compact and useful study of the religion of Israel in which Vriezen presents his understanding of the historical religion

123

which forms the basis of Old Testament theology. An English translation of this was published in 1967.

The references in the present essay are to the first English edition of *An Outline of Old Testament Theology* which is currently the most accessible presentation of Vriezen's views for English readers.

ARRANGEMENT OF OLD TESTAMENT THEOLOGY

The arrangement of Vriezen's theology consists of a basic division into two parts. The first part contains a general introduction to the subject, and the second offers a descriptive account of its content. This twofold division makes for convenience and orderliness, and enables a detailed study to be made of Vriezen's own understanding of his task. The second part is a coherent and systematic account of the nature and content of faith in the Old Testament. It is historical in its approach, critical in its treatment of the sources, and theological in its purpose. It provides a detailed presentation of the nature of Israel's religion and of the distinctive ideas which emerged within it. As such this section must be regarded as the fundamental text upon which a consideration of Vriezen's view of Old Testament theology must be based.

The first part, which contains a prolegomenon to the task of writing an Old Testament theology, deals with a variety of matters which have a formal, rather than a material, relationship to each other. There is a brief survey of the history of the church's use of the Old Testament, and some general observations on the historical character of the revelation which it contains. This is followed by a short survey of the spiritual structure of the various Old Testament writings in which the basic contents of the canon are analyzed. The particular interests and purpose of each of the books are noted, and the historical process by which the canon emerged in its Hebrew form as a threefold division is described. There follows a study of the use of the Old Testament by the Christian church in which importance is attached to the task of historico-critical exegesis, and the use of this approach in preaching.

The concluding chapter of this first part is by far the most distinctive and original in the whole book and sets out the author's view of the basis, task, and method of Old Testament theology. Here some of the most searching and fundamental questions are raised about the character of revelation in the Bible and the way in which this historical revelation can be described theologically. Vriezen argues that Old Testament theology must be a theological discipline, both in the method of its working and the object which it strives to attain. It thus forms a connecting link between dogmatic and historical theology. It differs from a study of the history of Israelite religion because its object is the Old Testament and not the religion of Israel, and because it proceeds beyond a phenomenological description of Israel's religious life and institutions to evaluate the message of the Old Testament. It is concerned with this message both in itself and in its relation to the New Testament. Thus Old Testament theology examines the characteristic features of the message of the Old Testament and especially seeks to elucidate the element of revelation which it contains. Because it works with theological standards which take their origin in the Christian message of the New Testament, Old Testament theology is able to work with a measure of freedom. It is not bound to deal with every aspect of Israel's religion, but can select only those aspects which are of particular importance. Similarly Old Testament theology is not tied unreservedly to the existing form of the canon, but remains free to exercise its own judgment upon it.

Nevertheless such a theology cannot restrict itself solely to the ideas which emerge in the Old Testament, but must concern itself with the whole reality of the revelation of God as this becomes evident in historical institutions and the written witness of the Old Testament. Thus every aspect of the modern study of the Old Testament—literary, philological, historical, and archaeological—comes within the scope of such a theological approach, and a continuous contact with the results obtained in each field of scholarship becomes important.

Two factors of special significance emerge from Vriezen's method of approaching his task. The first is his insistence that the proper subject matter is the Old Testament itself, and not the historical religion of ancient Israel (pp. 15, 40, 118, 121).[1] Thus, just as a certain selectivity is evident in the testimony which the Old Testament makes to the religion of Israel, so the Old Testament theologian maintains this

[1] All citations in parentheses are taken from Th. C. Vriezen, *An Outline of Old Testament Theology* (Newton, Mass.: Charles T. Branford Co., 1958). Quotations used by permission of Basil Blackwell, Oxford.

principle of selectivity in his evaluation of its message. The second factor which is strongly insisted upon is that Old Testament theology is a Christian discipline and must work with Christian theological standards (pp. 86f., 89, 91f., 121f.). Thus it must make the New Testament its starting point. It is concerned not only with the faith of Israel, but with the relationship of this faith to the New Testament. This kind of Old Testament theology does not evaluate its subject in an arbitrary fashion, but gives an insight into the revelatory content of the Old Testament on the ground of a Christian understanding of God. This confrontation with the New Testament need not be overtly expressed or elaborated, but it will be an underlying factor in the study and arrangement of the material. In fact, in the main body of Vriezen's outline of Old Testament theology a direct confrontation with the New Testament scarcely appears.

For the content of Old Testament theology Vriezen seeks a classification of the material which expresses an existential relationship between man and God, although he admits that this structure is not wholly satisfactory. Thus he deals with the doctrines of God, man, the relationship between them, and the ethical relationship between man and man. A concluding chapter deals with eschatology as one aspect of God's relationship to man and the world.

CONTENTS OF OLD TESTAMENT THEOLOGY

After this lengthy introductory section, Vriezen proceeds in the second part of his book to describe the actual content of Old Testament theology as an integrated whole. This theology may be described summarily as an account of Israel's communion with God. What Vriezen regards as the essential message of the Old Testament is not a disclosure of the Being of God as he is in himself, but rather a revelation of the nature and possibility of man's communion with God. Consequently, Vriezen never opens a consideration of the secret of God's own Being.

The starting point for this view of Old Testament theology is found in the Old Testament itself with its distinctive view of what the knowledge of God means. This knowledge is something altogether different from intellectual knowing, since it appeals to the whole life of man and must be expressed with the heart and will as well as with the mind. It is existential rather than ontological. An account of such a knowledge cannot therefore be given without relating it to the whole life of man. The fundamental presupposition of the Old Testament literature is its awareness of the reality of this immediate spiritual communion between God and man which ultimately rests upon divine revelation. *"This communion exists as a spiritual knowledge, revealed by God; as something Israel received in a special way in its covenant with Yahweh"* (p. 133). The formal expression of Israel's relationship to God is thus found in the conception of the covenant, which is the most influential idea of the Old Testament and which was disclosed to Israel through the prophets. "Israel owes this knowledge to the special revelation granted to the prophets, from the earliest times (Abraham or Moses) ; and it was preserved to the end by the prophets alone, who spoke the explanatory Word of God all through Israel's history" (p. 133). The continued danger that beset Israel was that of making this revealed knowledge into a natural assumption. The goal of revelation is thus seen by Vriezen as a knowledge of man's communion with God, which for Israel took the form of a belief in a covenant relationship existing between God and the people. The medium of revelation was prophecy, and the sphere of its operation was the whole of Israelite history. On a more individualistic basis the outstanding feature of the Old Testament conception of man is that he is created in God's image. When we inquire what the Old Testament discloses to us therefore, and what constitutes its fundamental message, we can summarize it briefly: God has, of his own free will, entered into a direct, complete relationship with man, thereby overcoming the distance between mankind and himself (p. 147).

Within this scheme describing the nature of the communion between God and man, which the Old Testament presupposes and to which it testifies, Vriezen is able to introduce the characteristic ideas of Israel's faith. His chapters dealing with the doctrines of God and man are based upon reconstructions of the thought-world of the Old Testament. God is holy and righteous, and yet because he is also gracious and merciful, he enters into fellowship with men. Although in the Old Testament this fellowship is primarily limited to Israel, it is never exclusively the possession of the one nation. The ultimate goal of the salvation of Israel is the sharing of this salvation with the nations of the world. There is a nationalistic limitation therefore in the

Old Testament witness to God's communion with man, but this is never absolute and is overcome through the greatest prophetic personalities.

In the doctrine of man, Vriezen deals with the fact of human sin and with the various ways in which the Old Testament describes this reality. He follows this discussion with a consideration of the relationship of the individual to the community and a study of the various institutions of Israelite society. The characteristic Israelite conception of the state was that of a theocracy, which ultimately took on an eschatological dimension as a belief in the future kingdom of God.

Questions of the nature and media of divine revelation are dealt with as aspects of the intercourse between God and man. "The essential meaning of all revelation is the COMMUNION between God and man; it is the most profound desire of individual piety, and the ultimate promise of the prophetic message" (p. 233). This revelation was not tied to certain unique moments in Israel's experience, but was a continuing fact. Its method of operation was that God entered into an immediate contact with certain individuals whom he chose and to whom he granted his spirit and his Word. In this way the relationship of God to man remained thoroughly personal.

The cult is also treated by Vriezen under the general heading of Israel's relationship to God. He fully acknowledges the important part played by the cult in Israel's religion and concedes that much of it bears a very close relation to that of neighboring nations. Israel was greatly indebted to its environment for the institutions and practices of its cultic life, yet whatever Israel borrowed was modified by its subordination to the idea of the covenant. "The cult exists as a means to integrate the communion between God and man which God has instituted in His Covenant, in other words, the cult exists for the sake of the atonement" (p. 280). Thus the sacrificial service of the sanctuaries enabled Israel to continue in communion with God through the provision of a means of atonement and reconciliation. Within the Old Testament we discern a growing moralizing and spiritualizing of the cult, which led to a deepening inwardness of spiritual life. At the same time we also observe the opposite phenomenon of a growing superficiality, in which the cult became a mere observance, and even a human achievement. Nevertheless Vriezen regards the cult as an indispensable aspect of Israel's religion, in which the major contribution which it has to make to an Old Testament theology is the idea of atonement which it upholds.

The distinctive features of Israelite morality are directly related to Israel's religion, since, as in all religions, the relation between man and man is fundamentally determined by the relation between God and man. Religion and ethics are thus closely bound together. The monotheistic belief of Israel contributed to its ethical achievement by showing that the one will of the one God dominates the whole of life.

The doctrine of creation is set within certain limits in the Old Testament, and its particular value for the religious life is a consequence of its connection with the history of salvation. Yet, just as Israel's deepening spiritual insight into life gave it a growing interest in God's relation to the world, so also did it lead to a growth of knowledge of the relationship between Israel and the world of nations. This knowledge found its expression in the conception of the kingship of God, leading to the idea of his eschatological kingdom. The expectation of this kingdom was founded on the absolute certainty of God's kingship now and ever.

In the Old Testament the hope of future salvation took widely different forms which cannot be brought into complete harmony with each other. All Israel's expectations of future salvation, however, arose out of its faith in the actual presence of the holy God as the God of salvation. Thus, the awareness of communion with God in the present gave rise to an eschatological vision of a kingdom of God which would be revealed in Israel for the sake of mankind. This eschatological vision expressed the belief that God, because he is the God of all human history, would bring history to its end in complete communion between himself and man, so he might be all in all.

RELATIONSHIP BETWEEN FAITH AND HISTORY

To evaluate the distinctive features of Vriezen's presentation of Old Testament theology, we must clarify as far as possible the underlying ideas of his work, and in particular the idea of the nature and method of revelation. We have already noted in the survey of the content of Vriezen's theology that he introduces the various media of revelation in Israel as features of its continuing spiritual communion with God.

The whole of Israel's life in fact was based upon revelation, since the founders of its faith were prophetic personalities through whom God spoke to men. Thus it is "an incontestable fact that the religion of Israel (at any rate as represented in the Old Testament) is fundamentally prophetic throughout and that the Old Testament revelation came to the people of Israel first and foremost through the intermediation of prophets" (p. 258). Thus, the primary feature of revelation in the Old Testament is that it is mediated through human personalities and is both founded upon a spiritual communion with God and testifies to this as its chief goal. Thus revelation has a truly spiritual character and is given directly and personally. The various material and external means of discerning the will of God, as in the sacred lot, play little part in the Old Testament religion of revelation.

A second important feature of revelation is its continuing and progressive character. "There is a spiritual development from Moses (or Abraham) to Deutero-Isaiah, the last of the great prophets in whom the knowledge of the revelation of God was deepened and broadened, with whom, in fact, Jesus Christ links up directly and to whom St. Paul goes back again and again in his Epistles" (p. 16). Revelation was thus not limited to certain unique events or to a few chosen individuals, but introduced a continuing spiritual growth throughout the whole period which the Old Testament covers. "Man is initiated further and further into the truth concerning God and he gains a more profound spiritual understanding of God which enables him to speak of God in new terms and purer forms" (p. 17). In this historical movement "Jesus Christ is . . . the last phase of the revelation of God in Israel" (p. 91).

Revelation therefore is an aspect of Israel's communion with God since this communion is founded upon it and, as a result of fellowship with God, a fuller revelation becomes possible. Furthermore the goal of this revealing action of God is nothing less than his disclosure to man of the possibility of communion with himself. Throughout Vriezen's work, therefore, we can recognize a conception in which revelation and communion with God are regarded as closely related facts of Israel's experience and give to the Old Testament its unique character. The substance of this revelation is to be defined not in abstract or dogmatic terms, but in a deepening consciousness of the nature and character of man's relationship to God.

When we come to inquire in what precise way Vriezen relates this revelatory element to the history of Israel, we find a rejection of any attempt to divorce revelation from the actual course of events or from the actual religious development which took place. The methods and tools of historical criticism are indispensable to a proper presentation of Old Testament theology. "As a result of the historical research of this century and the last . . . our insight into this progress of revelation has increased and deepened" (p. 16). Nevertheless, although we are committed to a critical historical reconstruction of the development of religion in Israel, this must not be allowed to become a mere historicism. Such historicism would fail to discern the spiritual factor which has been at work in Israel's history.

Because Israel was established in an oriental environment and participated in the growth of the ancient eastern civilized world, it inevitably developed in a living relationship to other oriental religions. From these religions Israel was often a borrower, so that the growth of religion in Israel was closely related to the development of the cultural and political situation of the world which formed its environment. There is therefore both an internal movement of religious development within Israel and also an external movement as Israel was influenced by contact with its Near Eastern environment. Neither movement, however, is able to account fully for the unique quality of Israel's religion, which is the result of a particular spiritual factor which interfered decisively in Israel's life again and again. It is this element of divine intervention at work in Israel's life which made its religion quite different from other Near Eastern religions, and which was ultimately responsible for the gift of the Old Testament to the world. The mode of operation of this particular force was the inspired preaching of prophetic personalities.

In the course of analyzing Israel's religious and ethical ideas, Vriezen argues at many points that we can discern a decisive break in Israel with the ideas and practices which were current among its neighbors. The implication is that this break is a consequence of the revealing activity of God so that, although we cannot now wholly endorse all of Israel's beliefs and actions, we can recognize in them a move towards a more spiritual understanding of mankind's communion with God.

Since an Old Testament theology must be based upon a careful critical reconstruction of the course of Israel's religious history, the continued contact between Israel and its environment must be fully recognized, and acknowledgment made of Israel's indebtedness to its neighbors. The theologian, however, is concerned with more than a purely historical reconstruction of the development of Israelite religion, which is the province of phenomenology, and seeks out the unique spiritual qualities which become evident in a study of this development and which have been preserved for us in the Old Testament. Vriezen argues that in these qualities the revelatory action of God is to be discerned. Thus revelation takes place behind and within Israel's religion, and we are in no way committed to an identification of every aspect of Israel's political and religious life with the will of God.

The basis of this view of revelation in the Old Testament is found by Vriezen in Israel's own understanding of the media by which God communicated his will to Israel. The authority of this revelation for us is validated in a number of ways, the most important of which is that provided by the inescapable relationship which the Old Testament shares with the New. "It [the Old Testament] is authoritative when it shares in the truth revealed in Jesus Christ—in other words, when there is an essential relation between the message of the Old Testament and the New Testament" (pp. 86-87). Thus the authority of the Old Testament is ultimately the authority which has been conferred upon it by Jesus Christ, and its unique quality is a result of the activity of the Holy Spirit which was revealed in him.

Vriezen is careful, however, not to remove altogether the validation of the authority of the Old Testament to a Person and an event which lie beyond its compass, as though it were not IN ITSELF authoritative. There is a historical continuity which binds the revelation of God in the Old Testament to the revelation in Jesus, and the reality of Israel's communion with God is in no way to be denied because that communion was raised to a new height in the Incarnation. Vriezen in fact sees a historical movement in which the coming of Christ represents the last stage of the revealing activity of God to Israel. The whole of this movement has a unique authority because of the reality of the communion with God on which it was based and to which it led. Consequently, the authority of the Old Testament is not a formal dogmatic claim concerning its historical infallibility, but is approved to our own moral and spiritual sensibilities because of what it says about God and man.

On account of this particular personal and spiritual quality of revelation it cannot be identified unconditionally with the contents of the Old Testament canon. There are some parts of its writings where the Christian can find the revelation of the Spirit of God only with great difficulty, if at all. Because this literature reflects the spirit and attitude of its own environment this historical limitation has to be acknowledged. Vriezen does not mean that the contents of the canon should be changed, but rather that they must be read with a theological and critical judgment. Questions about the authorship of the biblical documents and their claim to have been written by divine inspiration do not affect the vital issue of their authority as revelation. "With respect to the truth of a Biblical writing it is fundamentally of no importance whether the date of such a writing is earlier or later than the date attributed to it by the Old Testament tradition or actually coincides with that date" (p. 89). The doctrine of verbal inspiration must be regarded as a later historical reflection which came into being after the contents of the Old Testament canon had been defined.

In conclusion we may formulate a statement of the underlying conception of revelation which informs Vriezen's work. Revelation is essentially the outcome of a personal communion between man and God, in which a deeper and fuller understanding of the divine nature and character becomes possible. Such a communion with God existed in Israel in a unique way, through the gracious intervention of the Holy Spirit, in which the primary medium was provided by prophecy. We cannot therefore unreservedly identify every aspect of Israel's religion with this divine revelation, nor can we identify revelation wholly with the Old Testament canon. It is the task of the theologian to search out the element of revelation in the Old Testament through his own spiritual understanding which is made sensitive by the revelation of God given in Jesus Christ.

CRITIQUE

Our critique of Vriezen's work must consider his methodology, his conception of the canon, and his understanding of the relationship of revelation and history.

METHODOLOGY.

The first point which we need to raise in a critique of Vriezen's theology concerns the consistency with which he has applied his own methodology. A number of reviewers have noted a lack of harmony between the two parts of Vriezen's book, particularly in regard to the question of using the revelation of the New Testament as the starting point for an evaluation of the message of the Old.[2] Certainly it is true that his introduction seems to anticipate a rather different kind of theology from that which is actually given. The two parts do not harmonize very well, and the central issue is that of the confrontation with the New Testament. Vriezen stresses the need for such a confrontation in outlining the task of presenting an Old Testament theology and yet is able to write the substance of his work with virtually no further direct reference to this fundamental principle. Admittedly, he states that such a confrontation should be implicit rather than explicit, but if it is so fundamental the objection may fairly be raised that this approach is inadequate. If the ultimate authority of the Old Testament as revelation lies in the fact that it shares in the truth revealed in Jesus Christ, then this relationship should be demonstrated in the presentation of its theology rather than presupposed as subjectively guiding its apprehension.

The lack of unity between the two parts of Vriezen's theology may be partly accounted for by the literary genesis of the work. A comparison of the first Dutch edition with the second shows that in the latter the introductory material has been greatly extended without bringing it into complete harmony with the main body of theology. Vriezen has himself recognized this and made considerable changes in the third Dutch edition bringing the two parts into a closer relation, and presenting their contents with greater consistency. The question of the relationship between the two Testaments is more fully considered, and the idea of communion with God, which is fundamental to the main outline, is carried over into the introduction.

We may still question, however, whether Vriezen has succeeded satisfactorily in combining the theological and historical require-

[2] Cf. B. S. Childs, *JBL,* 78 (1959), p. 258: "His treatment seldom penetrates beyond a description of Israel's faith. The reader is left still wondering what is meant by an OT theology judged from the 'point of view of the Christian faith.'"

ments of an Old Testament theology along the lines which he has laid down. In presenting the Old Testament evidence Vriezen wholly aligns himself with a historico-critical method of approach, and yet in evaluating the theological and spiritual significance of this material he asserts that we must take as a starting point the revelation of Jesus Christ in the New Testament. In the light of this assertion we must ask whether the conviction of the theologian does not come into collision with that of the historian of religion, so that ideas and institutions of great importance to the Old Testament are neglected because of their rejection by the New Testament. Israel's cult with its elaborate forms of service is a particular case in point. Can the theologian claim as a starting point what was undoubtedly not so in a strictly historical sense without breaking the bonds of historical discipline? Since the New Testament is historically younger than the Old, to use it as the primary basis of an Old Testament theology must overstep the limitations of a strictly historical method. Because of his commitment to the historical method Vriezen is content to preserve the historical character of his theology without bringing it into a direct and explicit confrontation with the New Testament revelation. By so doing, however, he seems to take an approach which is inconsistent with his claim that the revelation of the New Testament must be recognized as a basic presupposition for a theological understanding of the contents of the Old. The methodological consequences of such a recognition are very far-reaching and, as a theological construction, would call for a more detailed demonstration than the historical requirements of Vriezen's Old Testament theology allow to be given. Certainly the main substance of his theological outline appears less dependent upon the New Testament than his statement of the principle anticipates.

CANON

In his conception of the Old Testament canon Vriezen raises several questions which call for further examination. After making the valuable distinction between a history of the religion of Israel and a theology of the Old Testament, Vriezen does not develop this distinction fully. He argues that the literature of the Old Testament arose out of the unique spiritual quality of Israel's communion with God, capturing its deepest insights and preserving them for mankind.

While this observation is no doubt true, it fails to explain sufficiently the motives that led to the production of an Old Testament canon. In what ways did Israelites and Jews believe that the collection of their sacred Scriptures would contribute to their own communion with God? Undoubtedly something more was involved than simply recording the insights of the past. One of the most remarkable features of the Israelite religion was its transition from a cultic to a scriptural piety. In this transition they moved away from a central emphasis upon communion with God in the cult to an emphasis upon a knowledge of God through the sacred Scriptures, for which the cult served as a medium of communication. The character of Israel's religion changed dramatically during the course of its history, and the formation of a canon of sacred writings is a most significant outcome of this change. By possession of the writings of the law and the prophets, Jews not only sought to preserve the spiritual insights of their past, but also believed that they had a guarantee of their own divine election and an assurance of a coming eschatological vindication by God.[3] In a theology of the Old Testament an examination of the particular religious and political pressures which contributed to the formation of the Old Testament canon would seem to require a larger place than Vriezen gives to it.

Another question may also be raised about the canon. Both historically and theologically, in the Old Testament canon the law has the primary position over the prophets and the still less important writings. Vriezen, however, claims that the Old Testament as a whole is truly prophetic in its spirit (p. 90), and throughout all its parts its spiritual content has been determined by its prophetic origin. This judgment is wholly consonant with Vriezen's particular conception of revelation, but it does not agree with the actual historical development of the canon nor with the normal emphasis of Judaism. The law was undoubtedly first, and although it is arguable that its contents are informed by the prophetic spirit, this spirit is certainly not as prominent as in the second division of the canon. It is hard to escape the conclusion that the conception of revelation which becomes evident in a study of the canon, and which Judaism has traditionally upheld, is different from that which Vriezen makes. In the Old

[3] Vriezen briefly draws attention to the influence of the fall of Jerusalem in 586 B.C. upon the formation of the Old Testament canon (pp. 40f.).

Testament this conception is not so rigidly prophetic as Vriezen contends.

HISTORY

We may put further questions to Vriezen's work about its conception of history, and the relation of history to revelation. We have already seen that Vriezen accepts the thesis that revelation is mediated through persons who stand in a close communion with God. He does not enter into any argument therefore about revelation through historical events and the role of human interpretation of such events. For Vriezen the primary emphasis lies upon the human interpretation of the divine will under the guidance of the Holy Spirit. Throughout its history Israel enjoyed a succession of prophetic personalities, beginning with Moses, through whom the divine will was made known. Thus through these persons Israel's whole history took on a revelatory significance. In criticism of this view, which is somewhat reminiscent of the views of Wellhausen and Duhm, we may argue that the Old Testament does stress the divine hand in historical events, e.g., the Exodus and the Exile, in a way which must be fully allowed for in any conception of revelation. One of the most distinctive features of the Old Testament is that its writings present an increasing emphasis upon the role of Moses as the supreme mediator of the knowledge of God, a role which placed him above the prophets. As the emphasis upon a received divine law increased, so the freedom of inspired prophetic individuals decreased, and this emphasis upon law belongs essentially to that development which produced an Old Testament. Thus the Old Testament itself presents us with a changing conception of revelation.

The question of historical growth and development is a besetting problem for any presentation of Old Testament theology. By taking a classification of basic ideas—God, man, the relationship between God and man and between man and man—it is extremely difficult to give adequate room to the great changes that took place in Israel's religion, particularly through the great turning point of the Exile, which affected each of these basic doctrines. Without an analysis of this historical development in Israel one cannot show the true significance of that spiritual movement which led to the formation of a canon of scripture on the one hand, and to the eventual dispensing with such fundamental institutions as the temple and sacrifice on the other. Indeed, one may argue that this spiritual movement is of paramount importance to an Old Testament theology because of its relation to the formation of the canon and to the claim of the New Testament to be the fulfillment of the Old.

Also in relation to the problem of historical development we may question Vriezen's treatment of Israelite eschatology. This discussion appears at the end of his work as an elaboration of the doctrine of God's relationship to the cosmos and the world of nations. He claims that eschatology arises out of the conception of God's kingship in the present and points towards a coming kingdom of God over the nations. Its basis lies in the communion with God which Israel experienced, pointing forward to a deepening of that communion and a sharing of it with other nations. In this way eschatology appears as an extension of Israel's faith into the future, providing a goal for its spiritual ambition. Vriezen offers a very judicious survey of the various theories which have been put forward to account for this eschatological hope, but it is questionable whether he has shown sufficiently its radical nature. The element of catastrophe in Israel's history, especially as it was experienced in the Babylonian exile, and the breakup of the earlier political and cultic assurances of God's present kingship contributed in no small measure to this hope. Faith in the future arose not simply out of Israel's present fellowship with God, but out of an experience in which that fellowship seemed placed in jeopardy. Thus every aspect of Israel's faith was affected by that threatening experience, and the various institutions and doctrines which testified to Israel's communion with God underwent great changes as a result of it.

In summing up, we may acknowledge Vriezen's great achievement in presenting a coherent, systematic, and spiritually discerning theology of the Old Testament. The influence of reformed dogmatics on the one hand, and of the great Dutch school of research into the history of religion on the other, may both be discerned. The greatest strength of Vriezen's work lies in his firm refusal to isolate revelation in any way from the actual religion of Israel. At no point will he concede that we can have revelation without religion, either by locating it in historical events which are anterior to the growth of the religion or by limiting it to the spiritual ideas which that religion engendered. Israel's religion, with the whole range of its cultic institutions, is claimed as a religion of revelation because it was founded upon and promoted that communion with God which makes revelation possible.

In the main outline of his theology Vriezen has refined existing approaches to the subject, rather than attempting a radically new approach, although the introductory part of his work points towards a very distinctive conception of the Old Testament theologian's task. The problem of harmonizing the demands of theological insight with historical discipline is evident here, as in other modern Old Testament theologies, and Vriezen has sought to maintain a critical exactness with a thoroughly theological purpose.

SELECTED BIBLIOGRAPHY

Vriezen, Th.C., *Onderzoek naar de Paradijsvoorstelling bij de Oude Semietische volken* (Diss. Utrecht). Wageningen, 1937.

————, "La tradition de Jacob dans Osée XII," *OS* (1942), pp. 64-78.

————, "La création de l'homme d'après l'image de Dieu, *OS* 2 (1943), pp. 87-104.

————, "Two Old Cruces (Ruth iv:5; Zech. ii:12)," *OS* 5 (1948), pp. 80-91.

————, "Oud-Israelitische geschriften" in *Servire's Encyclopaedie,* Den Haag, 1948; 2nd ed. as *De Literatuur van Oud-Israel,* 1961.

————, "De compositie van de Samuelboeken," in *Orientalia Neerlandica.* Leiden, 1948, pp. 167-189.

————, *Hoofdlijnen der theologie van het Oude Testament.* Wageningen, 1949; 2nd ed. 1954; 3rd ed. 1966; German translation 1957; English translation 1958.

————, "'Ehje ᵃšer 'ehje," in *Festschrift Bertholet zum 80, Geburtstag,* Tübingen, 1950, pp. 498-512.

————, "The Term Hizza: Lustration and Consecration," *OS* 8 (1950), pp. 201-235.

————, *Palestina en Israel.* Wageningen, 1951. 2nd ed. 1952.

————, *Die Erwählung Israels nach dem Alten Testament* (Abhandlungen zur Theologie des Alten and Neuen Testaments 24). Zürich/Stuttgart, 1953.

————, "Die Hoffnung im Alten Testament. Ihre Voraussetzungen und äusseren Formen," *ThLZ 78* (1953), cols. 577-586.

————, *De Bijbel I. Het Oude Testament.* Groningen, 1953.

————, "Theokratie and Soteriologie," *EvTh 16* (1956), pp. 395-404. Reprinted in *Probleme alttestamentlicher Hermeneutik* (Theologische Bücherei 11). Munich, 1956, pp. 192-204.

————, *Het Nabije Oosten in de branding,* Nijkerk, 1957.

—————, "Essentials of the Theology of Isaiah," *Israel's Prophetic Heritage,* B. W. Anderson and W. Harrelson, eds., New York/London, 1962, pp. 128-146.

—————, *Jahwe en zijn Stad,* Amsterdam, 1962.

—————, *De Godsdienst van Israël.* Zeist/Arnhem/Antwerp, 1963; English translation 1967.

—————, "Geloof, openbaring en geschiedenis in de nieuwste Oud-Testamentische Theologie," *Kerk en Theologie 16* (1965), pp. 97-113, 210-218.

—————, "The Credo in the Old Testament," *Studies on the Psalms* (Die Ou Testamentiese Werkgemeenskap in Suid-Afrika). Potchefstroom, 1963, pp. 5-17.

—————, "The Edomite Deity Qaus," *OS* 14 (1965), pp. 330-353.

5
Edmond Jacob
Theology of the Old Testament

by Robert B. Laurin

Edmond Jacob was born into a pastor's family on November 1, 1909, at Beblen-heim, France. He was educated in Strasbourg, Paris, and Jerusalem. After having served two pastorates, in 1941 he became Professor of Old Testament at Montpellier. In 1946 he moved to a similar position at the University of Strasbourg.

THE STRENGTH OF EDMOND JACOB'S *Theology of the Old Testament* lies in its concise and synthetic presentation of the basic ingredients of Old Testament faith. Although one would need Eichrodt or von Rad for a more comprehensive understanding of Old Testament theology, yet Jacob is not at all superficial. One of the delights of the book is the profundity of insight that is expressed in many a deceptively simple paragraph or sentence. But the book is brief, and often its profundity does not become clear until one has seen it in the perspective of further detailed study. The volume was first published in French in 1955, and then was translated into English in 1958.

A second edition in French appeared in the early part of 1968 with a new preface in which Jacob discusses some criticisms of the first edition, takes a look at von Rad's approach to theology,[1] and stresses the unique place of a "theology" of the Old Testament among studies of Israel's history, canon, and religion. He also adds a few

[1] Cf. Jacob's longer critique of von Rad in "La théologie de l'ancien Testament: état présent et perspectives d'avenir," *EThL,* 44 (1968), pp. 424-426.

new bibliographic notes. Apart from this preface, however, the book contains the same text as the first edition. Jacob quite rightly observes that more extensive revision would entail a completely new book, although he does suggest some changes he would make. Professor Jacob has written elsewhere on a diversity of topics in the field of Old Testament, including studies on various aspects of history, theology, criticism, and archaeology. The bibliography at the end of this chapter will provide guidance to materials that will elucidate more completely many of the topics which are so concisely discussed in Jacob's *Theology*.

ARRANGEMENT OF OLD TESTAMENT THEOLOGY

One encounters a difficulty with Jacob's approach to Old Testament theology in the opening statement of the book: "The theology of the Old Testament may be defined as the systematic account of the specific religious ideas which can be found throughout the Old Testament and which form its profound unity" (p. 11).[2] His work then is not a presentation of all religious phenomena, but only of the unifying ideas. The problem, of course, lies in the use of the expression "specific religious ideas." This seems to run counter to what we have been shown, particularly in the past generation, about the central historical orientation of the Old Testament, namely, that it is act-centered, rather than idea-centered. Certainly such an emphasis would be the opposite of von Rad's approach to theology as the kerygmatic recital of the acts of God. However, Jacob does not mean what the first impression suggests. As one continues to read he finds expressions like these: "The Bible contains not a timeless revelation, but a word of God for particular men in particular circumstances" (p. 27); "theology does not work with ideas, but with historical facts" (p. 28); "there is no history without theology and no theology without history" (p. 30); and "the Old Testament does not bring us ideas about God, but acts of God" (p. 32).

The confusion may be due, as J. Bright suggests, to the fact that two different French words have both been translated as "ideas"—

---

[2] Edmond Jacob, *Theology of the Old Testament*, Eng. trans. by A. W. Heathcote and P. J. Allcock (New York: Harper & Row, Publishers, 1958). All citations in parentheses are taken from this book.

notions (used in the initial definition on page 11) and *idées* (used in other quotations). Apparently these terms have different connotations in Jacob's mind.[3] For him, "specific religious ideas" *(notions)* means specific theological themes and descriptions which emerge out of God's relationship to history.[4] This historical-connotational understanding is confirmed by Jacob's statement that the book deals "only with God and his relationship with man and the world. Piety, religious institutions and ethics are not part of Old Testament theology's specific domain" (p. 32).

Two dominant themes provide the rubrics under which Jacob discusses Old Testament theology—the PRESENCE of God manifested as sovereign over the world, and the ACTION of God manifested as savior of the world. Part I of the book, entitled "Characteristic Aspects of the God of the Old Testament," deals with the "presence of God" revealed through his titles, his relation to other gods and powers, his forms of appearance, and his attributes of holiness, righteousness, faithfulness, love, wrath, and wisdom. Part II, titled "The Action of God according to the Old Testament," discusses the "action of God" through his Spirit and Word, in creation, in man, in history, and in institutional figures and forms. Part III, called "Opposition to and Final Triumph of God's Work," combines both themes of "presence" and "action" in a study of sin and redemption, death, the future life, and the consummation of God's work in history in the messianic kingdom. The brevity of this section is a major weakness.

Throughout all three parts Jacob stresses that the presence and action of God are "manifested," that is, are related to history and not simply to philosophical speculation about God's essence or to ideas about him. The word of God, writes Jacob, is to be understood "comme la parole d'un Dieu toujours en action adressée à un peuple toujours en marche."[5] This remark would seem to blunt, at least

[3] J. Bright, "Edmund Jacob's 'Theology of the Old Testament,'" *ET*, 73 (July, 1962), p. 305.

[4] Cf. E. Jacob, *La tradition historique en Israel* (Montpellier: 1946), for a penetrating study of Israel's historical perspectives. Cf. also his important word about the future of theology as a historical science in his previously-mentioned article in *EThL*, 44 (1968), pp. 426-427.

[5] E. Jacob, *Théologie de l'ancien Testament*, Deuxième ed. (Neuchatel: 1968), p. viii.

partly, the objection of Bright that placing the section on characteristic aspects of God before the one on the action of God will "convey to the unwary reader the impression that Israel's faith consisted first in a certain view of God, certain ideas about Him, and only secondarily in the awareness of, and response to, the divine action in history." [6] Perhaps so, but of course it is to be assumed that the "unwary reader" will study the text of Jacob's discussion. If he does, he cannot escape the constant reference by the author to the fact that these characteristic aspects of God are all seen within the context of historical experience.

There is, however, some further confusion. Jacob claims, as we saw, that "piety, religious institutions and ethics are not part of Old Testament theology's specific domain." But this cannot be true absolutely. [7] Certainly God does not reveal himself in such an abstract fashion that he simply discloses truths about himself. God acts so that man will respond in certain ways and through that response find fullness of life. A person can experience true humanity only when the revelation becomes a specific "I-Thou" encounter for him. Here again, however, Jacob's confusion stems not from his failure to comprehend the situation, but rather from the limitations of his initial definition. In claiming that one of the themes of the Old Testament is God's manifestation of his presence as sovereign Lord, Jacob states: "that is why the fear of God is at the basis of all piety and all wisdom" (p. 32). He then deals with the matter in his brief section on "The Imitation of God, the Principle of the Moral and Spiritual Life" (pp. 173-177). Furthermore he has a chapter on "God in Institutions" (pp. 233-279) in which he deals with the theological/secular character of such roles as king, priest, and such matters as cult and law.

RELATIONSHIP BETWEEN FAITH AND HISTORY

Jacob claims, as we saw, that "there is no history without theology and no theology without history" (p. 30). Why does he make this judgment? Simply because in the Old Testament faith is grounded in the fact that God really acted in the events of Israel's life. In his

[6] Bright, *op. cit.*, p. 307. Cf. also Arnold Rhodes' review of Jacob's *Theology* in *Interpretation*, 13 (1959), pp. 468-470, for a similar criticism.

[7] Jacob recognizes this briefly in the preface to the second edition, p. v. Cf. also his article in *EThL*, 44 (1968), p. 430.

chapter on "God the Lord of History" (pp. 183-232), perhaps the finest part of the book, Jacob spells out in detail what he means. He sees a double relationship between history and faith: History gives faith objective reality, while faith makes history understandable. On the one hand, as the credo shows (Deuteronomy 26:5-9), faith is a confession about a series of actual events; thus it is not mere speculation or philosophy. On the other hand, the prophets and historians describe the events of Israel's history as part of a divine plan. In his discussion of the acts of God in Israel's history Jacob needs more careful delineation of the dating of the various Old Testament texts that he quotes. The same criticism applies to his study of various biblical words. The tendency is to obscure the development of concepts in various periods of Israel's life. At this point Jacob makes clear his difference with any kind of theology that would dissolve history into an existential encounter. Faith is based on a series of events that are directed towards a goal. He points out that the unique element in the biblical view of history is not that God is the initiator of events; all religions hold to this. What sets the biblical revelation apart is that God has a purpose in these events which embraces all mankind. There is order and direction to universal history, but history is not merely mechanical, the unfolding of a plan fixed in advance. Rather Yahweh respects human freedom, "so history always appears to be a drama in which the two protagonists, God and men, call one another, flee from one another and finally become reconciled" (p. 189). Thus Jacob also takes his stand against a theology that would view history as a process in which God himself develops.

> The events of the history are far from being compared with God's presence itself. . . . God's presence in history is that of the hidden God whose intentions always remain full of mystery in men's eyes (Isaiah 45:15; 55:8), but the hidden God is also the one who comes at certain moments in time to demonstrate through certain events the totality of his being and of his action. This coming of God into history—we prefer the term coming, as being more dynamic than presence—is on God's side an action and at the same time an interpretation.[8]

In other words, God both acts and entrusts his word of interpretation to a prophet (Amos 3:7), so that the presence of a prophet is the sign of a crisis in history; something is being unfolded by God.

[8] *Ibid.* See also E. Jacob, *Grundfragen Alttestamentlicher Theologie.* Franz Delitzsch-Vorlesungen 1965 (Stuttgart: Kohlhammer, 1970).

The question of the relationship of God to the world has for centuries been a problem, yet there is a difficulty here with Jacob's description. Granted that God is not to be confused with all the events of history; what does Jacob mean by the "coming of God INTO history"? At first reading this sounds like a suprahistorical God, one who is unrelated to the normal course of events, one who only intervenes at crucial moments. Perhaps Jacob means this, but his stress upon history as a drama with two protagonists, God and men, would seem to deny such a conception of God. Would he go so far as to agree with the judgment of L. C. Birch that "God's purposes embody what is potentially possible for the world. They are not achieved by mechanical intervention but by the persuasive lure of value and purpose"?[9] Further clarification of this point would help.

The faith of Israel, says Jacob, is based on two main historical events—the Exodus and the Day of Yahweh. These two events are interrelated as two periods in the same history, so that the Exodus with the subsequent conquest bears a typological relationship to the Day of Yahweh. Between these there are "many interventions of Yahweh but they only serve to confirm and make explicit the initial revelation of the Exodus or to announce the future kingship of Yahweh" (p. 190). Thus, the Exodus with its cluster of events was the central element in Israel's confession of faith (Deuteronomy 26:5-9; 6:20-24; Joshua 24:2-13; Psalms 77:12-20; 78; 105; 136). Each generation considered that it too had experienced the deliverance (cf. Amos 3:2). Other elements were added to this in cultic usage, such as the Sinai and temple themes, but these were simply further expressions of the purpose and goal of the Exodus. Here Jacob follows von Rad and Noth in viewing the Sinai event, for example, as initially not part of the Exodus story, but added later out of a variant tradition. This point of view, however, is becoming increasingly more difficult to hold.[10]

[9] L. Charles Birch, *Nature & God* (Philadelphia: The Westminster Press, 1965), p. 96.

[10] Cf. Walter Beyerlin, *Origins and History of the Oldest Sinaitic Traditions,* trans. S. Rudman (Oxford: Basil Blackwood, 1965). Beyerlin argues persuasively for the original linkage of the Exodus and Sinai themes. Cf. also Murray Lee Newman, Jr., *The People of the Covenant: A Study of Israel from Moses to the Monarchy* (Nashville: Abingdon Press, 1962).

Then Jacob sees the Exodus cluster of events used typologically for the Day of Yahweh. The prophets, particularly the two great prophets of the Exile, Ezekiel and Second Isaiah, did not view the disaster of Israel's destruction as an invalidation of the ancient credo. "Both stress the point that the temporary loss of national independence is the result of multiple disloyalties to the covenant, but the punishment is only transitory, while the promise will have a still finer flowering than in the time of Moses" (pp. 192-193). There will be a new Exodus (Isaiah 54) with an invitation to drink at the well of living water (Isaiah 55:1), a new passage from death to life (Ezekiel 36–37), a new wilderness wandering (Ezekiel 20:35), and finally a new temple (Ezekiel 47). Thus, for Jacob, there is no contradiction between eschatology and history: "it is important to bear in mind that for Israel it is less a matter of the end than of the coming of Yahweh which marks the end of a period but which, because he is essentially the living God, inaugurates a new beginning" (p. 190, n. 1). History is ever moving onward toward a purposive goal, because history is not only a revelation by which God shows himself to man, but also a redemption by which he saves him. Here Jacob has rightly stressed the HISTORICAL character of typology; future events bear an analogical relationship to past events as parts of a historical process in which God's basic purposes remain the same. There can be a correspondence between the Exodus and the Day of Yahweh because they represent the same God at work in the world. Consequently, the historicity of the Exodus events is never weakened by the typological meaning they acquired in later times.

Jacob has difficulty regarding the relation to history of two elements in Old Testament tradition—the apocalyptic and the wisdom books of Job and Ecclesiastes. He feels that history has been weakened in the apocalyptic sections by its determinism and use of old mythical ideas. But is this so? Granted that the mythical trappings and the deterministic structure are there, is not this only another form of the same historical consciousness? Is not the use of a scheme of world ages another example of the utilization of a mythical framework, as in Genesis 1, to show the progress of history and to stress God's sovereignty over all of life? One must read the mythical framework against the background of Daniel 9 and Daniel's prayer of confession. There the foundation of Israel's life in its covenant is reiterated, and the petition is given for God to "give heed and act" (9:19), concepts reflective of the fact that Daniel truly conceived of history as "drama" where both man and God were involved.

In the wisdom literature, Jacob claims, "revelation through history is wanting" (p. 197). But again is this only an apparent contradiction? Certainly neither Job nor Ecclesiastes is based on an historical scheme (nor are Proverbs or Song of Songs for that matter), but is not their appearance in the canon an important foil which illuminates the Old Testament's historical orientation? Ecclesiastes' frustrated search for the *summum bonum* by investigating things "under the sun" is a demonstration of the Old Testament historian's point that life does not contain its own meaning apart from the judgment of faith received by revelation (a point made by Jacob on p. 149). And Job adds the important note that the full meaning of God's actions in the world is ultimately mysterious. Nonetheless one can be assured of God's gracious purposefulness. By pointing to his providence which cares for the natural order, God implies to Job a comparable purposeful care for mankind. Thus although history is hidden in these books, it is nevertheless there.

CONTENTS OF OLD TESTAMENT THEOLOGY

The three major sections of Jacob's work deal respectively with the presence of God, the action of God, and the opposition in the world which God ultimately overcomes.

CHARACTERISTIC ASPECTS OF THE GOD OF THE OLD TESTAMENT

The first major theme of Old Testament theology—the "presence of God"—rests on the basic affirmation that God exists as sovereign over the world. This assertion is expressed, however, not in the form of philosophical speculation or argument, but in illustrations taken from the experiences of Israel. God is predominantly one who is involved in history. Therefore, the stress of the Old Testament is always first on God's "life," and then secondarily on his "eternity." It was this "life" that guaranteed Israel's continued existence, for in contrast to all other gods, only the living Yahweh could fulfill his promises (Jeremiah 10:9-10; Ezekiel 17:19). This theme of a "living God" dominates the whole book, for Jacob attempts to show us that the unity of the Old Testament lies in its constant affirmation that only God's being and will bring life to the world, while all that opposes God brings death.

Jacob spends the rest of this section on characteristic aspects of God showing the three basic ways the presence of God has been expressed. The FIRST way has been through the DIVINE NAMES. As part of this section Jacob deals with the relationship of God to other gods. He discusses the usual terms for God, particularly El/Elohim and Yahweh, and shows the unique character which these titles had in Israel. Among the ancient Israelites, as among the Canaanites, there was an evolution from polytheism towards monotheism. In the process Yahweh gradually assumed the functions and names of other gods encountered in Canaan. Through it all the "presence" of God was emphasized by the primary and uniquely Israelite name, "Yahweh." Related to the idea of "existence," this name is not to be seen as a causative form of the verb "to be," nor as a present tense meaning simply "he is" and meant to imply existence and mystery, but rather as signifying the God who is constantly with men in active presence.

Jacob's arguments here are generally lucid and well balanced, but there are some problems. He speaks of a parallel evolution from polytheism towards monotheism in both Canaanite and Israelite religion, but leaves unmentioned the fact that this development reached quite a different conclusion in Canaan than in Israel. It never became true monotheism in Canaan; at best it was monarchism. El, and then Baal, became the supreme god, the head of a pantheon, a fact to which Jacob alludes later. Furthermore Jacob is misleading in his statement about the form of monotheism that developed in Israel. Although he states correctly that monotheism was not clearly expressed until Deutero-Isaiah, there could be misunderstanding when he writes: "One cannot speak of evolution within the faith of Israel towards monotheism, for from the moment when Israel becomes conscious of being the people chosen by *one* God it is in practice a monotheistic people" (p. 66, n. 1). Here a distinction between "incipient monotheism" and "theoretical monotheism" needs to be stated clearly.

The SECOND basic way that God's "presence" is expressed in the Old Testament is in its descriptions of the VARIOUS MANIFESTATION FORMS OF YAHWEH. Jacob deals with angelic beings, including demonic creatures, and with God's "face," "glory," and "name," showing in each case how these were utilized as means of reconciling the presence of God with his invisibility and transcendence.

The THIRD and final way of expressing God's "presence" is through his ATTRIBUTES of holiness, righteousness, faithfulness, love, wrath, and wisdom. What is of particular importance is that these are not speculative attributes, as in some forms of dogmatic theology, but rather are descriptions of Yahweh gained from his actions in history. Thus, for example, "holiness" expressing a characteristic of God, may be a surrogate for deity. But it always connotes the double idea of power and separateness in reference to God's "acts" in Israel's life.

"Righteousness" denotes basically "conformity to the norm," and although it may be used nontheologically (e.g., of a merchant's balances), it is applied predominantly to actions which are in conformity to the divine norm. The righteousness of Yahweh, therefore, is defined by his actions which conform to his character as holy, merciful, loving, and just. This is why "righteousness" may also be used in the sense of "grace" or "salvation," or in later Judaism of "almsgiving" and "benevolent works."

In his discussion of the righteousness of God, Jacob employs the French word *justice* to cover both "righteousness" and "justice," and so the translator has attempted to determine which is intended in a given sentence by employing either word. But this is often confusing, simply because "righteousness" is not "justice." Righteousness is conformity to a norm, while justice is only one action, albeit the most predominant, based on this norm. Thus when Jacob writes, "A person is righteous when he acts justly, he does not act justly because he is righteous" (p. 95) there is no question that this statement is correct, but it is not complete. Righteous behavior also involves mercy, faithfulness, love, as Jacob does indicate later.

"Faithfulness" is Jacob's translation of *chesed,* a word which has the primitive significance of "strength." [11] So *chesed* is used in various

---

[11] Henri Cazelles, in his review of Jacob's *Theology* in *VT,* 6 (1956), p. 328, argues that "strength" is not always the basic meaning, since one finds in such passages as Leviticus 20:17, Proverbs 14:34; 25:10 that *chesed* must be translated as "shame" or "reproach." But the argument is not well taken, since in those verses it simply connotes "strong feeling" used in a negative sense, but in the majority of Old Testament passages it has a positive meaning. Cf. my article on *chesed* in *Foundations,* 7 (1964), pp. 179-180.

contexts to stress "social obligation," "solidarity," and "covenant loyalty"—that is, in situations where the emphasis is on the strength of commitment to various relationships, and particularly to a covenant.

Jacob claims that *chesed* loses its sense of the bond upholding the covenant and must be translated as "love" or "grace" in those passages which describe Yahweh's action when the human partner has broken the covenant (Hosea 2:19; Jeremiah 3:12; Isaiah 54:7-8). Does not Jacob miss here the profundity of *chesed* in prophetic thought? Is not the point of the prophets that in spite of the normal expectations in a suzerainty covenant, where unfaithfulness by the vassal would destroy the bond, Yahweh is not the usual suzerain? Disloyalty to the covenant by man does not mean that Yahweh will ever abandon the relationship. It was given as an "everlasting covenant" (Genesis 17:7; Leviticus 26:42-45), and so the offer of the relationship is constantly made. This is just the point of Isaiah 54:10. So "love" or "grace" is implied in *chesed* in such cases, but lying behind this profound expression is also the concept of covenant loyalty on the part of Yahweh.

"Love" is the author's term for the Hebrew *'ahab,* a root "which serves to express the reality of love under the double form of *eros* and *agape.*" Love is the "spontaneous movement which carries one being towards another being with the desire to possess it and to find some satisfaction in that possession" (p. 108). "Love" is therefore different from "faithfulness" in that it expresses an ardent and voluntary desire unconditioned by any obligation. Jacob also says that *'ahab* is the attitude of a superior towards an inferior, and so the word "is not used for the attitude of a wife to her husband nor for that of children to their parents" (p. 108). However, in the prior paragraph he states that it is used once for a woman's love for her husband (1 Samuel 18:20; so also one should include Song of Solomon 8:6) and once for the love of a subordinate for his superior (Deuteronomy 15:16). He also mentions that it is often used of men's love for God. The question therefore arises: Why does he attempt to restrict the term to the superior-inferior relationship? Jacob's major emphasis in this section is rightly that *'ahab* combines the double idea of *eros* and *agape* (presumably meaning "strong emotion" and "commitment of the will"). Marriage thus povides an apt analogy of the relation established by God's "love" to which man responds with his own "love."

The second major theme of Old Testament theology—the "action of God"—develops out of the ways that Yahweh acts by Spirit and Word. "Spirit" *(ruach)* is used with reference to God's work in the physical reality of "wind" (e.g., at Exodus, Exodus 14:21; 15:8), in the biological reality of "breath," in the demonic reality of "spirit" (e.g., 1 Kings 22:21), but primarily in the divine reality "Spirit." In all senses the etymological meaning of *ruach* as "air" suggests the idea of power as well as mystery in the way Yahweh works. In each case the contextual usage shows that "the spirit is God himself in creative and saving activity" (p. 124). This is particularly so in the realm of history, where the spirit of Yahweh works for the fulfillment of the divine purposes in three ways—by coming upon individuals (e.g., judges) who perform mighty deeds, by anointing the prophets so they can speak the word of Yahweh, and by being poured out in the future on nature, on the servant of Yahweh, and on all men so that the messianic age will be achieved.

"Word" *(dabar)* is closely related to *ruach* both etymologically and contextually. The Word presupposes the Spirit (cf. Ezekiel 2:2; 3:24), so that *dabar* has a dynamic quality—it denotes thing/act as well as word, something happens as well as is said. Now this dynamic sense of *dabar* is not peculiar to Israel or the Old Testament, but there is a profound difference in the way it is applied.

> Whilst in Babylon and Egypt the divine word intervenes in isolated events which have no connection with one another, the word of God in the Old Testament directs and inspires a single history which begins with the word of God pronounced at the creation and which is completed by the word made flesh (John 1:14) (p. 129).

The dynamic sense of *dabar*, however, was forgotten in Israel when the Word was crystallized in writing and in hypostasis. Israel (and the church after it) became a "book" religion and obscured the active role of the word of God in its midst.

Jacob states that *dabar,* in distinction from *'amar,* "alone possesses creative dynamism" (p. 128). However, there is a danger in being too concerned about the explicit meaning of words which may have more than one meaning. Although it is true that *dabar* is the dominant term for this dynamic work of Yahweh, yet other terms, such as *'etsah* (Isaiah 44:26) and *'imrah* (Psalm 147:15, cf. Isaiah 44:27) also came to be used in this sense. As J. Barr has stressed, the basic unit of meaning is the sentence, not the word.[12]

In the rest of the section on the action of God, Jacob deals with the four basic ways in which God works through Spirit and Word. The FIRST way is in CREATION. To Jacob, one must not view creation apart from the covenant with Israel, for "the idea of creation is secondary to that of covenant, of which it is both the condition and the consequence" (p. 136). Yet the covenant with Israel must not be understood simply in terms of some localized concern; God's interest is worldwide. So in answer to the question, why did God create the world, the Old Testament would reply, "He has created it for the covenant, that is to say because of his plan of love and salvation for humanity by means of Israel" (p. 137). Thus, creation in the Old Testament is basically history-centered, that is to say, it is part of a movement in time, not a movement outside of time. When the Israelites turned to the creation myths of their day in order to describe creation, they subordinated the mythological elements to history.[13] What one finds in the theological reflection on creation (e.g., Genesis 1-2; Psalm 104) is a history of creation and not a myth of creation with cyclical return. So creation by Spirit and Word has a commencement ("in the beginning," Genesis 1:1; Psalm 33:6); it has a history (events and nature are continuously being created, e.g., Psalm 104:30; Amos 5:8); and it has an end or goal. In showing the movement of creation toward this goal, Jacob is particularly profound. He points out that the original stuff with which Yahweh began—the dark, watery chaos (there is no *creatio ex nihilo* in the Old Testament)—

---

[12] J. Barr, *The Semantics of Biblical Language* (London: 1961), pp. 144-147; cf. also his review of Jacob in *JSS*, 5 (1960), pp. 116-169, where he criticizes him for putting too much stress on etymologies. Barr's caution is well taken, but overall Jacob demonstrates both by example and by specific statement (p. 210) that he realizes this. Jacob comments to this effect in the preface of the second edition, pp. v-vi.

[13] In "La théologie de l'Ancien Testament: état présent et perspectives d'avenir," *EThL*, 44 (1968), p. 429, he adds that "en fait l'Ancien Testament a récupéré le mythe et lui donne son sens véritable en le débarrassant de la mythologie."

was only subdued at the beginning. Light was only separated from darkness, and the sea was only confined within certain limits. So it is that throughout the Old Testament these two "residues of the chaos" —darkness and the sea—are seen as continually menacing the creation. The world is still incomplete, and God must constantly show his creative power over these chaotic forces. The goal of creation awaits the new heaven and the new earth when darkness and the sea will have disappeared (Revelation 21:1; 22:5). Therefore creation is an eschatological conception. Thus the covenant idea embraces the narrower concept of Yahweh's covenant with Israel (the people were "created" as God's agents to fulfill his universal purposes, Isaiah 43: 1, 7, 15), and the wider concept of his covenant with all mankind.[14]

Jacob has been criticized for beginning his discussion of the action of God with creation rather than, as is popular today, with the redemption of Israel. Historically Israel experienced God as redeemer prior to her comprehension of him as creator. If creation is secondary to covenant, "will not the very fact that the material is arranged as it is tend to throw the picture of Israel's faith out of focus in the reader's mind?" [15] Presumably the fear is that creation will be viewed as cosmological speculation, rather than as part of a historical, redemptive movement. Certainly this has happened all too often in the history of interpretation, but I wonder if this is a valid objection to Jacob's work. On the one hand, the very fact that Jacob constantly affirms in this section the historical thrust of creation must surely make clear to the reader the proper perspective to take on this matter. And, on the other hand, how much can the arrangement of a theology of the Old Testament be guided by the Old Testament's own canonical structure? In the initial pages of his book where he writes about the early theologians in the Bible (Yahwist, Deuteronomist, Priestly school, Chronicler, Second Isaiah), Jacob states:

> We recall these early outlines because we hold that, even in the twentieth century, a theology of the Old Testament should be able to draw inspiration

[14] H. Cazelles, *op. cit.*, p. 329, has an intriguing suggestion in this regard when he writes: "Peut-on dire d'ailleurs que l'alliance est eternelle tandis que la creation prendra fin? Is. xxxiv 4 est suivi par Is. xxxv sur le nouvel exode. L'alliance, rompue (Os ii 4) sera remplacee par une nouvelle (Jer. xxxi 31) comme les cieux et la terre seront remplaces par terre et cieux nouveaux (Is. lxvi 22) : il y a similitude."

[15] J. Bright, *op. cit.*, p. 307.

from them so as not to fit the Old Testament into a modern scheme or explain it according to a dialectic that is fundamentally foreign to it (p. 12).

One must, therefore, ask the question: What were the shapers of the canon intending us to understand by their arrangement? Is it not possible that the canonical form teaches in a more compelling way than the approach in vogue today? Does not learning in any area take place more effectively by first beginning with a problem? The Old Testament begins with a description of the high destiny of man as the partner ("image") of a sovereign God involved in a creative process (Genesis 1–2). It then depicts the rejection of this destiny by man, and the cause of disorder in the world (Genesis 3–11). The rest of the Old Testament moves on to present the solution in the redemption and missionary call of Abraham and Israel.[16]

The SECOND way God acts is in regard to MAN. Basic to all of the Old Testament affirmations about man is the assertion that he shares in the feebleness and ephemerality of all creatures and therefore is dependent upon God (Isaiah 31:3). However, man is superior to the rest of the created order in that he has had special dignity conferred upon him by reason of his relation to God; he alone is God's "image." This is a functional, not an ontological relationship, for the purpose of an image is to represent someone. This representative role always involves man's entire being, since Israelite thought always views man as a totality. Man is a "soul," a "psycho-physical being," a creature both spiritual and physical, the result of God's animation of *basar* by his *ruach*. Man is also a "corporate personality" who has been created to enter actively into the world with other individuals and to function as the image by exercising dominion over physical and spiritual forces. Man's function can thus be expressed as an imitation of God; he is to "struggle along with God for the fulfilling of his plan" (p. 174). Therefore all of man's actions are to reflect his double obligation—toward God and toward the world.

Jacob's stress on the ontological and functional unity of man in the midst of a diversity of parts is a healthy corrective to the tendency in the church to adopt a Greek view of lower and higher elements. Man "is not a collection of separate organs but an organism animated by one single life and each organ can give expression to the life

---

[16] G. E. Wright also has criticized Jacob for his handling of creation in his review of the book in *JBL*, 79 (1960), pp. 78-81.

of the whole" (p. 157). Yet Jacob's explication of man's separate functions is not always clear. This is particularly so in his delineation of "soul," "spirit," and "heart." The basic elements are given, but the difference between them is not always clear. How, for example, is the "spirit" of man to be distinguished from God's "Spirit"? Jacob does say that sometimes *"ruach* ceases to be regarded as a power lent to man and becomes a psychological reality residing in man in a permanent manner and like *nephesh* able to be the seat of faculties and desire" (p. 162). The distinction between these psychological realities needs to be made clearer. Furthermore, what is the difference between "soul" and "heart," or what is the relation between "spirit" and "heart"? Here Eichrodt's discussion is more illuminating.[17] Perhaps Jacob is reaching too far when he claims that in understanding man as the "image of God," "the external appearance is perhaps even more important than spiritual resemblance" (p. 118). Admitting that no Old Testament text expressly connects bodily beauty with the image of God, Jacob argues that it is implied in Genesis 9:6, where "to touch man is to touch God himself, of whom every man is the image" (p. 169). But surely this is strained exegesis. The point of the verse in Genesis is not on the care to be exercised toward man because of his physical resemblance to God. Rather the point is on man's dignity and worth because of his unique function-bearing relationship with God. And, finally, can we really say that in Old Testament thought woman is subordinate to man because "man by himself is a complete being, the woman who is given to him adds nothing to his nature, whilst the woman drawn forth from man owes all her existence to him" (pp. 172-173)? Has not Jacob pushed the imagery of the rib too far, and failed to distinguish between "man" and "male"? Does not Genesis 1:27 state that "man" is male and female, so that the distinction is one of function, not one of worth or completeness?

The THIRD major way that God acts by Spirit and Word is in HISTORY. As we saw earlier, Jacob sees the special characteristic of biblical revelation in its proclamation that history is a drama with two protagonists—God and man—in which God is working for the salvation of all men. Integral to this process is God's election of Is-

[17] W. Eichrodt, *Theology of the Old Testament,* vol. 2 (Philadelphia: The Westminster Press, 1967), p. 148.

rael, that is "the initial act by which Yahweh comes into relation with his people and the permanent reality which assures the constancy of that bond" (p. 201). Actually, says Jacob, there were two elections, the first at the time of Abraham when Yahweh declared the existence of a people, and the second at the time of Moses when Yahweh commissioned that people for a special work. So in Old Testament theology election always carries with it the idea of service as its necessary corollary: "to be the 'am of Yahweh involves being his 'ebed" (p. 204). Hence, the election of Israel did not mean the rejection of other men, "for if certain ones are left outside the election it is only for the time being, in order to make more readily possible the accomplishment of God's plan" (pp. 206-207).

The claim by Jacob that there were "two elections," at the time of Abraham and at the time of Moses, in terms of "being" and "doing," although true overall, must not be stressed too strongly. The election of Abraham certainly concentrated on the promise, seen not only in the terms given to Abraham, but also in the "covenant of pieces" (Genesis 15) where God alone passed through the parts of the sacrifice. Yet at the initial time of promise (Genesis 12:1-3) the "doing" aspect is also very evident in the call to "go" (12:1), and also in the double sense of the imperative in verse 2: "so that you will be a blessing" also implies the command "and be a blessing." Throughout the patriarchal period, as the promise is reiterated, the point is made clearly that the fulfillment of election was conditionally based upon response to its terms (Genesis 17:1; 18:19; 22:18; cf. especially 26:5).

The specific way Israel's election was illustrated was by the covenant between Yahweh and Israel, a relationship that implied three particular things: a gift from Yahweh, a bond of communion, and an obligation in the form of law. The establishment of the covenant took place fundamentally at Sinai, and all covenant-makings following Sinai (e.g., at Shechem, Joshua 24:25; with David, 2 Samuel 23:5) were simply renewals or extensions of that covenant. Yet even though the Sinai covenant was so fundamental to Israelite faith, it is rarely mentioned in the Old Testament outside of the historical accounts. Instead the Exodus is given a central place. Jacob explains that this difference in emphasis is due to the strong historical interest of Israel's writers: "to stress the Sinai covenant might easily have led to a static conception of revelation and to a mythologizing against which Israelite religion always protested" (p. 214).

Jacob's explication of the covenant, although quite illuminating, suffers at two points in particular. First, the insights of recent discussion of Near Eastern treaty forms could have helped to clarify the distinction he makes between covenants between humans and those between God and man. Jacob claims that in covenants between men "the truth almost always points to a covenant between two partners who are on an unequal footing; it is the stronger who proposes the *berit*" (p. 210). Perhaps his emphasis is on the words "almost always," but most of the examples which he gives, on closer investigation, seem rather to be treaties between equals, the so-called "parity covenant" form.[18] In the discussion regarding covenants between God and man, the illumination provided by the "suzerainty covenant" form would have added a great deal of clarification. Second, the great amount of controversy over the feast of covenant-renewal needs more space than the one sentence allotted to it on page 213.

Israel's election also meant missionary duty for the people, and the manifestation of miracles and providence by Yahweh. The call to worldwide service was given initially at Abraham's election and confirmed at the time of Moses. It was grounded in the conviction of the superiority of Yahweh over the gods of the nations and in his jealousy to guard this sovereignty.

The FOURTH way God acts by Spirit and Word is in Israel's INSTITUTIONS. First of all, there were four institutional offices or ministries by which God's presence among his people was represented—king, prophet, priest, wise man. "The ministry's objective is to show in concrete form an activity which is assumed in a perfect form by God himself" (p. 233). Thus,

> the king guarantees God's rule on earth, the prophet expresses by his person and his message God's action in history, the priest, through the administration of sacred things, gives reminders of God's sovereignty over time and space, lastly, the wise man shows and teaches still more that there is no happiness possible outside God's love (pp. 253-254).

[18] Cf. G. Mendenhall, *Law and Covenant in Israel and the Near East* (Pittsburgh: 1955), pp. 24ff.; D. J. McCarthy, *Treaty and Covenant.* (Rome: 1963); also his *Der Gottesbund im Alten Testament* (Stuttgart: 1963). Jacob speaks of the need for further discussion of this subject in the preface to the second French edition, p. v.

Jacob's discussion of the prophet, priest, and wise man follows the standard lines of interpretation, but his examination of the king calls for some comment. Denying the point of view of Mowinckel and the Uppsala school that the king was the god incarnated, who through cultic drama at a New Year festival assured the continuity of the pattern of nature, Jacob stresses the history-oriented, representative role of the king. The king was chosen by God and people to safeguard the people's interests by being a strong leader who reflected the presence of God on earth. The two forms of kingship—charismatic (Israel) and dynastic (Judah)—both show this dependence upon and subordination to Yahweh. Thus, even though the terms "son of God" (Psalm 2:7) and "God" (Psalm 45) were applied to the king, the use of these terms never deified the king, but only indicated his close relationship to God. Thus the king could be the channel of divine blessing and could take the role of high priest. He was a mediator and so bore great responsibility for the manner of his life; he represented the rule of God, the true king, on earth.

Jacob's stress on the Israelite king's nondivine, vicegerent role is important, but he has apparently misjudged Mowinckel. As Mowinckel points out, the Pharaoh was considered to be deity incarnate, but in Mesopotamia and Canaan the king was a man, perhaps sometimes a "demigod" but not a god. The real lord was the god of each city, and the king was his specially endowed and empowered vicegerent. The king was a sacral figure, not a divine figure.[19] One has to be careful to allow a nonliteralistic interpretation of phrases in Babylonian and Canaanite literature, as well as in the Old Testament. So when in Babylonia the king says to God, "I have no mother, thou art my mother; I have no father, thou art my father," [20] this may well express not an ontological relation to the gods, but a relational one. Indeed, as Mowinckel mentions,[21] even though the Assyrian king Ashurnasipal says of himself that he was "born among unknown mountains," and that the goddess Ishtar "brought him forth" to be a shepherd of men, yet we know elsewhere that he was born in the royal palace as a legitimate son of Shamshi-adad. Thus

---

[19] Cf. the discussion in S. Mowinckel, *He That Cometh* (Oxford: Basil Blackwell, 1956), pp. 21-95.

[20] *Gudea Cylinder,* A, II, pp. 6-7.

[21] Mowinckel, *op. cit.,* pp. 36ff.

when Mowinckel writes of the Israelite king that he was a "super-human, *divine* being," [22] although the wording may be misleading, a survey of the context shows that he means only that the king was set apart and endowed with a special relationship to God and with resultant special power.

Apart from the institutional offices, God also acted in various institutional settings. First, the sacred place was identified in an attempt to resolve the tension of God's remoteness and nearness. Although Yahweh's dwelling was clearly in heaven (a concept expressing not so much distance as totality or omnipresence), yet God chose to dwell temporarily in various places. The sacred place could be a stone, a mountain, a tent, an ark, but primarily it was the sanctuary or temple. Here the realization of God's transcendence was never forgotten. The freedom of God to manifest himself anywhere was symbolized by the references to his presence in his *alter ego* or "name," by the movable ark, and by the palm trees and cherubim (reminders of paradise).

Because the temple became conceived of as a sort of talisman which guaranteed security, the prophets spoke of its destruction as a sign that the personal relationship of the Israelite to God was more important. Nevertheless the prophets looked to the restoration of the temple when Israel had been cleansed. Thus even the temple became part of God's revelation in history.

A second institutional setting for the relationship with God was the cult. Although utilizing Canaanite forms, Israel radically changed the concepts of the cult. On the one hand, time was substituted for space in that Yahweh was not permanently limited to the sanctuary or to nature. In the midst of its remembrance of particular moments in the year (New Year Festival, new moon, sabbath), Israel's theologians never forgot this emphasis upon God's actions, although often popular practice did. On the other hand, history was substituted for myth and its cyclical renewal. The cult was a revelation of God's actions past, present, and future. By dramatic representations of the great events of the past, accompanied by sacrifice, each worshiper was brought into present relationship with God. "We envisage the sacrifice as the act through which God reveals and communicates his life-force" (p. 269). The cult also looked toward the future and Yah-

[22] *Ibid,* p. 62.

weh's final consummation of his kingdom by challenging the worshiper to make a decision about his ethical behavior in the light of God's judgment. Thus the main forms of worship had the purpose of affirming God's sovereignty and demanding some response to it.[23]

A third institutional form was the law. Integral to the covenant relationship from the beginning, law had "the object of permitting those who have been the object of the choice to lead a life conformed to the new situation into which they have entered" (p. 271). There are many terms for law in the Old Testament, but the supreme one is *torah,* which has the sense of "pointing out a direction." There were two stages in the development of law. At first it was given as a revelation to those in the covenant, but later, law became severed from the covenant. Because Israel failed to keep the law, the covenant was broken and punishment was inevitable. Yet the prophets saw the day coming when the covenant would be restored, and law became the condition for its restoration. "The law is no longer given by merely belonging to the chosen people, but one belongs to that people only by accepting the law" (p. 274). Jacob has traced the proper outline of "law" in the Old Testament, but he has failed to deal adequately with the question of apodictic and casuistic law (the two terms are used in passing on p. 129).[24]

OPPOSITION TO AND FINAL TRIUMPH OF GOD'S WORK

The double themes of the "presence" and "action" of God are brought together in the third and final main section of the book. FIRST of all, Jacob deals with SIN AND REDEMPTION. He defines sin basically as the breaking of a relationship with God: "God is the one who enters into relationship and who makes the covenant, sin is a breaking of this relationship" (p. 281). This sin is caused by two elements

[23] One wonders if the important question of the "enthronement festival" does not deserve more detailed discussion than a footnote (p. 266, n. 1), and if the various forms of sacrifice do not require more than a sentence to make their meaning clear (pp. 268-269). Indeed the whole discussion of priesthood and sacrifice is much too brief.

[24] One should also consider the illuminating discussion in E. Gerstenberger, *Wesen und Herkunft des 'apodiktischen Rechts'* (Neukirchen: 1965), and also in his article "Covenant and Commandment," *JBL,* 84 (1965), pp. 38-51. He suggests that the terms "apodictic" and "casuistic" should be abandoned in favor of "genuine legal clauses" and "prohibitives" and "commands."

in man. First, sin stems from man's created nature as a feeble being, apart from any fall into sin. It is in this sense that Psalm 51 asserts the universality of sin and man's propensity towards it. But, secondly and primarily, sin stems from man's will. Although sin is not intrinsically inevitable, yet man acts as if it were. He wants to be the equal of God ("the knowledge of good and evil"), and as a result of his continual movement in this direction eventually receives a "hardened heart" that renders his personality insensitive to God's call to a dependent, obedient relationship. Therefore, any remedy for man to achieve his created role as God's partner must lie in a future special intervention by God who will circumcize man's heart. This insensitivity to God explains also why any present relationship with God is an act of divine grace. Thus although sin places each man in a state of guilt before God and brings its punishment, God's creative purpose for man is never forgotten. There is always divine mercy in the midst of punishment. Consequently, the essential stress of sacrifice, as we saw, lies on the bestowal of life to man, not on the death of the victim.

Jacob's explication of sin and redemption is profound and inclusive, and provides an important background to the point in Ephesians 2:8-9 that even man's faith in God is a gift of divine grace that breaks through man's hardened heart. Yet Jacob also writes that man's grasp at "the knowledge of good and evil" is an attempt to gain

> total knowledge and, since for the Hebrew mentality knowledge is more dynamic than intellectual, a total power which would have made him like Elohim. To know anything is to have power over it; now Yahweh does not wish man to be his equal, because that would rupture the relationship and the filial bond which should remain as the one binding man to God (p. 284).

However is not Jacob pushing the idiom and the story of Genesis 3 too far? The "knowledge of good and evil" clearly means "total knowledge," but in the context of Genesis 3 it carries the further sense of "adulthood" (as it does in Isaiah 7:15-16 and the Qumran scroll 1QSa 1:10-11). Thus the point is not so much that "Yahweh does not wish man to be his equal, because that would rupture the relationship," but rather that Yahweh does not wish man to be independent of him (symbolized by adulthood) simply because man is a feeble creature and cannot live in this state without destroying himself (the point of Genesis 4–11).

The SECOND part of this final section deals with DEATH AND THE FUTURE LIFE. The Old Testament presents two views regarding the afterlife. The first or analytical approach shows death as nonexistence; man's flesh returns to dust (Ecclesiastes 3:20; 12:7) and his spirit departs to God. However the second or holistic approach is more dominant; it depicts death as the entrance of the whole man into a shadowy existence marked by weakness, where he bears some physical resemblance to his original self, but where the forces of life are at their lowest intensity. Yahweh himself is absent from the abode of the dead (Isaiah 38:9-19). Therefore, "the Old Testament never presents death as a liberation or as a gateway giving access to perfect felicity" (p. 299). Sheol, the place to which the dead go, is in the depths of the earth, a part of the original dark chaos. In the majority of texts describing Sheol, there is no real differentiation in moral order. Although Isaiah 14 and Ezekiel 32 suggest a division between righteousness and wickedness, even in these passages no rewards or punishments are suggested. Was there any hope of escaping death? There are only the rare exceptions of Enoch and Elijah, and perhaps Moses, who were translated to heaven. But what of individual resurrection? Although there are pale gleams of hope in Job 19:26 and Psalm 73, two late passages give the first clear statement (Isaiah 26: 18-21; Daniel 12:2). A successive series of disasters to the nation and to innocent martyrs finally led Israel to formulate resurrection as a necessary outworking of Yahweh's law of restitution. Thus it was faith in Yahweh's power and righteousness, and not wishful thinking, that constituted the basis for the belief of Israel in resurrection.

The THIRD area of Jacob's concern in this final section is the CONSUMMATION. The first part concerns the eschatological drama. Eschatological hope did not arise out of disappointment over the realization of Yahweh's kingship, as Mowinckel has suggested, but was based on the conviction of Yahweh's sovereignty. The basis of hope was "solely the certitude that their God Yahweh, whose name evokes being and presence, was more powerful than all other gods and that he would come and establish his kingship" (p. 317). However, this coming would truly be an eschaton or rupture; the present world would come to an end. Yet even in this conception history is dominant, for:

> On the one side the God who will reveal himself by a grandiose theophany at the end of time has already manifested himself and does not cease manifesting himself in the course of history; and on the other side all historical events are already charged with eternal significance (pp. 318-319).

Eschatology did not arise in postexilic days, as held by some scholars, but is inherent in Israel's whole concept of the historical process. Jacob's denigration of the role of disappointed kingship in the formation of eschatological hope is perhaps overstated. Certainly the basis of eschatological belief was faith in Yahweh's sovereignty, but the failure of Israel's kings could not help but speed the process of messianic formulation.

The second part of the consummation is concerned with the messianic kingdom. The expectation of the Messiah always plays a subordinate part to the hope in Yahweh and does not truly develop until the time of the monarchy. Yet the messianic theme has its roots in earlier times. It is based partly on the belief in Ur-man (Genesis 1:26; 3:15; Ezekiel 28:13; Isaiah 14; Job 15:7ff.; Psalm 11), which was applied especially to historical figures (e.g., Jacob, Moses, Gideon, David), and partly on the messianic oracles of Balaam and Jacob. But the monarchy and the centrality of David's rule gave messianism its distinctive foundation. God's future reign is linked with David's dynasty. Therefore the abolition of the monarchy did not nullify the hope itself, for the hope was ultimately founded on faith in the creative power of God in history. Therefore, Deutero-Isaiah and Ezekiel both proclaim restoration, not as a return to the past but as a new creation by God. This theme is particularly seen in the Servant Songs which offer us a theology of history. The Servant, who sums up the history of Israel as "the elect, the wretched, the missionary, the glorified one" (p. 338), will succeed where Israel failed. This Servant, who must be an individual in the last song, and who is described occasionally by elements taken from the pagan cults, is essentially the *'ebed* who fulfills all the basic roles of Israel as king, prophet, and priest.[25] How is the Son of Man in Daniel related to the Messiah and Servant? Although he represents primarily the tradition of "primordial man," and through this stress on transcendence helps to keep

[25] The discussion of the Servant Songs (pp. 338ff.) shares in the general weakness of the third part of the book in being much too brief. The whole problem of identification of the Servant of Isaiah 40–55 is virtually passed over.

the messianic idea from becoming simply a political hope, he is not in absolute opposition to the Messiah. "The Son of Man is, then, a real king, his function overlaps the Messiah's but by giving him the title of man the author of the book of Daniel seeks to disentangle Messianism from national ties and to link it with the universal outlook of Genesis" (p. 342).

RELATIONSHIP BETWEEN THE OLD TESTAMENT AND THE NEW TESTAMENT

Apart from an occasional sentence (e.g., pp. 61-62, 112) Jacob limits discussion of the relationship between the Testaments to only a few statements in the Introduction. Thus, although his general position is clear, he leaves various questions unanswered, particularly in regard to the pattern of relationship. Jacob states boldly:

> A theology of the Old Testament which is founded not on certain isolated verses, but on the Old Testament as a whole, can only be a Christology, for what was revealed under the old covenant, through a long and varied history, in events, persons and institutions, is, in Christ, gathered together and brought to perfection (p. 12).

Elsewhere he states: "A line not always straight, but nonetheless continuous, leads from the anthropomorphisms of the earliest pages of the Bible, to the incarnation of God in Jesus Christ" (p. 32).[26] What he means is simply that in spite of diversities the twofold theme of the Old Testament—the presence and action of God—carries on into the New Testament. The Old Testament shares with the New the basic message of the same God who is present in the world and who comes to save. For this reason Jacob can point out that one often needs the Old Testament to complete the message of the New. The Decalogue is the finest expression of Christian ethics, the psalms of Christian piety, and the prophets of Christian eschatology (p. 31).

Jacob takes his stance, then, on some form of promise and fulfillment. The purposefulness in history, of which he speaks at length, finds its greatest and ultimate fulfillment in Jesus Christ. The pattern

---

[26] In the preface to the second French edition Jacob writes: "L'Ancien Testament compris comme une histoire qui est l'histoire du salut, nous mène non seulement jusqu'au seuil du Nouveau Testament, mais englobe même ce dernier" (p. ix). He also speaks here of the difficulty of understanding the place of the intertestamental literature in this history of salvation.

of God's actions shown in the Old Testament is typical of his work illustrated in the New. Thus apart from the New Testament the profundity of the Old cannot be seen, for the New Testament is itself a theology of the Old Testament. Therefore, Old Testament theology "can only be Christology," and presumably a theology of the Old Testament written by a Jew would have some basic differences from Jacob's theological formulation. However, one could wish for more clarification, although Jacob expressly states that he does not attempt to deal with the permanent or Christian value of the Old Testament (p. 32). The claim that Christian ethics, piety, and eschatology have no better expression than in the Decalogue, psalms, and prophets is somewhat confusing. If the New Testament is the fulfillment of the Old Testament, then in that very fulfillment there is something new. What are the new elements and in what sense, if any, do they abrogate the Old Testament? Jacob does show how the early church, in its battle against Marcion and the Gnostics, absorbed the Old Testament into its canon by allegorical exegesis; but only by implication does he suggest the legitimate role the Old Testament may play in the life of the church.

Looking back over Jacob's *Theology,* one appreciates anew the excellent way he has brought together the variant elements of Old Testament faith, and focused our attention on their central themes. The book's relatively brief scope (334 pages), its solid scholarship, its balanced judgments, and its lucid style, all combine to make it a reliable and penetrating study. The bibliographies that follow each chapter provide helpful guides for more detailed research. One can only regret that the second French edition did not bring them up to date more thoroughly. Inevitably in a work of this size there are lacunae or discussions that are too brief to be clear, but overall the unifying religious ideas of the Old Testament have been spelled out and shown to be derived foundationally from the "presence" and "action" in history of the "living God."

SELECTED BIBLIOGRAPHY

Jacob, E., *La tradition historique en Israel.* Montpellier, 1946.
————, *Theologie de l'Ancien Testament.* Neuchatel, 1955. Deuxième edition, 1968. Eng. trans. based on first edition, by A. W. Heathcote and P. J. Allcock, *Theology of the Old Testament.* New York, 1958.
————, *Ras Shamra-Ugarit et l'Ancien Testament.* Neuchatel, 1960.

————, "Osée," *Osée, Joël, Amos, Abdias, Jonas.* Neuchatel, 1965 (Commentaire de l'Ancien Testament xi a).

————, *L'Ancien Testament.* Paris, 1967 ("Que sais-je?" Le Point des Connaissances Actuelles No. 1280).

————, "L'Expérience prophétique d'Esaie d'après le Chapitre 6 de son livre," *EThR* 16 (1941), pp. 616-673.

————, "L'Idéal de paix dans les espérances d'avenir de l'Ancien Testament," *EThR* 19 (1944), pp. 3-13.

————, "A propos de l'interprétation de l'Ancien Testament: Méthode christologiques ou méthode historique?", *EThR* 20 (1945), pp. 76-82.

————, "L'Ancien Testament et la prédication chrétienne," *VC* 4 (1950), pp. 151-164.

————, "Le prophètisme israélite d'après les recherches récentes," *RHPR* 32 (1952), pp. 59-62.

————, "Considérations sur l'Autorité canonique de l'Ancien Testament," *Le Problème biblique dans le protestantisme* (J. Boisset, ed.). Paris, 1955, pp. 71-85.

————, "Histoire et Historiens dans l'Ancien Testament," *RHPR* 35 (1955), pp. 26-35.

————, "Quelques remarques sur les faux prophètes," *TZ* 13, 1957, pp. 479-486.

————, "L'Ancien Testament et la vision de l'histoire," *RThP* 7 (1957), pp. 254-265.

————, "Les bases theologiques de l'ethique de l'Ancien Testament," *Congress Volume, Oxford 1959* (P. A. H. DeBoer, ed.). Leiden, 1960, pp. 39-51 (Supplements to Vetus Testamentum. vol. VII).

————, "Abraham et sa signification pour la foi chrétienne," *RHPR* 42 (1962), pp. 148-156.

————, "L'Heritage cananéen dans le livre du prophète Osée," *RHPR* 43 (1963), pp. 250-259.

————, "Der Prophet Hosea und die Geschichte," *EvT* 24 (1964), pp. 281-290.

————, "The Biblical Prophets: Revolutionaries or Conservatives?", *Interpretation* 19 (1965), pp. 47-55.

————, "Possibilitiés et limites d'une théologie biblique," *RHPR* 46 (1966), pp. 116-130.

————, "La théologie de l'Ancien Testament: état présent et perspectives d'avenir," *EThL* 44 (1968), pp. 420-432.

6
George A. F. Knight
A Christian Theology of the Old Testament

by John I. Durham

George A. F. Knight was born in 1909 at Perth, Scotland. He holds major degrees from the University of Glasgow in Scotland and the University of Melbourne in Australia. He has been deeply involved in Jewish-Christian relationships, and served a parish in Glasgow from 1942-1946. In 1947 he became Professor of Old Testament Studies at Knox College, Dunedin, New Zealand. He returned to Scotland in 1959 as lecturer on Old Testament at St. Mary's College, University of St. Andrews. From there he moved to McCormick Theological Seminary, Chicago, in 1960 as Professor of Old Testament. At present he is the Principal of Pacific Theological College at Suva, Fiji, a post he has held since 1966.

SOME MIGHT SAY, AND WITH JUSTIFICATION, that G. A. F. Knight's *A Christian Theology of the Old Testament*[1] is neither a proper

---

[1] Though the bibliography of Knight's published works continues to grow, and though each of his works casts at least some light upon his understanding of Old Testament theology, the present essay will treat in detail only his most extensive and comprehensive work on the subject, *A Christian Theology of the Old Testament* (Richmond: John Knox Press, 1959). Hereinafter this work will be referred to in footnotes as CTOT. All citations from this book will be identified by the page numbers in parenthesis in the text.

Special mention must also be made at this point of: (1) *From Moses to Paul: A Christological Study in the Light of Our Hebraic Heritage* (London: 1949), to some extent more christological in its treatment of the Old Testament, as the subtitle would indicate, than the present, more mature work; (2) *A Biblical Approach to the Doctrine of the Trinity* (Edinburgh: 1953), especially the first three chapters, pp. 1-59, each of which deals with some aspect of "Hebraic thinking"; and (3) *Law and Grace: Must a Christian Keep the Law of Moses?* (Philadelphia: The Westminster Press, 1962), a more homiletical work than any Knight has written, clearly designed primarily for the nonspecialist, and concerned with "the present-day trend . . . to integrate 'Law' and 'Gospel'" (p. 10).

theology of the Old Testament nor a really Christian work in orientation and approach. Certainly, there is in this work nothing like a theological system. Its references to Christianity seem to come more from impulse than from an ordered bias, occurring as they do in concluding paragraphs, footnotes, and appendices. One may legitimately ask, therefore, why this work should be allotted space in a volume of essays about contemporary treatments of Old Testament theology in which some special attention is given to the relation of Old Testament thought to the Christian faith.

The answer to such a question is not difficult. To begin with, Knight's work, with all its inadequacies, is surely the most serious and extensive effort to deal with Old Testament theology as the formative framework of New Testament theological statement which has yet appeared during what R. C. Dentan has so aptly called "a Golden Age" in the production of works on Old Testament theology.[2] Again, Knight has kept his work within the mainstream of contemporary discussion of Old Testament theology by avoiding, for the most part, the christological approach of Wilhelm Vischer.[3] For example, Knight states: "The assumption that the Old Testament is the Word of God to the Church . . . is not the same thing as the inference that may be drawn therefrom, *viz.*, that the Old Testament must be understood christologically" (pp. 7-8).

Further, both hermeneutics and typology, subjects of such crucial importance in the study of Old Testament theology today, form a central part of Knight's treatment; the latter, more than Knight seems willing to admit.[4] These reasons alone would make the in-

[2] Robert C. Dentan, *Preface to Old Testament Theology,* rev. ed. (New York The Seabury Press, 1963), pp. 72 ff., dates the beginning of this "distinct turning point" in the history of the study of Old Testament theology at 1949. Cf. Brevard S. Childs, "Advance, but Not Arrival," Review, *Interpretation,* **14** (1960), pp. 202-204.

[3] Wilhelm Vischer, *Das Christuszeugnis des Alten Testaments,* vols. 1-2, third ed. (München: 1936). For briefer treatments, see his "Everywhere the Scripture Is About Christ Alone" in *The Old Testament and Christian Faith: A Theological Discussion.* B. W. Anderson, ed. (New York: 1963), pp. 90-101, and *Die Bedeutung des Alten Testaments für das Christliche Leben, TS,* **3** (Zürich: 1947).

[4] Cf. Samuel Terrien, Review, *USQR,* **15** (1960), p. 329; Howard N. Bream, Review, *LQ,* **12** (1960), pp. 174-175.

clusion of Knight's work mandatory in any serious assessment of Old
Testament theology in contemporary discussion.

ARRANGEMENT OF OLD TESTAMENT THEOLOGY

A Christian Theology of the Old Testament is not a definitive work;
Knight himself would not claim that it is more than "a theology of the
Old Testament." (p. 7). Some critics would even deny that it is a
theology.[5] Nor is Knight's work well-organized or comprehensive;
it is by no means exhaustive even on those subjects it treats; and not
a few subjects which are of vital and perhaps crucial importance to
any thorough consideration of Old Testament theology, such as doctrines of the presence of God, the cult, and the laity, are either given
a cursory treatment or ignored altogether. All in all, the book is quite
uneven in quality: there are times when Knight makes his point with
thoroughness and vigor but there are other times when he makes it
poorly or not at all. Too often, the reader is faced with unnecessary
digressions, with sections which stop short of a satisfactory or even a
relevant conclusion, and with a surprising number of *non sequiturs*,
especially in the abundant biblical references.

At the same time, there is no denying Knight the honor due him
for producing a work which is creative, nearly always stimulating,
and quite often eloquent. He has included in this book a large number
of exceedingly helpful insights into Hebrew thought and some most
imaginative word studies. For the most part he has done his exegesis
carefully, lapsing only occasionally into eisegesis, and his arrangement of supporting passages is many times both fresh and brilliant.
The strengths of *A Christian Theology of the Old Testament* far
outweigh its weaknesses, and perhaps the finest compliment to be
paid it is to say that this interpretation of Old Testament thought
will provoke in the careful reader as many new ideas again as the
book itself sets forth. Even if these new ideas are contradictory to
his own, Knight will have had an ample reward in having stimulated
them.

The reviews of the book bear out what is here said by the very
range of their estimate of its value; they run the gamut from en-

---

[5] See, for example, H. D. Hummel, "Survey of Recent Literature," in *The
Old Testament in Modern Research,* H. F. Hahn, ed. (Philadelphia: Fortress
Press, 1966), p. 303; M. G. Kline, *WTJ,* 22 (1960), pp. 195-196.

thusiastic approval[6] through qualified admiration[7] and reserved appreciation [8] to puzzled dissatisfaction,[9] disfavor,[10] vigorous demurrer,[11] and complete disavowal.[12] While it is not appropriate to call Knight's statement controversial, only a thought-provoking book could call forth such a variety of scholarly opinion.

One of the things Knight's reviewers complain about is his organization of the material at his disposal;[13] while others undoubtedly would have ordered the treatment differently, a part of a man's presentation is the skeleton upon which he hangs his argument and conclusions. In the summary which follows, therefore, Knight's own outline is followed as closely as possible.

Having made clear his presupposition that the Old Testament "is nothing less than Christian Scripture" (p. 7), that it must be understood in its totality, and that the same God speaks in both Testaments through his Son (Israel and Jesus, respectively), Knight then presents his argument in four parts: "God," "God and Creation," "God and Israel," and "The Zeal of the Lord." Aside from the first part, which deals exclusively with the Old Testament concept of God, the traditional "God and Man" categories of Old Testament theology are not followed, and the classical, though probably artificial, subcategorization of the systematic theologies of the Old Testament is rightly abandoned altogether.

[6] Alan Richardson, *JTS*, 11 (1960), pp. 376-377; L. A. Whiston, Jr., *JBR* 29 (1961), pp. 244-245.

[7] N. H. Snaith, *SJT*, 13 (1960), pp. 90-91; Terrien, *op. cit.*, pp. 329-330; Childs, *op. cit.*, pp. 202-204.

[8] Norman Porteous, Society for Old Testament Study *Book List* (1960), pp. 37-38; H. H. Rowley, *ET*, 71 (1959), p. 73; J. D. Smart, *JBL*, 79 (1960), pp. 290-291; J. Hempel, *ZAW*, 72 (1960), pp. 96-97; C. A. Keller, *TZ*, 16 (1960), pp. 483-484.

[9] D. G. Hill, *Theology*, 63 (1960), pp. 82-84; *Biblica*, 41, p. 449, which accords CTOT only an indifferent two sentence note.

[10] H. S. Gehman, *TT*, 17 (1960), pp. 390-391; Dentan, *op. cit.*, pp. 77-78.

[11] Kline, *op. cit.*, pp. 193-196; Bream, *op. cit.*, pp. 174-175.

[12] James Barr, *Biblical Words for Time*, Studies in Biblical Theology, Series 33 (Chicago: Alec R. Allenson, 1962), pp. 61, 114, 129-133. Cf. his criticism of *A Biblical Approach to the Doctrine of the Trinity*, in *The Semantics of Biblical Language*. (Oxford: 1961), pp. 15-19, 23, 28-29, 89f., 252-254.

[13] See Snaith, *op. cit.*, pp. 90-91; Childs, *op. cit.*, p. 203; Smart, *op. cit.*, pp. 290-291; Bream, *op. cit.*, p. 174.

For Knight, Hebrew man thinks in concrete terms and employs "pictorial language," activistic and related to God alive and man alive. Such thinking also characterizes the New Testament; indeed, "Pictorial thinking is the essence of the whole biblical revelation" (p. 80). A theology of the Old Testament conceived in Christian terms is therefore best set forth, Knight has obviously concluded, upon the basis of a collection of these theological pictures into a unified showing with like periods placed loosely together, side by side. It is just this which *A Christian Theology of the Old Testament* attempts to do, and this accounts in part for its often disjointed and sometimes forced quality.

RELATIONSHIP BETWEEN FAITH AND HISTORY

Knight's approach to his subject is topical, and sometimes his topics are misleading. He is convinced of the importance of history for an understanding of Old Testament theology, and says in fact that "Exegesis remains exegesis, only so long as we cling faithfully to history" (p. 215). He does not, however, tie his argument to any definite historical framework, and tends consequently to attach far too much importance to the Exile and to see connections where perhaps none exist. Further, Knight takes an approach to literary criticism which is far too naive, and he too often sets forth only the view which supports the point he wishes to make. In fairness, however, one must add that he argues in this manner from his view of the unity and consistency of Old Testament thought across many years, and not from a determined proof-text methodology *per se*.

CONTENTS OF OLD TESTAMENT THEOLOGY

Knight arranges his theological pictures under four topics for the reader's consideration: "God," "God and Creation," "God and Israel," and "The Zeal of the Lord."

GOD.

The first gallery of pictures is concerned with how the living God makes himself known to man. His revelation is wrought out in history and in relationship to one specific people who were no people until they became a people in God's purpose for his service. Indeed, Old Testament theology is to be discovered in the "historical sequence" of "the development of the relationship between the *living* God . . . and that empirical People" (p. 18).

So God reveals himself in speech, in action and in his image, which is in man and is man. The fluidity in Hebrew thought between the one and the many is present also in thought about God.[14] God pictures himself as man, in totality in his own being and in totality in society. God's name, which he himself gives, is the nearest Old Testament approach to a divine self-description. Involved in this revelation is the declaration of God's Word in connection with visible phenomena. For Knight, this revelation is God's "emptying" himself "in total humility into Moses' hands" (pp. 44-45). However, one wonders whether the action depicted in Exodus 3 is not rather a confident, even arrogant assertion of divine sovereignty, and even more profoundly, a placing of the divine "presence" in the midst of the chosen people.[15]

God is known in the active participial forms which describe his continuing activity, particularly in his "being with" and "becoming with" his people (pp. 52-56). "Yahweh is the God who is 'with' his people because he is in their midst" (p. 56). The spoken word for the Hebrew had an objective, concrete quality; man's word, "spoken with intent, was always becoming 'incarnate'," and so also with God, who must always "speak with intent" (p. 60). God's name and God's word are his *alter egos* and at the same time part of his unity of being, and through them "he was immanent" (pp. 61-64).

God also makes himself known to Old Testament man through his "family." Among names other than Yahweh, the most significant is *'elohim,* "a quantitative plural," quite likely referring to "the living hosts of heavenly beings" (pp. 65-68). Included in such "hosts" are the various manifestations of God, his "sons," his "messengers," his "angels," his "powers," and his theophanic visitations.[16] Also included

[14] In addition to the basic sources on "corporate personality," cited by Knight, see the important article by J. R. Porter, "The Legal Aspects of the Concept of 'Corporate Personality' in the Old Testament," *VT*, 15 (1965), pp. 361-380.

[15] Cf., e.g., Gerhard von Rad, *Studies in Deuteronomy,* Studies in Biblical Theology 9, trans. David Stalker (Chicago: Henry Regnery Co., 1953), pp. 37-44.

[16] Knight's *seriatim* listing of "the various Old Testament theophanies," CTOT, pp. 75-78, made in the context of his discussion of the angel, is perhaps for that reason limited. One wishes both that he had defined what he

in the list of heavenly beings are the "Angel of the Covenant" (p. 80) and the "Angel of his presence" (pp. 80-83).[17]

A further manifestation of God is to be seen in the movement of his Spirit through the life and times of Old Testament man. The Spirit of God, indeed, "is no less than God himself" (pp. 85-86)—a statement which is no doubt correct, but one which Knight proceeds to undermine by his rather debatable exegesis of Psalm 51:11 and Psalm 139:7. On the surface these passages seem to identify the presence of God with the Spirit of God.

The Old Testament, says Knight, does not "provide us with any speculative ideas" about God; we must rather find God as he reveals himself in his own heavenly life and in his actions in the world, and clues for the search are to be found not in "abstract nouns" but in "verbs or active participles" (pp. 88-89, 101).[18] At the same time, Knight claims, "the essence of God is divinity" (p. 89), and the Old Testament employs two significant words to describe "what God is like in himself"; *qdsh,* holiness, and *kbd,* glory. Holiness refers to the fact that God is "wholly other" (p. 90) and possesses an "awe-ful otherness" which separates him from man as man and from man as sinner (p. 93). Glory is that "living" manifestation of God, covering many aspects of his essential nature, through which "the hidden God

---

means by "theophany" and more, that he had given much fuller attention to this important aspect of Old Testament theology. Cf. Jörg Jeremias, *Theophanie: Die Geschichte einer alttestamentlichen Gattung* (Neukirchen-Vluyn: 1965), WMZANT 10; J. K. Kuntz, *The Self-Revelation of God* (Philadelphia: The Westminster Press, 1967); Claus Westermann, "The Epiphany of God" in his *The Praise of God in the Psalms* (Richmond: John Knox Press, 1965), pp. 93-101.

[17] Though Knight's discussion of *panim* and *panah* and his question "God or the angel?" in reference to Isaiah 63:9 (pp. 80-83) seem to miss the point: the angel and God must surely be identical here as at so many other places in the Old Testament.

[18] The similarity of Knight's argument here and in *A Biblical Approach to the Doctrine of the Trinity,* pp. 8-17 (and to some extent *passim* in both works) to the argument set forth in much greater detail by Thorlief Boman in *Hebrew Thought Compared with Greek* (Philadelphia: The Westminster Press, 1961), esp. pp. 27-51, 58-67, 72-113, is worth noting. Though Knight depends heavily upon Johannes Pedersen, *Israel, Its Life and Culture* (New York: Oxford University Press, 1926-1940), he seldom refers to Boman's work—see, for example, CTOT, p. 163, n. 1.

of the Old Testament principally expresses his essential Self to man" (p. 97).[19]

GOD AND CREATION

The beginning of the victory of God on behalf of his people is the defeat of a primal chaos-monster (pp. 108-116). The writers of the material of the early chapters of Genesis, who incidentally, are far too intimately connected with the Exile by Knight, "moralized" mythological concepts at their disposal, and retold the story of beginnings in terms of "purpose." This chaotic principle is manifest in the waters of *tehom*, in the oppression by Pharaoh and the land of Egypt, in the desert, in abyss/Sheol, and in the disorder and agony of the individual's personal existence.[20] Creation thus comes, in a very specific sense, to be equated with redemption.

Man is a creature among creatures, but differs from other creatures in his authority to rule over them and, so far as Israel is concerned, in his Exodus-redemption. Even though sinful, man is yet able to have fellowship with God. The image of God which is set within man has become defaced with man's fall, but not eradicated. Man has free will, but somehow *tohu*, chaos, gets the uppermost hand within man, implanting "the tendency towards disintegration" (Knight's translation of *yetser*). Thus sin, "a breaking off of relations with the living God," becomes a disruptive factor in God's original "plan" (pp. 124-127).[21] This rebellion, further, is in evidence throughout

---

[19] It should be mentioned in passing that Knight's treatment of *qdsh* is much too superficial, particularly with regard to what he calls its "moral content." The reader is referred to Otto Procksch, "The Use of the Term Holiness in the Old Testament," *TDNT*, vol. I, pp. 89-97 and to James Muilenburg, "Holiness," *IDB*, vol. E-J, pp. 616-625. Further, Knight's statement that God's *kbd*, however conceived, is "objectively separable from God himself" (p. 95) is not borne out by the Old Testament: see Exodus 33:22; Leviticus 9:4, 6, and 23; Psalm 113:4; Zechariah 8:2, for example, and cf. G. Henton Davies, "Glory," *IDB*, vol. E-J, pp. 401-403.

[20] Though Knight goes entirely too far in suggesting that the waters struck by Moses from the rock (Numbers 20:11) were none other than the *tehom*-waters (p. 115), and that Jesus when calming the waters of the Sea of Galilee (Mark 4:35-41) was claiming to be Lord "of the Chaotic-Deep" (pp. 116-117, n. 3).

[21] Knight never defines precisely what this "plan" was.

the universe—even the "angels in heaven" are involved (pp. 127-128), and God's task is therefore both vast and urgent.

As a consequence of this sinful rebellion, God's wrath is visited upon his creation and upon no one more fully than his special people, whose special blessing gives them a special responsibility. This "wrath of God" is yet another aspect of the active, living God, and the Old Testament makes it clear that this wrath is directed at the sinner, not at the sin (pp. 132-134). The instruments of wrath are represented pictorially—angels of destruction and Satan, variously conceived and manifested—and they are all under the sovereignty of God. Man's rebellion, in time made inevitable by his hardness of heart, has infected his environment and brought the whole earth under God's curse. But this rebellion, too, is under God's sovereignty. He is merciful and gracious, actively manifesting his love for Israel, and able to make good even of "man's inner *yetser* towards rebellion" (pp. 143-145).

GOD AND ISRAEL

The revelation of God mediated to the world by Israel (and to Israel by Israel) is inseparably wed both to history and to the interpretation (and reinterpretation) of that history. For Knight, "The Sinai event must have been historical" (p. 150). Yet the Old Testament writers were concerned not with "objective history," but with setting forth the "significance of the events" in regard to God's purposes for his people. However, the interpretation becomes inseparable from the historical event and, "in reality . . . as much part of the divine event as the original historical occurrence itself" (pp. 152-155). There is, further, an essential unity to all the successive interpretations and retellings which both attests the validity of the historical core and leads to the corollary that "the whole cosmic purpose of God . . . hinges upon the historical fact of God's choice of empirical Israel" (p. 157). So God's action, Israel's response to it, and a collection of interpretative descriptions of both are the makings of the Old Testament, and the response of the Christian man makes a suprahistorical revelation of the historical core and all the layers of interpretation in the Old Testament (pp. 157-159).

The first great historical event in the history of Israel as a people is, of course, the Exodus-deliverance; it was in this event, indeed, that Israel came into being. But the Exodus in Old Testament theology is fused with the concept of creation, both symbolically and actually. Because of the Exodus Abraham's fatherhood takes on a special significance, and the Exodus can even be described, says Knight, as the moment of birth not only of the nation, but even of the cosmos, "already lying waiting to be redeemed through Israel" (pp. 165-166). So again the need for "empirical Israel" is seen; without Israel, no Exodus could have taken place, as, paradoxically, there could be no Israel without Exodus. All this line of interpretation, of course, makes the Old Testament an almost incredibly Israel-centered revelation, which is the view which Knight is trying to establish.

The Old Testament sets forth Israel's own theological understanding of herself through a number of figures, in keeping with the Hebrew penchant for concrete pictorial language. The figure of the vine and the vineyard, "as the type of effervescent life," represented both the *totum corpus* of Israel ("one Vine") and also the individual sons and daughters of Israel ("twigs and shoots"), planted by God (pp. 167-169). The figure of the Son of God similarly has reference to Israel as a *corpus* and to individuals within Israel; the son is unique not by virtue of any physical relationship to the Father, but because of the "adoption" of Israel "at birth" in the Exodus-deliverance (pp. 169-174). So also the figure of the Son of Man, "Man in his very essence," is a description of "the empirical Israel of the Old Testament story," and refers both to the "chosen" and "beloved" representative of Israel and to the whole of Israel, separately and/or simultaneously (pp. 174-177).

Though there is some question about the exact meaning of the figure "Bride," says Knight, there can be no doubt that for Hosea, particularly, the "Bride of Yahweh" is "the whole body of Israel, empirical, sinful Israel" (pp. 177-178). Israel, through idolatry, had become a harlot, subject to *ba'al,* "master"; Yahweh is prepared to forgive and restore her to relationship with him as *'ish,* "husband." In fact, holy Yahweh is proposing to become "one flesh" with harlot Israel (Hosea 2:16 and Genesis 2:24),[22] a figure which approaches

[22] The "two dicta" of these two verses were set "side by side in the one sacred Scripture" by the people of Israel, says Knight, and "regarded . . . as the Word of God to be believed, accepted and made incarnate in their com-

"blasphemy" except for those "who see the completion of the Old Testament in the New Testament" (pp. 179-181). This figure has, in reference to the union of Yahweh and his Bride, an eschatological aspect: Knight proposes the theory of a marriage at Sinai, followed by a wilderness honeymoon, and anticipating a "marriage" yet to be experienced "in all its true and deep sense and meaning," and involving the "total surrender" of the Bride (pp. 181-184).

Israel also thought of herself as a rock; as God is a Rock in whom she hides and takes refuge, so she is to become in the "messianic future" a "refuge to the weary and the worn" and also a God-hewn "rock of offence" to the Gentiles (pp. 184-189). Finally, Israel is presented in the Old Testament as a Servant, "slave . . . who belongs to a master," and this Servant-figure can be seen to represent Israel *in toto,* the "faithful element within Israel," and also in the person of an individual (pp. 189-192). Each of these six figures, indeed, can be seen to refer to Israel as a whole and in individual extension of the whole; and each one sets forth the "unique relationship that obtains between God and Israel," a suggestion of what Israel "was to be to the Gentiles" (pp. 192-193).

THE ZEAL OF THE LORD

The final major section of *A Christian Theology of the Old Testament* is given to a consideration of the question of God's purpose in this unique and "strange" relationship which he established with his special people. In this final section the majority of Knight's specifically Christian implications of Old Testament theology are set forth; but even here, they are in fact far less frequent than Knight's title would lead one to expect.

In view of the covenant which God has made with man, he cannot "go back," even in the face of Israel's perversity and rebellion. Thus he devises a new plan, which will be operative within history and will "enfold within his purpose" a certain segment of sinful mankind, using even a limited allegiance to his end (pp. 197-200). God moves this plan forward in a series of "moments," each of which

---

munity life" (CTOT, p. 179). Such comparisons are quite typical of Knight's methodology; and in cases such as this one, one wonders whether "the people of Israel" ever saw these two verses as complementary. Cf. Childs, *op. cit.,* p. 203.

contains his active judgment and mercy, and each of which has "relevance for the End of the total plan" (p. 201).[23]

These moments are five in number, and the first three of them—birth, marriage, and death—correspond to the three great moments in the life of mankind. God gave birth to his people in the Exodus, when he called Israel into being as his son, married Israel at the foot of Sinai, and put Israel to death in 587 B.C. by permitting the Babylonians "not only to lay the Holy City in ruins, but also to take into Exile the Body itself which once had been actually wed to God its beloved Husband." This "crushing experience" is interpreted in Old Testament theology as "an act of well-merited punishment," and one which would seem to mark both the end of God's people and the failure of God's "second plan" (pp. 203-207). But as "one flesh" with God, Israel had still somehow to be alive, and so there comes a fourth moment, establishing continuity as a repetition of the first moment: out of the death of Exile, the WHOLE body of Israel is re-created. The fifth moment takes its form in the historical return of Israel to the Holy Land, but is conceived primarily in eschatological terms as the moment when God's purposes will be brought to a successful conclusion and "all creation" will be reconciled and brought home "to the Promised Land" (pp. 210-213).

Four corollaries of biblical theology may be seen in the light of this "five moment" interpretation, says Professor Knight.[24] First, Israel's five moments "correspond exactly with a like five 'moments' in the work of Christ." [25] Second, a new content for eschatology is established which includes meaning beyond life as well as meaning

[23] Cf. Gerhard von Rad's "openness to the future" discussion in his *Old Testament Theology,* vol. 2 (New York: Harper & Row, Publishers, 1965), pp. 410-429. See also H. W. Wolff, "The Understanding of History in the Old Testament Prophets," in *Essays on Old Testament Hermeneutics,* ed. Claus Westermann (Richmond: John Knox Press, 1963), pp. 336-355.

[24] These corollaries, which are imaginatively typological, constitute the most important statement in CTOT of Knight's understanding of the relation between the Testaments. Strangely, in view of his prefatory remarks (pp. 7-10) and his not infrequent typological allusions (see above, n. 4), Knight makes a curious and weak apology for the typology of the corollaries on the grounds that Paul did the same kind of "exegesis" (pp. 215-217).

[25] A fact which for Knight solves "the problem of the Apocrypha": since the two Testaments contain "the total knowledge of God's saving purpose for the cosmos," the apocryphal books can be ignored (p. 213).

here and now.[26] Third, the "pattern of God's dealings" with the historic Israel, with the second Israel or Christ, and with the third which is the church, "is seen to be identical," and thus "Israel" represents a " 'continuum' of revelation in the one Body spoken of from Genesis to Revelation." Finally, the Old Testament can be seen as "the divinely given commentary upon the New Testament" which assists the individual believer in an understanding of his own relationship to God (pp. 214-215).

One of the results of these significant moments (particularly the second) in the relationship between God and his people is the covenant, an "idea" which "dominates the whole Old Testament." [27] Five analogies can in fact be made between marriage customs among men and the special covenant-marriage with God, and as with any human marriage, the covenant preserves the aspects of a legal contract *(berith)* and a promise of faithfulness and loyalty *(ḥesedh)* forever. This *ḥesedh* is to be characteristic both of God, unswervingly faithful to his people, and also of Israel, cleaving loyally to Yahweh alone and manifesting this loyalty in obedience, which is a result not a prerequisite of forgiveness.

God's commandments and statutes constituted the "Book of the Covenant" which kept the covenant a living reality for the people and provided them with a means of expression of their *ḥesedh*. The requirements of Torah were specifically related to the individual and community life of the people, as the primary feasts of the cult were related to the actions of God which established his faithfulness and required theirs. Comprehensive in reference, the covenantal obligations involved the preparation of God's people to be like him and prepared for his task, out of love, not fear or flattery (pp. 230-241).

God is considered by Old Testament theology to be really present in the midst of his people, "as the Forgiver of Israel," creatively involved in the establishment of his *mishpat*, "justice itself," and making

---

[26] CTOT, pp. 213-214. Cf. C. H. Dodd's "realized eschatology" in his *The Parables of the Kingdom,* rev. ed. (New York: Charles Scribner's Sons, 1961), *passim,* but esp. pp. 34-80, and note G. A. F. Knight, "Eschatology in the Old Testament," *SJT,* 4 (1951), pp. 355-362.

[27] Though Knight also considers covenant a "secondary" issue in the Old Testament (CTOT, p. 9), his sparse use of the work of Walther Eichrodt is surprising. See esp. the latter's *Theology of the Old Testament* (Philadelphia: The Westminster Press, vol. 1, 1961; vol. 2, 1967).

his holiness "visible" through his *tsedheq,* "righteousness," in "putting right" and "prospering" Israel (pp. 242-246). In this process, God acts within the history of Israel, within the life of the remnant in Israel, and within the lives of specific individuals in Israel to create *shalom* among men and between himself and men and so to bring men, "through *tohu,* into his promised *shalom*" (pp. 247-267):[28] a process of which the life of David may be considered something of a paradigm. As not all of Israel was responsive to God's covenantal call, the concept that within Israel there might be obedient remnant and disobedient *goi* arose, and after the Exile the remnant concept became more and more "individualized" in the person of the "*ḥasidh,* . . . the true believer" (pp. 260-262).

The imagery of the Old Testament, portraying pictorially the active God, both "objectified" the Word of God and had in its own right a certain power. This imagery remained "constant throughout" the history of Old Testament man and was believed by him to be given originally by God. The Word of God in the Old Testament may thus be considered more and more inseparable from the Thing or Deed of God. God is seen, for example, as a consuming Fire, something which is ever active in its essence. So God is in the midst of Israel and in the world: burning, refining, destroying (pp. 273-278).[29]

A sacrifice for atonement, the Old Testament cult came to see, would be required if sinful Israel was to be made able to approach this "living God of Fire." The normative rituals of the established cult could not meet this need because the people who performed them were often impure of heart; nor could any "heavenly or spiritual" being fulfill the need: "it could only be one of flesh and blood," as the sins were the sins of the flesh and blood people of God. Thus God's "own Servant and Bride" became the elected medium, and so

---

[28] Though Knight is careful (p. 250) to point out that more than "peace," in its English sense, is meant by *shalom,* he comes nowhere near plumbing the depths of its meaning (pp. 250-253, 263-266). This is regrettable, particularly since *shalom* in the Old Testament often refers to "completion, fulfillment of promise"—a concept which would suit Knight's purpose nicely.

[29] Both here and on pp. 73-74 and 98-100, Knight fails to give proper attention to fire as a theophanic symbol in the Old Testament. At the same time it can hardly be maintained, on the basis of the Old Testament evidence (or even Knight's own theology), that ". . . the unspeakably Holy God can be present in the midst of Israel only in the form of Fire or Furnace" (p. 276).

Israel came to be "crucified." Upon the basis of the three Servant-poems in Isaiah 42, 49, and 50, Knight posits the view that God burns in his fire and wrath the body of his harlot-Bride, makes her in the process the *'asham,* "sin offering," for the redemption of the Gentiles, and then takes her to himself. Then, in the fourth poem, Isaiah 52: 13–53:12, the body of Israel has become "one flesh" with God's glory, "that entity employed by God to show forth his relationship to the world." [30] Though Israel was crucified and resurrected (brought into new life and restored to her land), she did not become in any sense "the Savior of the world"; yet, says Knight, "the pattern had indeed been set" (pp. 289-293).

Israel's convictions about a living active God had implications for the future which involved meaning in history, "rather than the last of all calendar dates in time," and these implications are expressed in a messianic hope for the Day of the Lord when "God's total purpose for his world" shall have been accomplished "through the instrumentality of Israel." Once again the "language of imagery" is the means of expression, and Knight singles out some seventeen images which together express "the whole eschatological hope of Israel." This looking toward the future in Old Testament theology is not to be understood, says Knight, as "a 'preview' of the Jesus of the New Testament"—it rather is a characteristic of the Old Testament "as a whole" (pp. 294-296). This view, incidentally, separates Knight sharply from Wilhelm Vischer, who takes precisely the opposing view that "the theological exposition [of the Old Testament] . . . can be nothing other than Christology." [31]

Some of Knight's eschatological images are treated, in different contexts, in other parts of his *Theology:* the holy city (pp. 243 f.), the bride (pp. 177 f.), the servant (pp. 189 f.), the new covenant (pp. 219 f.). As images looking to the future end of God's purpose, however, they are all seen to have the same point as interwoven strands of the same rope. Together, they give assurance of the success of

[30] Cf., as Knight in fact does, Gerhard von Rad, "Typological Interpretation of the Old Testament" in *Essays on Old Testament Hermeneutics,* ed. C. Westermann (Richmond: John Knox Press, 1963), esp. pp. 30-32.

[31] Wilhelm Vischer, *The Witness of the Old Testament to Christ,* Eng. trans. A. B. Crabtree (London: 1949), of vol. 1 of *Das Christuszeugnis des Alten Testaments* (see n. 5), p. 29. On the infelicities of this translation, see J. R. Porter's review in *Theology,* 53 (1950), pp. 192-193.

God's promise and even suggest the shape of the fulfillment to come. Examples are the promise of David's line; the rule of God which will bring order out of chaos and establish God's *shalom* in God's land and God's city; the intervention of God which will save his people and "individualize" *shalom;* and the coming of a new covenant "to fit the new situation" being brought by the outpouring of God's Spirit (pp. 296-333).

The inadequacy of Old Testament ideas about a life beyond this life, coupled with the experience of death and resurrection in the Exile and return, led Old Testament thinkers, says Knight, to the view that God must be planning a resurrection of the whole creation, a final victory "over sin and 'chaos' in both 'earth' and 'heaven'" (pp. 334-343). "At that day," God will marry (and thus transform) the land and will consummate his marriage with the bride, the people of Israel, considered "in reality one great corporate *nephesh.*" A *nephesh,* indeed, which might be "summed up in one man alone": a man who, "according to the genius of Hebrew thought . . . would still be the Lord" (pp. 343-347).[32]

RELATIONSHIP BETWEEN OLD TESTAMENT AND NEW TESTAMENT

Knight concludes his work with a brief appendix entitled "Israel and the Church." In view of the promise of his title and the always imaginative, sometimes creative, work of the first 348 pages of his book, one comes to this last bit expecting great things only to be disappointed. Three points are made: (1) The church is both a *continuum* of Israel, as the Old Testament people of God, and discontinuous in the new existence through Christ. (2) Christ "is the Remnant of Israel in himself," discontinuous in sinlessness, but the "'inclusive representative' of Israel, both old and new" (pp. 350-352). (3) The Jews, still the people of God, are no longer the "eschatological Israel of God," and thus they wait, "the shadow Church," for their *"raison d'être* to become apparent" (pp. 353-358). This latter section on "Israel and the Jews" exemplifies Knight's disconcerting habit of digressing into interesting but not always relevant

[32] Though the New Testament implications of this point are obvious, see Knight's further clarification in CTOT, pp. 347-348, n. 1: "human Son of Man upon earth . . . epitome of historical Israel."

material; and one's sense of regret is heightened at the brevity of the preceding four sections. The material which has been compressed in this final appendix to five pages most certainly deserves a much more central and extended treatment in a work such as this one; however, so compressed and incomplete a treatment of so interesting a subject is quite typical of many other sections of the work as a whole. The title and Introduction to this book promise far too much in the light of what follows.

There is a sense, certainly, in which Knight's work is little different from other Old Testament theologies written by Christians. Knight does not define a CHRISTIAN theology, or, for that matter, even an OLD TESTAMENT theology, though some words on these matters would undoubtedly have made his purpose and approach clearer to his readers. However, Knight has promised only "*a* Theology of the Old Testament" (p. 7), one man's approach written from the point of view of a Christian who believes the two Testaments to be organically and dynamically related. And this much he has plainly delivered.

Knight's approach differs from other Old Testament theologies by Christians in his desire to depict Old Testament theology as a kind of loom which sets in advance the pattern of New Testament theology. For him, the Old Testament is not the promise of which the New Testament is the horizontal fulfillment. Rather, it contains a "vertical" revelation which is paralleled by a similar "vertical" revelation in the New Testament. Both Old and New Testaments are "Word of God" and they show him working "in the same way, and towards the same ends, at all periods in the history of man" (p. 214). Thus the Old Testament establishes the pattern, in a sense, for both the form and the content of the New Testament and is therefore essential for our understanding of the latter.

Knight has served us by introducing into the contemporary discussion of Old Testament theology a number of stimulating ideas. Even if one expresses chagrin that he has treated some vital subjects too cursorily or not at all, he has given us some more of what Professor Rowley has called a deep penetration into the thought of the Old Testament.[33] Most of all, however, Knight has raised seriously the question of the dependence of the thought-patterns of the New Testa-

[33] Rowley, *op. cit.*, pp. 72-73.

ment upon Old Testament theological statements, has taken one step toward the answer, and has provided Old Testament scholars with some guidance about which way to take to find a fuller answer.

SELECTED BIBLIOGRAPHY

Knight, G. A. F., *From Moses to Paul: A Christological Study in the Light of Our Hebraic Heritage.* London, 1949.

_____, *Ruth and Jonah: The Gospel in the Old Testament.* London, 1950 (Torch Commentaries); cf. esp. pp. 9-12, 77-91.

_____, *A Biblical Approach to the Doctrine of the Trinity.* Edinburgh, 1953 (Scottish Journal of Theology Occasional Papers No. 1).

_____, *Esther, Song of Songs, Lamentations.* London, 1955 (Torch Commentaries); cf. esp. pp. 14-17, 57-59, 100-114.

_____, *Hosea: God's Love.* London, 1960 (Torch Commentaries); cf. esp. pp. 20-36.

_____, *Prophets of Israel* (1) *Isaiah.* New York, 1961 (Abingdon Bible Guides); cf. esp. pp. 88-96.

_____, *Law and Grace: Must a Christian Keep the Law of Moses?* Philadelphia, 1962.

_____, *Deutero-Isaiah: A Theological Commentary on Isaiah 40–55.* New York, 1965.

_____, and F. Neumann (eds.), *Jews and Christians: Preparation for Dialogue.* Philadelphia, 1965; cf. esp. pp. 36-56, 108-123, 123-136.

7

Paul van Imschoot
Theology of the Old Testament

by David A. Hubbard

Paul van Imschoot was born in Ghent, Belgium, on September 17, 1889. After studies at the Jesuit college of Ste. Barbe, and at the seminary in Ghent, he went to the Gregorian Institute in Rome in 1907. Here he received his doctorate in philosophy and theology in 1914. From 1919-1948 he was Professor of Exegesis (Old Testament and New Testament) at the Major Seminary of Ghent. In 1948 he became chaplain at the Maison St. Pierre in Ghent. He retired in 1963, and died in 19—.

PAUL VAN IMSCHOOT's work [1] is the first major Roman Catholic theology of the Old Testament since the publication of *Divino Afflante Spiritu* by Pope Pius XII in 1943 nudged Catholic exegetes to give careful attention to theological doctrine and moral teaching in biblical studies as well as to historical, archaeological, and philological matters. Van Imschoot's work is the basis of this survey, although the slightly older theologies of Paul Heinisch[2] and P. F. Ceuppens[3] are referred to on occasion, along with the later, briefer works of A. Gelin,[4] J. Guillet,[5] and J. Giblet.[6]

[1] Paul van Imschoot, *Theologie de l'Ancient Testament* (Tournai) Tome I, *Dieu*, 1954; Tome II, *L'homme*, 1956. English translation of Volume I by Kathryn Sullivan and Fidelis Buck (Tournai: Desclée & Co., 1965).

[2] Paul Heinisch, *Theology of the Old Testament*, trans. William Heidt (Collegeville Minnesota: The Liturgical Press, 1955). Translated from a revised edition of *Theologie des Alten Testaments* (Bonn: 1940).

[3] P. F. Ceuppens, *Theologica Biblica*, 4 vols., Rome, 1938ff.

[4] Albert Gelin, *The Key Concepts of the Old Testament* (New York: Paulist Press, 1955). Copyright 1955 by Sheed and Ward, Inc., New York.

[5] J. Guillet, *Themes of the Bible* (Notre Dame: Fides Publishers, Inc., 1960).

[6] J. Giblet, *The God of Israel, The God of Christians* (New York: Paulist Press, 1961).

193

The Roman Catholic view of the Old Testament canon immediately sets off van Imschoot's approach from that of the Protestant theologians. Though there are passing references to the books of Maccabees, Judith, Tobit, and Baruch, the lion's share of references to the apocryphal or deuterocanonical books is from Sirach (Ecclesiasticus) and Wisdom of Solomon. This choice is to be expected since the apocryphal wisdom books have more in common with Proverbs and Ecclesiastes than do any other apocryphal books with the canon.[7]

ARRANGEMENT OF OLD TESTAMENT THEOLOGY

Like the works of E. Sellin and L. Köhler, whom he cites, van Imschoot develops his theology topically and systematically rather than chronologically and historically. His declared aim is to "bring about a synthesis of the doctrines of the Old Testament" (I, p. 3),[8] and in so doing he groups the doctrines under three main headings: (1) God and his relationships with the world and especially Israel; (2) Man—his nature, his duties, his sin; and (3) Divine judgment and salvation. Unfortunately, he was unable to complete the third section before his death. In choosing this systematic, synthetic approach van Imschoot deliberately veers away from a chronological exposition of the religion of the Old Testament, which he holds to be a "strictly historical discipline" (I, p. 1). The chronological approach tends, he feels, to ignore the "profound unity which binds the old revelation to the new" (I, p. 2). Furthermore, he contends that the relationship between the Testaments, both in continuity and discontinuity, may be seen more clearly where a logical order is followed in unfolding Old Testament doctrine.

Van Imschoot is not unmindful of the historical character of biblical faith. But history is not his main concern. It is an ancillary discipline like exegesis and literary criticism.[9]

[7] A. Gelin, *op. cit.,* also makes substantial use of the deuterocanonical writings, especially in his sections on otherworldly retribution and the origin of sin (pp. 79-91).

[8] References to volume I use the paging of the English translation; those to volume II, the original French edition.

[9] Somewhat in contrast, A. Gelin, *op. cit.,* pp. ix-xiv, takes great pains to show how central history is to biblical faith: "The Old Testament is the history of the people that lived the great realities—Election, Promise, Covenant, Kingdom, Exile, Community" (p. ix).

The deep conviction which underlies his method is the basic unity both within the Old Testament and between the Testaments. He is not blind to the various emphases of the individual authors, but he places strong emphasis upon the divinely ordered unity which he considers the necessary result of the revelatory process. This unity makes it possible to isolate and group into a synthesis ideas from the various authors without slighting the differences in their viewpoints.

The progressive and fragmentary nature of Old Testament revelation (Hebrews 1:1) means that no one author was given a complete picture, but together the various pieces form a whole. Since the Old Testament itself follows a historical and not a systematic outline, van Imschoot contends that it is his duty to introduce a pattern "that will permit the logical arrangement of doctrines" (I, p. 4).

Van Imschoot is probably more conscious of the relationship between biblical and systematic theology than any other of our contemporaries whose work is assessed in the present volume. Much of his scheme is drawn from the pattern laid by Aquinas' *Summa Theologica* and followed by and large by Catholic theologians ever since. P. F. Ceuppens, for instance, in his multivolume *Theologica Biblica* makes it his stated aim to follow as closely as possible the format of the *Summa*.[10] And van Imschoot's outline, especially in dealing with the doctrine of God, is not much different. Indeed one of his reasons for following a systematic approach is to supply theologians with the "revealed facts which are the objects of their science" (I, p. 4).[11]

In the section on the doctrine of God, the dogmatic shadow under which van Imschoot works seems most pervasive. The author's hand is tipped by the first main heading: "God Considered in Himself" (I, 6). In treating the existence, the names, and the character of God separately from the sections which deal with his revelation and his

[10] P. F. Ceuppens, *op. cit.,* vol. 1, p. viii.

[11] Guillet, *Themes of the Bible,* breaks with this traditional Catholic approach and surveys several of the main ideas of the Old Testament. Using the basic Hebrew vocabulary as a tool, he seeks to open up the concepts of grace, justice and truth, sin and damnation, hope and inspiration. In no sense a full-blown theology, Guillet's work does have the merit of treating sensitively and devoutly some central ideas of the Old Testament, especially the impact of the Exodus, while also demonstrating how they are brought to fruition in the Christian revelation.

relationship to the world and to his people, van Imschoot veers from the track that the main line of biblical theology has taken well before the publication of G. E. Wright's *God Who Acts*.[12]

This attachment to the methods of dogmatics becomes even clearer when we turn to the section on the attributes of God and meet "metaphysical attributes" and "moral attributes" which are then followed by the "sentiments of God": love, repentance, jealousy, anger. These neat categories provide for effective analysis but raise major questions, given the Old Testament's reluctance to speak about God abstractly.

Not surprisingly, van Imschoot uses the Catholic canon as the basis for garnering his Old Testament materials. Though he applies the customary label "deuterocanonical" to the seven additional works (Tobit or Tobia, Judith, Wisdom, Sirach or Ecclesiasticus, Baruch, 1 and 2 Maccabees), he draws from them freely and makes no distinction between their authority and that of the thirty-nine other books. He does distinguish clearly between the deuterocanonical writings and the Apocrypha, which includes works like Psalms of Solomon and Ascension of Isaiah. Citations from the Apocrypha are not included in the bulky (over thirty pages) index of biblical references, which, incidentally, is one of the great assets of the English translation of volume I.

His commitment to the authority of the deuterocanonical works shows itself both in the number of citations and the crucial part they play in his theological discussions. In volume I alone there are over a dozen references to Tobit, about twenty to the Books of Maccabees, and nearly one hundred and fifty to the sapient writings, Wisdom and Sirach. Van Imschoot's interest in these latter works can be amply illustrated. For instance, in his discussion of Adam's sin the last two pages are given to an account of the ways in which Wisdom and Sirach interpret the temptation and fall. The lavish place given to deuterocanonical materials marks a chief difference between van Imschoot's work and that of Protestant theologians like Köhler whose style and structure is otherwise quite similar.

CRITICAL APPROACH

Given the wide range of critical viewpoints embraced by contempo-

[12] G. E. Wright, *God Who Acts* (Chicago: Alec R. Allenson, 1952).

rary Old Testament scholars, van Imschoot's approach is quite conservative. While keenly aware of theories more radical than his own, he manages most of the time to strike a happy balance between excessive skepticism and glib naïveté. Perhaps the best way to demonstrate this approach is to take a sampling of his critical observations.

He seems to take delight in opposing the evolutionary theories of Wellhausen, particularly the view that the moral character of God was a late (eighth and seventh century) development in Hebrew thought. Hand in hand with this attitude is his insistence that the decalogue in its primitive form (which he ventures to reconstruct) stems from Moses. Similarly he holds that the divine name YHWH was known to some Israelite tribes, e.g., Levi, before the time of Moses and was given new significance at the time of Moses' call. The Kenite hypothesis of the origin of the divine name he considers unproved.

His basic confidence in the accuracy of the early traditions is further revealed in his contention that the idea of a covenant ("a mutual relation of solidarity, originated by a pact, concluded at a given time") goes back to Moses and even to the patriarchs (I, p. 238). Van Imschoot's conservatism appears again in his discussion of the puzzling passage where Zipporah circumcises Moses' son (Exodus 4:24-26). With zeal he seeks to refute the theory of P. Volz and E. Sellin that God's anger against Moses was a manifestation of a "demonic" trait in the God of the early Hebrews (I, p. 83). Our author sees it, rather, as the wrath of a righteous God directed at Moses' failure to obey a ritual precept (Genesis 17:10, 14).

In contrast to some theologians, notably von Rad, who base their interpretations of pentateuchal theology on some form of documentary hypothesis, van Imschoot makes only infrequent reference to the documents (Yahwist or Elohist) as he deals with the narrative materials in Genesis and Exodus.

Though he accepts K. Galling's opinion that there existed two independent traditions of Israel's election—one tracing the election to Moses' time, the other to the patriarchal period—he rejects Galling's theory that the Yahwist invented the patriarchal narratives for political purposes: "Neither the Yahwist nor the Elohist have created the substance and the persons of their accounts; it has been handed down to them by tradition" (I, p. 247). In the case of the laws in

Exodus 34:13-27, the so-called "ritual decalogue," he admits that some elements may come from J and have been incorporated in the present text by a redactor. Van Imschoot recognizes considerable diversity in the origin and dating of the various legal sections. Parts of Exodus 34:13-27 he considers very ancient, though many of the injunctions presuppose a sedentary agricultural society after the conquest of Canaan. Without assigning a specific date to the "priestly code" (Exodus 25–31; 35–40; Leviticus; Numbers; Joshua 13–22), he notes that it contains a much older "holiness code" (Leviticus 17–26) which appears to have taken shape before the sixth century.

Turning from law to cult, we find that van Imschoot rejects Mowinckel's theory that the feast of tabernacles was a New Year Festival, celebrating the kingship of Yahweh. He, with many others, finds it incredible that a feast so central would escape mention in the historical and legal texts of the Old Testament. The Babylonian New Year Festival and a few cryptic verses in the psalms are an inadequate base on which to build so elaborate a structure.

In light of our author's skepticism about the New Year Festival, it is not surprising that he rejects the thesis of H. Zimmern and L. Dürr that the portrait of the suffering servant in Isaiah 52:13–53:12 is a reflection of the ritual of humiliation which the Akkadian kings underwent as part of the annual festival. Evidence for ascribing royalty to the servant is slim. Besides, the humiliation and suffering of the Babylonian king were purely ritualistic, while the servant's experiences are actual and historical.

There is little discussion of the dating of biblical writings. Van Imschoot seems to assume, for instance, an exilic date for Isaiah 40ff., although he makes no effort to review the evidence for this nor does he allude to Second or Deutero-Isaiah as far as I can discover. He calls Isaiah 40ff. "the book of the consolation of Israel" (I, p. 250), but most of the time ascribes passages from this section to Isaiah without tackling the problems of authorship.[13]

In the case of the Book of Esther, our author does discuss the historical background and date. He cites two possibilities for the origin of the book and its connection with the feast of Purim: a mythic

---

[13] In contrast, A. Gelin, in J. Giblet, *The God of Israel, The God of Christians,* does not hesitate to speak of "the triumphant accents of the Second Isaias" (p. 213).

origin (proposed by Zimmern, Winckler A. Lods, *et al.*) in which the chief characters are named after Babylonian and Elamite deities, and a legendary origin based on an historical event which cannot be pinned down with precision (cf. Eissfeldt, Weiser, Bentzen, *et al.*). In any case van Imschoot dates the feast of Purim after 200 B.C. on the grounds that Esther and Mordecai are not mentioned in the catalog of illustrious worthies in Sirach.

All in all van Imschoot's approach to critical, historical, and introductory problems reveals the caution and balance characteristic of all his work. He goes off on almost no tangents and admirably resists the temptation to build his theological superstructure on shaky critical hypotheses.

Still he is considerably more open to critical theories than is his fellow Catholic, Heinisch, whose work pays only modest attention to the studies of other scholars. Mosaic authorship of the Pentateuch and the unity of Isaiah are implied by Heinisch, who develops his theology independent of the main lines of critical scholarship.

RELATIONSHIP BETWEEN FAITH AND HISTORY

The historical character of revelation is central to van Imschoot's theology. Yet he makes no attempt to develop anything like a *Heilsgeschichte*. There is no effort to develop a theology based on a recital of the acts of God as G. E. Wright and John Bright have done. And there is certainly nothing of the elaborate scheme of promises and fulfillments so crucial to G. von Rad's theology.[14]

At the same time van Imschoot treats the historicity of revelation in the Old Testament with full seriousness. Rather than frame a detailed structure relating faith and history, he readily and constantly assumes that history is the matrix in which revelation takes place.

[14] A. Gelin, *The Key Concepts of the Old Testament,* makes history central as he tries to give the "feel" of the Old Testament. "In particular, it is the history of a number of great personalities who typify and direct their age— key personages, giants of the Spirit, mystic builders incarnating the upward movement of faith, taking religion forward, sensing the future and linking it with the past" (p. x). Their history is divided into "essential stages": the election of Abraham (c. 1800?); the experience of the kingdom, especially under David (c. 1000), of the exile (587-38), and of the postexilic theocracy (pp. xi-xiii). Gelin's point is that each stage made a major contribution to the development of the key concepts in Israel's faith.

No major Old Testament theologian is more sturdily committed to the historicity of the events in the life of Israel than our author. He spends little time justifying this pillar in his theology but everywhere builds his structure on it.

Divine revelation takes place "in a successive and fragmentary form" (I, p. 4) because it takes place in a sequence of historical events. That this pattern of revelation is unique to Israel is one of van Imschoot's strongest contentions. "The obvious superiority of the Israelite doctrine [of God] over that held by theologians of peoples who were older and much more advanced in arts and knowledge . . . can only be explained by the revelation that God entrusted to His chosen people" (I, p. 98).

His staunch defenses of the uniqueness of Israel's faith often lead van Imschoot to play the role of apologete. A case in point is his emphasis on fulfilled prophecy as a proof of the divine origin of Israel's faith: "No other people of antiquity provides, as does Israel, a series of precise prophecies, plainly prior to the events and fully confirmed by them" (I, p. 169). His view of revelation in history obviously includes both the prophesying of events yet to come and their subsequent historical fulfillment.

Miracles are also examples of divine activity: "Yahweh's startling interventions in nature and history manifest His glory; they are the revelation of the holy and almighty God" (I, p. 107). The miracles of the prophets, like Isaiah's reversing of the shadow on Hezekiah's sundial (Isaiah 38:7-9), are special signs to confirm the prophet's authority and the divine origin of his message. Here should also be mentioned the appearances of the angel of the Lord in the times of the patriarchs, Moses, and the judges. Van Imschoot gives no indication that he treats these narratives as other than historical events in which the will and ways of God are revealed.

Van Imschoot makes no overt judgment on the historicity of the patriarchal narratives. But despite the fact that he recognizes various traditions which have transmitted the stories, he treats them consistently and implicitly as factual.[15] He seems carefully to eschew terms like "legend" and "saga" when dealing with them. And, of

[15] So does J. Giblet, *The God of Israel, The God of Christians*. For example: "One day, more than four thousand years ago, God suddenly intervened in the life of a man called Abraham" (p. 24).

course, the word "myth" is almost exclusively reserved for the polytheistic religions of Israel's neighbors.[16]

Further evidence of van Imschoot's firm commitment to the historical veracity of Israel's faith is found in his treatment of Moses' role. In contrast with those who see Moses as a fuzzy figure on the horizon of history, van Imschoot views him as the founder of Israel's faith: "All the books of the Old Testament make Moses the true founder of the religion of Israel" (I, p. 34).[17] And unlike M. Noth and G. von Rad, our author links tightly the call of Moses in the desert, the deliverance from Egypt in the Exodus, and the giving of the law at Sinai.

Both the nucleus of the law and the ark of the covenant are considered Mosaic. In addition, the stories about the ark in the Books of Samuel are treated as historical.

One could wish that van Imschoot had been more deliberate in sketching the relationship between faith and history in the Old Testament. But perhaps it is to his credit that he resists attempts either to synthesize a structure which would be forced or strained or to theorize from data which are often inadequate and sketchy. At least he takes the biblical accounts with a seriousness intended by their authors. And this attitude is no bad thing.

SPECIFIC THEOLOGICAL INSIGHTS

The reason for dealing with van Imschoot's theology in terms of INSIGHTS rather than SYSTEM is obvious. There is no great principle that ties his observations together into a cohesive doctrinal unit. Choosing not to take a strictly historical approach, as von Rad does in his explication of redemptive history, and avoiding a central theme like Eichrodt's focus on the covenant relationship between God and his people, van Imschoot deals with his two main subjects, God and man, by dividing them into their logical sub-topics: God considered in himself, God and the world, nature of man, duties of man, etc.

---

[16] Where mythological elements have been borrowed by Israel, according to van Imschoot, they are always stripped of their polytheistic character and molded to suit Israel's monotheistic faith (e.g., I, pp. 88, 95).

[17] A. Gelin, *op. cit.*, p. 17, concurs: "The witness and human artificer of this decisive change [in religious faith] was Moses. . . . [whose] religious revolution was based . . . on elements drawn from the past."

The overall result of this approach is to compartmentalize the materials. Obviously, any attempt to treat Old Testament teaching systematically has to do so, but at the same time one hopes for help in seeing the links and transitions among the various sections. This hope is at least partially disappointed in van Imschoot's work.

What we do have, however, are a vast number of fruitful comments on a host of topics. Especially effective are the disciplined philological and lexical observations which attempt to take careful account of the contexts in clarifying meanings of words. Thus, our author avoids some of the pitfalls pointed out by James Barr, inter alia, who warns against wrenching words out of their contexts, defining them only by their root meanings, and blowing up words into concepts.[18]

Perhaps the most accurate way to describe van Imschoot's work is to call it a compendium of brief essays on Old Testament subjects. Were the articles in alphabetical rather than logical order, they would come close to comprising a dictionary of Old Testament themes. The section on sexual morality, for instance, could well stand on its own as a worthy summation of the Old Testament regulations on adultery.

All of this is not to say that van Imschoot lacks theological conviction. Although he has chosen a topical approach which often diverts attention from the unity of the Old Testament, he assumes a deep and binding consistency despite the diversity of the various traditions which are combined in the Old Testament.

The ground of this consistency is the INSPIRED AND REVEALED CHARACTER OF THE SCRIPTURES. The unity and continuity of the two Testaments "are manifest because they are both the work of God. . . . It is the same God who has spoken through the prophets and through His Son . . . the same God who has communicated His thought and especially His will to men" (I, p. 2).

The revelatory character of the Old Testament is everywhere assumed in van Imschoot's two volumes. But his principal, systematic treatment of it is found in volume I, pp. 134-223, where he concentrates on the means of revelation: theophanies, angels, oracles, dreams, prophets, etc. Despite the traditional Roman Catholic em-

---

[18] J. Barr, *The Semantics of Biblical Language* (London: Oxford University Press, 1961).

phasis on natural revelation, van Imschoot resists the temptation to read this philosophical approach back into the Old Testament. Instead he puts the stress on divine intervention, not natural reason: "If man knows God, it is because God has manifested Himself to him: the origin of this knowledge is always due to an initiative of God" (I, p. 134). And again, after a discussion of words used to express revelation *(ra'ah, yada', galah),* he affirms: "All these verbs signify that God made known that which man ignored. He revealed that which had been veiled" *(loc. cit.).*

Van Imschoot exerts little effort in defending or proving his doctrine of revelation, except in the frequent comparisons which he makes between Israel's faith and the religions of her neighbors. And he makes no attempt whatever to define the relationship between the acts of revelation in Israel's history and the inspired record of those acts in the Scriptures. This task, apparently, is left to the dogmaticians, although van Imschoot seems to assume their work in all that he says.

Perhaps the best way to convey some of his theological insights is to dip into his work from place to place and summarize what he says. Take THE DIVINE NAMES, for instance. Commenting on Exodus 3:14-17, a passage crucial to our understanding of the meaning of "Yahweh," van Imschoot stresses the meanings "to become," "to be in activity." This meaning he contrasts sharply with the causative ("cause to be") and ontic or essential ("absolute being") explanations. The name Yahweh "was intended to remove the people's doubts, because they wished to know the name of the God who sent Moses so as to be sure that this God would be capable of achieving this deliverance" (I, p. 16).

The title *Yahweh Seba'oth* describes God as Lord of all heavenly and earthly forces. Van Imschoot comes to this conclusion after surveying various theories which would link the term *seba'oth* too narrowly either to the armies of Israel or to the celestial hosts, the stars, which fought against Sisera (Judges 5:20). The use of this title by the prophets is particularly appropriate to their polemics against the astral deities revered by Israel's neighbors. The prophets, in effect, are saying that the stars are not gods at all but part of God's great army whose troops man both earth and heaven.

In dealing with the nature of God, van Imschoot wisely gives a

good bit of attention to GOD'S HOLINESS: "holiness is what characterizes divinity to the point that holiness constitutes the essence of divinity" (I, p. 40). After he discusses at some length the ritual and
moral aspects of holiness, he treats the attributes and sentiments of
God, frequently linking them to the theme of holiness which is so important in his approach.

Two comments are in order on THE SENTIMENTS OF GOD. First,
van Imschoot's attempt to relate the sentiments to specific attributes
seems superficial: "Love is the manifestation of goodness, repentance
of mercy, jealousy of the personality and unicity of God; anger and
hatred are associated with divine holiness . . ." (I, p. 75). Fortunately,
he does not restrict his comments within this tidy arrangement, but
proceeds to deal with God's sentiments in a richer, rounder way than
his pat analysis implies.

Second, he views these sentiments as human qualities attributed to
God. But should he not state this the other way around? Love, repentance, jealousy, anger, and hatred are certainly qualities found
among men but always in mixed and marred form. Theologians go
to great lengths to show how these qualities exist in perfect and
noncontradictory fashion in God, and van Imschoot agrees. Would it
not be more consistent with his view both of creation and of revelation for our author to see these sentiments as essential expressions of
God's character which man, created in God's image, shares in
broken, partial form?

The author's commitment to the uniqueness of Israel's faith comes
through strongly in his sections on GOD'S COVENANT WITH AND ELEC-
TION OF ISRAEL.

> By these two properties, namely its gratuitous as well as its moral and con-
> ditional character, the covenant of Yahweh with Israel differs from cove-
> nants and natural relations which unite other peoples with their national
> gods (I, p. 232).

And again:

> In those religions [of the ancient East] the bond which unites each people
> with their gods originated from the nature of things; in the Old Testament
> and in Judaism this bond is born from an act of the will and intelligence of
> the personal God, since it is the result of a gratuitous choice and based
> solely on love; it began at a given moment of history and is attached to
> certain historical events, which appear as special interventions of Yahweh in

the course of human things and as manifestations of His particular benevolence (I, pp. 254-255).[19]

Thoroughly aware of the complexities of the covenant traditions as given in the Pentateuch and elaborated by the prophets, van Imschoot has aptly captured the threads which tie the Old Testament together and give it its uniqueness.[20]

Nowhere does van Imschoot's competence as philologist and exegete stand him in better stead than in his discussion of THE NATURE OF MAN. Rightly he sees man *('adam)* as basically a collective or generic term used primarily to distinguish the human species from the animal world on the one hand and from God on the other (II, pp. 1-2). And rightly he shies away from the more speculative questions of the dichotomous or trichotomous nature of man, concluding rather that man in the Old Testament is viewed synthetically as a physico-psychic organism (II, p. 35).[21]

Again, he takes pain to show how the Hebrew view of "flesh" does not correspond with our Western concepts, influenced as they are by Greek thought. After sketching the intimate relationships between flesh and soul and between flesh and heart, van Imschoot reminds us that the narrative does not speak strictly of the creation of the body, the flesh, or the soul, but of man infused with the breath of life. Therefore, he feels that debates over dichotomy or trichotomy in the Old Testament are irrelevant, except in the sapient literature where Greek influence is more prevalent.[22]

---

[19] Apparently van Imschoot did not have access to the writings of G. Mendenhall and D. McCarthy on the relationship of the Israelite covenant and laws to the Near Eastern, and particularly Hittite, treaty patterns. In his supplementary bibliography they are mentioned without comment (I, p. 300).

[20] J. Giblet, *op. cit.*, pp. 3-42, begins his book with fertile studies on election and covenant. His approach underscores the priority of these themes and spotlights the way in which God made himself known to his people.

[21] In his treatment of the nature of man, van Imschoot is indebted to the works of H. W. Robinson and A. R. Johnson among others. In contrast, Heinisch's discussion of this topic shows almost no evidence of interaction with contemporary biblical theologians. He is content (p. 169) to sketch quickly some Old Testament passages and to conclude: "Hence a survey of Old Testament doctrine shows no evidence for considering man trichotomous." The basic unity of man's psychosomatic nature is given short shrift by Heinisch.

[22] In my opinion, van Imschoot overstates the impact of Greek philosophy on Ecclesiastes (vol. II, pp. 13-14).

Like Heinisch, van Imschoot denies that the Old Testament alludes to the PREEXISTENCE OF THE SOUL. Discussing the two passages which purportedly imply preexistence (Job 1:21 and Wisdom 8:19-20), he insists that exegetes have misinterpreted both. Job's point is that he will die as bereft of human goods as he was born, not that he will return to some previous state of existence. The author of Wisdom is not reflecting a Platonic view of preexistence as some have claimed. Rather, van Imschoot holds, he is using Greek terminology, while expressing basically Jewish ideas. For Plato, the soul's captivity within the body was a kind of punishment defiling to the soul. In contrast, Wisdom describes "Solomon's" birth as the union of a good soul and an unsullied body.[23]

In the length and detail of his discussion of AFTERLIFE in the Old Testament, our author's concern for Catholic orthodoxy shows itself quite clearly. Wisely he distinguishes among three facets of the topic of afterlife: survival of man after death, in which virtually all the ancients believed; retribution in the hereafter, which appears in the later books of the Old Testament; immortality of the soul, which is clearly taught first in Wisdom and in the New Testament.[24] And wisely he warns against the imposing of a rigid uniformity upon the diverse data on afterlife found in the Old Testament. While recognizing a certain process of development in Israel's views of survival after death, he sternly insists that it not be explained by a rigid evolutionary theory like that of Wellhausen (II, pp. 45-46).

After a thorough discussion of Sheol, van Imschoot notes the two factors which shaped the gradual development of Israel's belief in life beyond the grave: experiences in life which rocked their faith in the justice of retribution in the here and now, and the devout faith of some Israelites who dared hope for a lasting fellowship with God (II, pp. 57-58). He concludes, after studying Psalms 16, 49, 73, and Job 19 in some detail, that none of these passages, with the possible ex-

[23] Heinisch, *op. cit.*, pp. 166-167; van Imschoot, vol. II, pp. 24-25. The fact that both authors grapple with this question seems to suggest a certain defensiveness about the canonicity of Wisdom. Protestant scholars have sometimes used an alleged Platonic doctrine of preexistence as an argument against the inclusion of this apocryphal work in the canon.

[24] Heinisch, *op. cit.*, p. 171, tends to read the later understanding of immortality in the earlier stages of biblical history: "Israel at all times firmly believed that the soul, when separated from the body, does not cease to exist."

ception of Psalm 49, does much more than prepare the way for a full-blown doctrine of afterlife by challenging the traditional teachings on retribution in this present life.

Turning to the topic of RESURRECTION, van Imschoot suggests that Ezekiel's use of resurrection as a figure for Israel's restoration (Ezekiel 37) is a testimony to God's power to raise the dead, though a general resurrection of all men was not in view in Ezekiel's time. Isaiah 53:10 seems, in his opinion, to imply the resurrection of the servant of the Lord, while making no connection between his resurrection and a state of eternal life (II, pp. 66-67).

In the well-known crux, Isaiah 26:19, the bodily resurrection of the Israelite dead not only is seen to be a symbol of Israel's restoration, but also is "announced as a future reality." Participation in this resurrection is restricted to the dead who belong to Yahweh, i.e., the Israelites, although it is possible that all righteous persons are included (II, pp. 67-68).

Following a discussion of Daniel 12:1-3 and some deuterocanonical writings, van Imschoot draws one of his characteristic contrasts between Israel's faith and the religions of her neighbors: In the Persian religion the resurrection of the dead is universal, stemming from a belief in the destruction and the renewal of the world; for the people of Israel it is limted to the righteous or the elect, because it is born of their faith in the justice of Yahweh and in the messianic age with its program of restoration (II, p. 71).

Van Imschoot's handling of this whole topic is typical of his combination of scholarly balance and theological conviction. He resists the temptation to read too much New Testament theology into the earlier texts; at the same time, he strongly affirms the part that the Old Testament passages played in blazing the trail for Christ and the apostles. Characteristic, too, is his zeal to distinguish biblical faith from the other religions.[25]

Time and again van Imschoot's theological insights combine with his own devout faith to produce passages which penetrate to the heart of Israel's beliefs. For instance, in his discussion of the FEAR OF GOD, one of man's religious duties, he rightly perceives the intimate

---

[25] Van Imschoot's treatment of resurrection so closely parallels Heinisch's that one gains the distinct impression that he is dependent on the briefer, earlier work of Heinisch which first appeared in German in 1940.

connection between man's fear of God and his confidence in God's grace. The awesome sovereignty of God's grace in granting forgiveness is itself the greatest ground for fearing him (II, p. 99).[26]

Again, his sketch of THE KNOWLEDGE OF GOD merits comment. More practical than theoretical in perspective, knowing God is recognizing him for what he is in sovereignty, might, goodness, and faithfulness and then responding in worship and obedience. For this reason the knowledge of God is virtually synonymous with the fear of God (II, pp. 102-103).

One of van Imschoot's outstanding contributions is the section on SACRIFICE. He not only treats in some detail the various sacrifices, analyzing the meaning of their ingredients and ritual, but he also tries to grapple with their theological purposes. In addition to re-establishing fellowship with God and causing the sins of the people to disappear, the sacrificial system was intended to appease the wrath of God (II, p. 141). Despite the trend in biblical scholarship to play down the element of propitiation, van Imschoot properly recognizes the major role it played in Israel's worship.[27]

In the final section of volume II dealing with SIN, van Imschoot returns to the subject of ATONEMENT, as touched in the final servant song (Isaiah 52:13–53:12). Clearly distinguishing the suffering of the servant from that of the many psalmists who despair of life, van Imschoot tries to isolate what is new and unique in the picture of expiation wrought by the servant. Neither expiation by substitution nor intercession sets this song apart. Rather, the distinguishing characteristic is the sinless servant's voluntary acceptance of suffering, as God charges him with the sins which the people had committed. In addition to the fact that this sacrifice is so freely given is the conviction that it is part of the divine plan of salvation (II, pp. 329-333).

If van Imschoot does not draw out the messianic implications of the servant's sacrifice, it is probably because his projected volume III on salvation was never published. This unhappy fact accounts for

---

[26] This passage is based, of course, on Psalm 130.

[27] For contrasting approaches to this subject, see C. H. Dodd's *The Bible and the Greeks*, second ed. (Chicago: Alec R. Allenson, 1954), where expiation is stressed; and see Leon Morris' *Apostolic Preaching of the Cross* (Grand Rapids: Eerdmans, 1956), which makes a strong case for the propitiatory nature of atonement.

the truncated nature of his work which closes on the note of sin, and bypasses completely the major themes of messianism and eschatology.

From Heinisch's work, whose structure throughout closely resembles van Imschoot's and may well have served as a paradigm for it, we can reconstruct the themes which probably would have been sounded in volume III. Heinisch calls his last section REDEMPTION and divides it into three parts: judgment, the new kingdom of God, and the Messiah.

There is nothing sentimental in Heinisch's view of JUDGMENT. Whether God is judging the Gentile nations or Israel, the ultimate purpose is God's glory. By judgment "His honor, violated through sin, was repaired." [28] And again, "by disciplining Israel to the brink of annihilation, satisfaction was made to Yahweh's holiness and justice." [29] Not that the correcting or restoring ministry of judgment is overlooked, but it is linked to God's glory in the fulfillment of his sovereign purposes, not to a concern for man's convenience.

The section on the NEW KINGDOM OF GOD concentrates on the restoration of Israel and the conversion of the Gentiles; it concludes with a discussion of the messianic kingdom. As usual, Heinisch does little more than compile a topical concordance of the pertinent passages, especially from the prophets.

An exception is his survey of some of the difficult prophecies. Here he makes a number of helpful suggestions to aid in interpretation. For example, he reminds us that the prophets do not usually depict the future in chronological sequence. Events in God's future redemption merge so that it is difficult to sort out what may take place in the near future from end-time happenings. Helpful, too, is his reminder that prophecies of the future are usually couched in language influenced by the place and time in which the prophet lived.

Heinisch's discussion of the MESSIAH reveals his deep commitment to the unity of the Bible. For instance, the promise in Genesis 3:15 "is true of all men, but in a unique manner applies to Christ who, as Eve's child, delivered us from the serpent's power." [30] Again, he interprets Isaiah 7:14 as a direct prophecy of the virgin birth, no aspect of which is fulfilled in Ahaz' time. The terms "mighty God"

---

[28] Heinisch, *op. cit.*, p. 279.
[29] *Ibid.*
[30] *Ibid.*, p. 304.

and "son of God" in Isaiah 9:5 and Psalm 2:7 are considered clear proofs of the Messiah's divinity.

The value of Heinisch's work is seriously compromised by his almost simplistic approach to the subject of messianism. He makes no attempt to tackle the technical questions which swarm around the topic in the Old Testament. Does the term Messiah ever occur in the Old Testament as a title of the coming king? In what sense are the royal psalms, which describe Israel's kings in ideal terms, to be understood messianically? Is there a connection between the royal office of the Messiah and the suffering servant?

In short, Heinisch skirts most of the problems whether theological, historical, or exegetical and contents himself with brief expositions of passages which traditionally have been given a messianic slant. His motive may be commendable, but his method is questionable. Disservice is done the study of both Testaments when New Testament interpretations are read back into the Old Testament passages in such a way as to ignore their setting and context. We cannot force on the Bible a unity that does not flow out of its own texture.[31]

What van Imschoot would have done with messianism we can only guess. But it is safe to say that his characteristic caution and balance would have served his church and all of us more effectively than Heinisch's somewhat doctrinaire presentation.

RELATIONSHIP BETWEEN THE OLD AND NEW TESTAMENTS

The work of van Imschoot is a Christian theology of the Old Testament in every sense of the term. Hebrews 1:1-2 is a paradigm for his understanding of the relationship between the Testaments. As we have seen, the basic unity is provided by the one God speaking throughout the Bible: "It is the same God who has spoken through the prophets and through His Son, that is to say, it is the same God who has communicated His thought and especially His will to men" (I, p. 2).

[31] Much more satisfying is A. Gelin's brief essay "The Messias of God" in J. Giblet, *The God of Israel, The God of Christians*, pp. 199-218. Gelin is much more sensitive to the subtle developments in messianism and the way in which the New Testament braids several Old Testament strands together: suffering servant, son of man, royal messiah, priestlike Melchizedek, new and final Adam.

The New Testament completes and crowns the Old: "The old revelation was necessarily incomplete and imperfect because it was advancing toward the complete and final form which the Son was to give" (I, p. 3). Because of his emphasis on this pattern of progressive revelation, van Imschoot goes on to state its importance for biblical theology: "while paying scrupulous respect to the special characteristics of the Old Testament, biblical theology will bring about a synthesis of the doctrines of the Old Testament with a view towards the new revelation, since the new crowns the old and testifies to the final pattern God was following in the old economy and throughout the vicissitudes of Israel's religion" (I, p. 3).[32]

Heinisch is even more direct and specific about the preparatory role of the Old Testament. The conclusion of his work is titled "Old Testament Religion Perfected in the New." Though the nature of God and his demand for loving worship provide continuity between the Testaments, the coming of Christ marks a new beginning which both deepens our knowledge of God and sharpens our sense of obligation to him and others. Both in granting freedom from the Mosaic law and in offering full forgiveness through the cross, the New Testament goes far beyond the old, while building on its foundation.

To Heinisch, "The Old Testament was designed to condition men's minds for Christ," as the law "preserved Israel from being assimilated by her pagan environment, inasmuch as it imposed self-mastery, kept alive a consciousness of sin and fostered a yearning for salvation."[33] But when Christ came, God no longer needed Israel. "He willed to retain the imperishable religious content of the Old Testament for His new kingdom, but first He detached his new foundation from ancient moorings lest Israel continue to impede His plan."[34] Perhaps the need for terseness is to blame, but Heinisch here seems

---

[32] A. Gelin, *The Key Concepts of the Old Testament*, p. xiii, makes Christian involvement in the Old Testament pointedly personal: "This history is ours, since, as St. Paul says, we are Abraham's descendants; and its great themes, its great constants, must be returned to again and again." All this is true because "The Old Testament is one vast prophecy whose governing principles are not at first apparent; a land of mystery in which we have to learn to discern the royal roads that lead to Christ. It was to Christ that God's secret but powerful influence led Israel" (p. xi).

[33] Heinisch, *op. cit.*, p. 372.

[34] *Ibid.*, p. 373.

both to underplay the organic unity between the Testaments and to overlook the part that Israel is yet to enjoy in God's redemptive program according to Romans 11.

In addition to the section on the Messiah noted above, two other parts of Heinisch's work speak volumes about his view of the relationship between the Testaments. First, in his discussion of the nature of God he devotes over twenty pages to "Preparation for the Mystery of the Most Holy Trinity." While stressing the Old Testament's teaching on the unity of God in contrast with the polytheism that continually threatened to seduce Israel, Heinisch holds: "Nevertheless, the greatest mystery of Christian faith [the Trinity] should at least have been foreshadowed in the Old Testament." [35]

Setting aside some of the more extravagant interpretations of the Fathers of the first Christian centuries, he surveys a number of themes which in his view prepare the way for the doctrine of the Trinity: the angel of the Lord, Wisdom, the Spirit of Yahweh, and the Word of God. It is only fair to note that Heinisch shows considerable discretion in his study of these concepts and refrains from reading New Testament ideas back into them, though he does take pains to show their New Testament development.

The second passage which indicates Heinisch's views on the relationship of the Testaments is his "Critique of Old Testament Morality." "Since the Old Testament is only an anteroom to the New Testament," [36] later New Testament standards of conduct should not be expected. In the laws of marriage and divorce, in the ban *(herem)* which demanded the destruction of the enemies of Yahweh, in the attitude toward foreign nations which often degenerated into hatred, Heinisch finds the teaching of the Old Testament and the reactions of Israel definitely inferior to the standards of the New Testament. Still, he notes, the Old Testament itself often provides corrections to some of these abuses. And compared with the morality of her neighbors, Israel's standards had a certain loftiness that reflected the uniqueness of her revelation.

Far less frequently than Heinisch does van Imschoot show how an Old Testament idea is picked up and developed in the New Testament. When he does, the reference is usually terse and almost off-

---

[35] *Ibid.*, p. 102.

[36] *Ibid.*, p. 212.

hand. For instance, to a discussion of the relationship between God's justice and his mercy, van Imschoot adds: "This doctrine will be taken up by St. Paul" (I, p. 71).[37]

At other times he cites the New Testament in order to show how it sought to correct Jewish misunderstanding of an Old Testament theme:

> The Jews . . . forgot that the divine election was addressed to the nation, not to the individuals; they interpreted the love and the promises of Yahweh toward their ancestors as a blind partiality . . . so that eventually they believed that . . . belonging to the race of Abraham would assure the salvation of their descendants. Against this deformation of the doctrine of election rose up John the Baptist, and Jesus, and St. Paul (I, p. 255).[38]

No doubt van Imschoot's inability to publish his projected third volume has robbed us of the best resource from which to draw conclusions about his view of the relationship between the Testaments. As it is, he has left us little evidence of the precise ways in which the new revelation completes the old. There is, of course, an historical connection as the Old Testament events prepare for those of the New Testament and then give way to them. And there is a thematic connection as the New Testament picks up ideas from the Old, adjusting and expanding them in the full light of Christ's advent.

But neither the historical nor the thematic connections are spelled out in detail by van Imschoot. Though he is a thoroughly Christian theologian, his writings, unlike those of von Rad, Eichrodt, Knight, Vriezen, and others, do not tell us specifically how he ties the Testaments together. The index of passages to van Imschoot's first volume indicates his relative paucity of reference to the New Testament: for forty pages of Old Testament references, a page and a half of New Testament. The revelatory process of Hebrew 1:1-2 may be his paradigm, but van Imschoot has not done enough conjugating with it for us to see clearly what he means.[39]

---

[37] Cf. also I, p. 100 for a similar note in regard to the new heaven and new earth, and II, p. 16 in regard to the use of "flesh" as the seat of human sin.

[38] Cf. also II, p. 197, where van Imschoot shows how the New Testament challenges the Jewish interpretation of the sabbath.

[39] Happily, other French-speaking Catholic scholars have teamed together to produce a book which does show how a number of themes develop through both Testaments: J. Giblet, *The God of Israel, The God of Christians*. In a simple yet sensitive way, the book deals with five clusters of concepts—God's

SELECTED BIBLIOGRAPHY

van Imschoot, P., *Théologie de l'Ancien Testament.* Tournay, *Tome 1,* 1954; *Tome 2,* 1956. English translation of vol. 1 by K. Sullivan and F. Buck, Tournay, 1965.

————, "Le veau d'or (Ex. 32,1 ss.)," *CollGand* 14 (1927), pp. 113-116.

————, "Le prophète Michée et son temps," *CollGand* 17 (1930), pp. 176-182.

————, "De oraculo Isaiae 2,2-5," *CollGand* 18 (1931), pp. 149-152.

————, "De libri Sapientiae scriptore. De loco et tempore compositionis libri Sapientiae," *CollGand* 20 (1933), pp. 117-121, 181-183.

————, "La Sagesse dans l'Ancien Testament est-elle une hypostase?," *CollGand* 21 (1934), pp. 3-10.

————, "La composition du livre des Juges," *CollGand* 21 (1934), pp. 153-160.

————, "La composition des livres de Samuel," *CollGand* 22 (1935), pp. 141-148.

————, "L'action de l'esprit de Jahvé dans l'Ancien Testament," *RSPT* 23 (1934), pp. 533-588.

————, "L'esprit de Jahvé, source de vie dans l'Ancien Testament," *RB* 44 (1935), pp. 481-501.

————, "La révolte d'Absalom," *CollGand* 23 (1936), pp. 3-10, 101-106.

————, "Le règne de Dieu dans l'Ancien Testament," *CollGand* 23 (1936), pp. 254-258; 24 (1937), pp. 3-9.

————, "L'esprit de Jahvé et l'alliance nouvelle dans l'Ancien Testament," *EThL* 13 (1936), pp. 201-220.

————, "Sagesse et esprit dans l'Ancien Testament," *RB* 47 (1938), pp. 23-49.

————, "Lesprit de Jahvé, principe de vie morale dans l'Ancien Testament," *EThL* 16 (1939), pp. 457-467.

————, "Psalmus 8," *CollGand* 27 (1940), pp. 5-10.

————, "De creatione hominis in Gen. 2,7," *CollGand* 30 (1947), pp. 223-227.

————, "De serpente tentatore," *CollGand* 31 (1948), pp. 5-10.

————, "L'alliance dans l'Ancien Testament," *NRT* 74 (1952), pp. 785-805.

————, "L'esprit selon l'Ancien Testament," *BVC* 1 (1953), pp. 7-24.

---

plan, God's revelation, God's demands, man's sin, God's victory. The dogmatic slant, so characteristic of earlier Catholic writings, is far less noticeable, and a concerted attempt is made to deal with the themes within the mood and methods of biblical rather than systematic theology. Though less technical than H. H. Rowley's *The Unity of the Bible* (London: The Carey Kingsgate Press, Ltd., 1953), the work of Giblet and his colleagues drinks at the same stream of confidence that one God is recording and interpreting his revelatory and redemptive mission through the whole Bible. And the deep devotional impact is an added bonus.

————, "L'esprit de Yahweh, source de la piété dans l'Ancien Testament," *BVC* 1 (1954), pp. 17-30.

————, "Heilige Geest," "Genade," "Liefde," "Offer, Offermaal," "Verbond," "Vleesch," "Vloekpsalmen," "Zegen," "Ziel," in *Bijbelsch Woordenboek*. Roermond, 1939*ff*.

Index

INDEX OF SUBJECTS

217

Son of Man, 108, 167, 182, 210
Spirit, 39, 98, 133, 154-158, 179, 212

Tabernacle (tent), 82f., 102, 162
Theology, and history, 26ff., 30f., 47-
55, 73-77, 94f., 129-133, 137ff.,
145-150, 158ff., 177-183, 199-201
methodology of, 16ff., 26-31, 43-47,
73-77, 93f., 124-126, 134f., 144ff.,
175ff., 194ff., 201
and New Testament, 19, 38f., 55-61,
76f., 86-88, 116f., 118f., 125, 126,

135, 167ff., 173ff., 176f., 184ff.,
188ff., 210-213
and religion, 30-32, 36f., 47-50, 94f.,
97, 125ff., 131f., 144f.
unity of, 30, 42ff., 56f., 167f., 181,
195, 202
Traditions-history, 65-73
Typology, 30f., 49, 58f., 149, 174, 184

Vine, 182

Wisdom, 39, 98, 109, 114, 149f., 212
Word, 39, 76f., 98, 154f., 186, 212

INDEX OF AUTHORS

Anderson, B. W., 20, 75, 77
Aquinas, T., 195

Barr, J., 80f., 155, 176, 202
Bentzen, A., 199
Bernard, J. H., 76
Beyerlin, W., 148
Birch, L. C., 148
Boman, T., 179
Bream, H. N., 174, 176
Bright, J., 69, 146, 156, 199
Bultmann, R., 56

Cazelles, H., 152, 156
Ceuppens, P. F., 193, 195
Childs, B., 134, 174, 176, 182
Clements, R., 68, 123-139

Davies, G. H., 65-88, 180
Dentan, R., 16, 21, 77, 95, 117, 174
Dodd, C. H., 185, 208
Durham, J., 173-190
Dürr, L., 198

Eichrodt, W., 25-62, 117f., 143, 158,
185
Eissfeldt, O., 199

Fohrer, G., 77
Freedman, D. N., 75

Gabler, J., 74
Galling, K., 197
Gehman, H., 176
Gelin, A., 193f., 198f., 201, 210f.
Gerstenberger, E., 163

Giblet, J., 193, 198, 200, 205, 210, 213f.
Gilkey, L., 17
Gottwald, N., 25-61
Guillet, J., 193

Heinisch, P., 193, 199, 205ff., 209, 211f.
Hempel, J., 176
Heschel, A., 20
Hill, D. G., 176
Hubbard, D., 193-214
Huffmon, H. B., 71
Hummel, H., 74f., 175

Imschoot, P. van, 193-214

Jacob, E., 17f., 143-169
Johnson, A. R., 40, 87, 205

Keller, C. A., 176
Kline, M., 175f.
Knight, G. A. F., 173-190
Köhler, L., 20, 194, 196

Laurin, R., 15-21, 143-168
Lods, A., 199

McCarthy, D., 160, 205
Mendenhall, G., 160, 205
Miskotte, H., 15
Mowinckel, S., 161f., 165
Muilenburg, J., 74, 180
Murphy, R. E., 70, 75

Newman, M. L., 148
Noth, M., 148, 201

INDEX OF BIBLICAL PASSAGES